L
L
I
N
G

H
A
R
D

FALLING HARD

A Journey into the World of Judo

MARK LAW

TRUMPETER
BOSTON
2009

Trumpeter Books
An imprint of Shambhala Publications, Inc.
Horticultural Hall
300 Massachusetts Avenue
Boston, Massachusetts 02115
www.shambhala.com

© 2007, 2009 by Mark Law

Revised edition of *The Pyjama Game: A Journey into Judo.*
Published by arrangement with Aurum Press Ltd.

9 8 7 6 5 4

Printed in the United States of America
∞ This edition is printed on acid-free paper that meets the
American National Standards Institute z39.48 Standard.
♻ Shambhala Publications makes every effort to print on recycled paper.
For more information please visit www.shambhala.com.

Distributed in the United States by Penguin Random House LLC
and in Canada by Random House of Canada Ltd

Library of Congress Cataloging-in-Publication Data
Law, Mark.
Falling hard: a journey into the world of judo / Mark Law.
   p.   cm.
Rev. ed. of: Pyjama game: a journey into judo.
Includes bibliographical references.
ISBN 978-1-59030-715-1
1. Judo. I. Title.
GV1114.L385 2009
796.815'2—dc22
2008044900

To judoka—in every place, in every time

CONTENTS

ACKNOWLEDGMENTS

Many knowledgeable guides have accompanied me on my journey into judo. Nicolas Soames, my former colleague on *The Times* and the *Daily Telegraph,* has worked tirelessly under various pseudonyms, most notably that of Philip Nicksan, to keep judo coverage alive in the British press. His personal experience and knowledge, his journalism, and the books he has written or published under the Ippon imprint that he founded, have all been invaluable sources for which I am profoundly grateful. Bob Willingham has given me much help with numerous aspects of the modern tournament scene, and I have his kind permission to use material from his magazine, *The World of Judo.*

The late Dickie Bowen was a fount of knowledge about the origins of judo, its dissemination, and its early years in Europe. Chris Holmes and Ben Andersen have steered me through the complexities of Japanese history, culture, and philosophy, as well as shedding light on the practice of the sport in modern Japan. John Goodbody of *The Times* and Barnaby Chesterman of Agence France Presse and the International Judo Federation have provided valuable material and expertise from their long experience in covering major tournaments. Simon Hicks who, before his tragic death just as this book was being completed, gave me what he realized was his most precious commodity: time. I would like to record my gratitude for all his advice and knowledge and also for access to the Fighting Films archive.

I acknowledge a particular debt to *Judo: A Sport and a Way of Life* by Michel Brousse and David Matsumoto, which carries a beautifully assembled verbal and pictorial account of the early days of judo and its spread to the West. I have drawn heavily from *A Life in Judo,* written by Neil Adams with Nicolas Soames, which tells in rare detail of the exigencies of a top-level competitive career; as does *Judo Champion* by Karen Briggs, also written with Nicolas Soames, and a key source for the chapter on U.K. women's judo. My researches have benefited from the insights and experience garnered from Roy Inman's spoken and written words, of the latter notably *Olympic Judo* (written with Nicolas Soames) and *Women's Judo*. I thank Mike Callan, director of Judo at the University of Bath, for help based on his wide knowledge of technical and fitness training in Japan and the West, and for great practical assistance and advice at major tournaments.

Brian Watson's biography of Jigoro Kano, *The Father of Judo,* proved an important source. Neil Ohlenkamp's Judo Information Site (www.judoinfo.com) has made accessible much obscure but valuable writing on the subject. This includes Masahiko Kimura's *My Judo,* originally published in 1985 but translated by "pdeking" and posted to the Judo Forum on Neil Ohlenkamp's site in March 2000, which sheds so much light on the man and his era.

I have received valuable help from Tony Sweeney on aspects of technique and the history of U.K. judo; David Finch has enlightened me on the modern tournament scene, Chris Bowles on aspects of British judo, and Andrew Moshanov on the development of the sport in Russia. From my colleague Sir John Keegan, the defense editor of the *Daily Telegraph,* I learned much of the military history of Japan from his conversation and his book *A History of Warfare.*

Keith Perry and the staff of the *Daily Telegraph* sports desk, who commissioned and handled my copy, and gave me the opportunity to cover a number of major international tournaments. I would like to thank Matthew d'Ancona, the sometime Captain of the London Area Schools Judo Team, for his kind permission to use material from an article which appeared in *The Spectator* magazine, which he edits, and I am also grateful to his predecessor, Boris Johnson, for commissioning my writing. My thanks go also to Craig Neff at *Sports Illustrated* in New York; Lizzie Richmond at the University of Bath, for access to the Bowen collection; John Bowen in Tokyo; Roland Oswald, Dr. Roland Regner, and Dr. Harold Tünneman at IAT, the Leipzig sports science institute; and Robert van der Geest in Holland. Diana Donovan has kindly granted me permission to use the late Terence Donovan's portrait of Yasuhiro Yamashita.

Graham Coster, editorial director of Aurum Press, has given me wise advice and constant support throughout as has my agent, David Luxton. I thank my editor, Steve Gove, to whom I owe a debt rather larger than I care to admit. I am grateful for much helpful advice on the manuscript from Andrew Harrison, Bruce Holmes, and Tim Willis. The project reached them as the result of the early encouragement and help of Mick Brown, my colleague on the *Daily Telegraph*.

I have to thank all my colleagues at The First Post for their support while this book diverted me from my duties.

I could not have made my journey without all the patient encouragement of my instructors. Colin Savage, Lee Gonzalez, and Tony Sweeney have borne the brunt of the task of teaching me, and to them I owe an enormous debt. Of those at the Budokwai, Peter Blewett, chief instructor; Ray Stevens, manager; and Roy Inman have given me much kind help. I would like to thank others among the club's instructors: Paul Ajala, Ben Andersen, Eric Bonti, Steve Fraser, Ron Isaacs, Danny Kingston, Danny Murphy, and Darcel Yandzi. Elsewhere, I thank Syd Hoare at the London Judo Society and Chris Holmes and Percy Sekine at the Judokan. Sadly both clubs are now closed.

I also had the privilege of being taught by three distinguished champions from Japan who came to the Budokwai as visiting instructors: Hidetoshi Nakanishi, Hirotaka Okada, and Kenzo Nakamura. In the course of training at the club, I have made occasional forays into the Brazilian jujitsu classes in the downstairs dojo: I thank Maurizio Gomez, Roger Gracie, and Felipe Souza for their welcome and their instruction.

I offer my special thanks to my regular training partners and the other countless people I trained with: from the mightiest in the world, who gave me their time, to absolute beginners who gave me a chance—and all those somewhere in between. I acknowledge a debt to the staff of the Budokwai and all those committee members past and present who have given their time to the fabric and the administration of the club.

Dreas Reyneke's miraculous Pilates classes made it possible for me to embark on this sport at an age when any sensible person would be giving up. A number of members of the medical profession enabled me to keep going. Scott Glickman, a Budokwai member and surgeon, saw me through a tricky time, as did physiotherapists Kate Hunt and Andrew Ferguson. Diane Thaal gave me enormous assistance. The unqualified help of Sean Cochrane rescued my fortunes at a crucial moment.

My personal trainer, Duke, a mongrel, now deceased, dragged me into the park and rushed me around it at speeds and levels of enthusiasm I would not have attained without him.

Finally, my greatest gratitude goes to Joan, who has borne the burden of my journey into judo.

To her and all these many people: Thank you.

HAJIME!

My legs are leaden, my throat is dry, and I feel slightly sick with anxiety. As I make my way toward the arena the roar of the crowd gets louder. This is my first major tournament and to say I am nervous is an understatement. I think it is because of the uncertainty of what I will face out there. One question keeps edging into the small part of my mind that is functioning normally: What on earth are the combatants going through if I feel like this when I've just come along to watch?

"*Rei!*" It always starts like this, courteously, with a bow. Next the referee shouts "*Hajime!*" which means *Begin!* and that's pretty much the end of any courtesy for the next few minutes. One in white, one in blue, the contestants circle each other, searching and darting in for their grip—a handful of collar, a fistful of sleeve. They break off, re-engage, and begin a violent and dazzling dance that zigzags and whirls around the mat, fingers darting like daggers, feet sweeping like scimitars.

The contest, which has a strange springy, elastic quality, is a fight of enormous speed, fury, and Herculean effort. Bodies twist, somersault through the air, stumble and crash, as each tries to whisk his opponent off his feet and whack him onto the floor with all the force he can unleash. Sometimes both contestants go down and the pace slows to a grim grapple on the ground, and it's hard to see what is happening in this strength-sapping entanglement of limbs. But somewhere in that jumble of cloth, fingers are inching their way around a windpipe, searching for a choke, a submission.

And what variety there is among these combatants: huge heavyweight men, tiny lightweight women, and every size in between—and every color too, every skin tone in the palette from the blackest of Africa to the whitest of the polar lands, from Mongolia to the Mediterranean Sea, and from the Indies West to East. Scarcely a nation is unrepresented, and so this tournament is a place of Babel, a cacophony of languages in the crowd and among the coaches bellowing instructions to their battered, gasping charges. But in all, there seems to be one common language, a language of fighting like no other. The spectators are reading it; the fighters are speaking it even though their mouths, livid with effort, are for the most part silent. This is a vernacular of colliding and twisting torsos, of sweeping legs and whipping wrists, of assertions written in the air with flying bodies. The end will be marked by a gestured judgment from a shoeless man with an expressionless face; it may be a sudden death in a whirlwind of a throw, or a slow death as a strangle does its work. Either way, the victor waves his arms and bounces about like a jubilant macaque, and on the floor the vanquished lies, inert, apparently lifeless. Then the next pair of combatants are brought in to take and make their chances on the mat.

This goes on all day, sometimes for days—wave after wave of athletes waiting to stride from the gloom of the tunnel into the glare of the arena and the crowd's roar. And when it's all over, they return home where their achievements will be unremarked by almost all but others in the sport. The reason? Their art is too hard to understand. Anyone can manage to follow a soccer match and make some plausible remark. But judo? It leaves most people uncomprehending and speechless. It is far too fast, too subtle, too foreign.

As everyone prepares to leave town, as they pull down the banners and take up the mats, a scent of the danger and aggression of the past few days still hangs in the air. There is a sense, even, that beneath the carnival trappings of a great sporting tournament lies an atmosphere of menace, because at the heart of every judo contest resides the vehement desire to inflict symbolic death. For this reason the place feels not so much like a modern stadium but rather an ancient amphitheater, and we sense that we have been watching nothing less than the latest disturbing display by the highly trained gladiators of an international traveling circus.

Two things drew me to judo: some pictures and some words. The pictures were of people in white flying through the air—not just falling, but traveling apparently with a very clear sense of direction and in some haste. The words were "In judo you can throw people over your shoulder." They both seem potent, magical. But as a youth I was always an indolent sportsman, convinced that I would never be able to cope with the rigors of such a game. Late in life a physical transformation wrought by Pilates following an injury made me reconsider. And then one of those milestone round-figure birthdays began to loom, and it was a case of now or never.

I went to my nearest judo club and, fearful of making a fool of myself in front of others, arranged to have some private lessons to see if I could cope. I was given the number of Colin Savage, a former member of the British national judo squad and a Commonwealth champion. "I'm going to be fifty in a few weeks," I explained over the phone, "Do you think I can do this?" In a slightly unsettling way, a deadpan Belfast voice replied, "There's only one way to find out."

After a month of Savage's laconic encouragement and unconcealed amusement, I joined the general class for beginners, but I continued to have my weekly private lessons. During these sessions, while he waited for my lungs to recover from a succession of traumas, Savage would tell me tales of the international competition circuit. As one who had never followed any sport at all, I found these particularly astonishing. But as he told me more, and as the months passed, I met and, more bizarrely, found myself training in close proximity to various international competitors. I came to suspect that, even in sporting terms, this was an extraordinary world. And I had landed in the middle of it. Almost every session I attended shed a little more light on the life of high-level contestants. One day, I was in the Tuesday beginners' class when Danny Kingston, then a middleweight in the British squad, was teaching us a new strangle. He finished his demonstration, got up from the floor, and called out, "Right, pair up and try it for yourselves. I think you'll find it works." And then in a muttered aside said to me, "Well, it worked for me on a Russian in Moscow over the weekend."

Moscow? Over the weekend? Danny was going all the way to Moscow for the weekend to strangle people? And now he was back here in Chelsea teaching the beginners' class. What sort of life was this? I soon understood that not only did the rest of the sporting world know little of the realities of the judo circuit, but many who practiced at the club didn't have much of an idea either. Certain members would disappear to return after the weekend, sometimes looking a little battered. It turned out they'd been to some competition in Stockholm or Tiblisi or wherever, and few in the club seemed aware of just what they'd done.

I began to take notes, not with any clear idea in mind, but merely because, as a journalist, I have been conditioned to write down interesting things. I talked to people who had competed or officiated or witnessed some of the great tournaments, and questioned those who had been to Japan and trained in some of its most celebrated dojos under the tutelage of legendary fighters, and had even fought people who had fought the early gods of judo. I overheard a lot of conversations, scoured quite a lot of books and magazines, and I started going to big tournaments myself, sometimes as a reporter for the *Daily Telegraph*.

Although there was a welter of literature on the techniques of judo, I was surprised that little else been written. Here was an untold story of unsung heroes. And it was one which I realized could only be written by a judoka; moreover, the people who were best qualified to tell this story had never gotten around to it.

Those who ask what right I have—I, who know nothing—to take the task upon myself have a good point. I would only say that I have written down what I have seen and what I have been told and what has been written by people who know what they are talking about. I have, of course, drawn some of my own conclusions, but in doing so have taken some care for health insurance. I know of a big room in Chelsea with hard walls and a soft floor full of people who are only too ready to draw disobliging links between my readiness to write about judo and my woeful shortcomings in practicing it. They would be delighted to offer forthright literary criticism in the way that they know best. I hope they will all bear with me for the following reason.

On some evenings down at the club, an awkward situation can arise when, during *randori,* the period of free fighting or sparring, the next batch of people go onto the mat and form a line. They must stay there for, say, four bouts of three or four minutes each and take on anyone who comes out to stand in front of them. Sometimes a very good judoka, maybe an international player, will be standing there and, because the challengers feel too tired or too intimidated, no one will come out to face him. This reflects badly on the club. It is better that anyone comes forward, however inexperienced, than that someone is left without a partner. An incompetent judo player can at least provide a bit of target practice until someone better comes along. So, when it is absolutely certain that no one else is going to volunteer, one must step forward.

This is done not out of courage—one soon learns that the best players are usually by far the safest—but because it must be done.

That is the spirit in which I have stepped forward to write this book: to tell a story that was standing there waiting impatiently to be told.

So now our *randori* is about to begin.

To fight, as we shall see, is to take part in a kind of dialogue and, in some senses, that is what you and I are going to have. If you know nothing of judo and are stepping onto the mat for the first time, my task is to convince you that, in spite of your doubts, this thing called judo is a subject worthy of your time. But I must warn you now that you will encounter more exhaustion and more anxiety than you expect, and, likewise, more elation and despair.

In the course of our encounter, you will come across some Japanese words. Do not regard them as a blurry obstacle and canter around the side of them like a riderless horse in a steeplechase. Japanese is one of the easier languages to pronounce. Just break each word down into its syllables and say it out loud to yourself, but giving each syllable equal stress. The chances are that you have got it pretty much right. *Randori,* for instance, sounds more or less like *tandoori.*

Now it may be that you are a high-grade player with many great competition victories to your name, in which case my task is a hard one, because you not only know of what I write, but you know more than I do, and you may resent my attempt to tell you anything. In your case, I'd hope that you have not heard at least some of the tales I recite and that I may be able to introduce you to some people you have not met. I even hope that, in a way that is new and unfamiliar to you, I might express and explain this sport which in our own very different ways we share.

However, as I look around, it seems you are something of a mixed bunch. As well as high-grade competitors and some good club players, I can see that quite a lot of you have never even worn a *judogi*—a judo jacket—before, let alone been on the mat. It is going to be difficult talking to you all at once, so I must ask you to be patient. The experienced and knowledgeable must bear with me while I write about what they know; the newcomers must not be put off by the occasional complexities.

So, please, whoever you may be, step forward onto the mat. When the *sensei,* the instructor, shouts out the command of "*Hajime,*" we must take our grip. You, I suspect, will probably favor the double lapel grip, which is not so good for footsweeps but ideal for holding the pages of this book. I will try and reach out to grasp your curiosity and your imagination.

But we cannot begin until the *sensei,* calling us to bow, shouts "*Rei!*" At that point you must bow to me as I will now bow to you, to show mutual respect. Place your feet nearly parallel and close together, then, tucking in your chin, bow gently from the waist, letting the tips of your fingers slide down the sides of your legs and come around lightly to touch the front of your knees; not too deep, not too shallow—just a modestly respectful bow.

"*Rei!*"

I feared as much. Some of you have not bowed. Perhaps you thought the request was merely rhetorical, a literary device. It was not. Perhaps you were embarrassed, thinking you might be seen, in which case you may do it later in private. But do please bow, I beg you. I have bowed to you and if you do not do the same, you are failing to observe the spirit of judo and it is probably better that you leave the mat now; it may not be dignified, but it would be honest. All sorts of things are about to happen and before we can go on, we must insist on this simple mutual expression of respect. I promise you one thing: if you do as I have asked, you will feel differently about yourself and everything that follows. Thank you.

Now that we have both have done this, we wait for the cry, "*Hajime!*" And now we can begin.

2

BEGINNER'S LUCK

I am on a southbound flight path low over Central London, heading in the direction of Gatwick. Heathrow is to starboard and I am passing over Chelsea. Down there the trophy babes are slinking their way from Holmes Place Health Club around the corner, back to their little zillion-dollar stucco palaces. I am traveling at an altitude of some twenty-two feet above one of the many tributaries of Fulham Road, in the main dojo on the second floor of the Budokwai Judo Club. I am flying over someone's shoulder. I am somersaulting in the air and am about to crash. It is at around this time that I find myself concurring with the proposition that it is better to travel hopefully than it is to arrive.

A white belt in the dojo is like a toddler at a tea party and demands a similar etiquette: People must take turns to play with him; it is incumbent upon everyone to encourage him, praise his simplest achievements, and not laugh when he falls over.

I am in a maelstrom. This is my first open class. There are about thirty people in the dojo with belts of every color, but none is as white as mine. I am struck by the mayhem created by the combatants as they scuffle, skeeter, somersault, and hurtle through the air to crash to the floor. I am entranced by this childish exuberant abandon; this is part ballroom, part bar brawl, and part bouncy castle.

Towards the end of the session I find myself wondering why all these entangled pairs hurling each other around the room never actually collide. I have time for these thoughts because I have been thrown and am trapped on my back. I am like a rider who has come adrift during a steeplechase and is wondering whether he will be trampled upon. Quite soon after making this observation, I see a pair locked in hostile embrace come hurtling across the floor from the far corner of the dojo. Just before they get to me, one of them manages to turn in for a throw with enough force to bring them both crashing down. Their point of arrival coincides with the precise location of my outstretched left knee. There is a terrible sound like a boulder smashing through a sack of kindling. The pain is indescribable. The man whose spine landed on my leg stays on the floor for several minutes; I, miraculously, have come out of it better and am able to get up and hobble around, but I am suffused by a mixture of extreme pain and wild rage. Why me?

And that ended my newfound enthusiasm for a few weeks. But something important had happened before that incident. A black belt had dutifully agreed to give me a practice and, as is the custom, had left the beginner to make most of the attacks. I did my utmost to follow what Colin Savage had taught me. My opponent nonchalantly countered most of my efforts, but just once I came in for a throw; he flew through the air and landed smack on his back. And that was it. I was hooked. I had thrown a black belt. I was convinced I was a natural. Thus did the sport seize my mind in its grip.

It took six weeks for my knee to recover enough to return to the dojo. It took me slightly longer to accept that the black belt had duped me. I hadn't thrown him, of course; he'd "jumped." This cleverly convincing performance is just one of several devices the dealers use to get newcomers addicted to judo. The other is colored belts. And I was soon hooked on those too.

I did not admire sportsmen. I was bored by the seriousness with which they take their sport, by their obsessive pursuit of their ridiculously unimportant victories. I despised their absurd little superstitions, but most of all I despised their tears. As if it mattered. This, then, was pretty much my attitude when I embarked upon this journey.

I myself was never a sports enthusiast of even the humblest kind. At school, my idea of a sporting triumph was to avoid going on a cross-country run. In my youth, exercise consisted of some languid horsemanship. In my thirties, I did some vigorous vegetable gardening, and in my forties I did a bit of skiing. And then in my fifties came judo. When, in the twilight of this undistinguished sporting career, I find myself in a state of near-collapse on the dojo floor, I do seriously wonder if I might have played my cards in the wrong order.

Yet my time in the dojo provided an escape from one reality into another. The sheer urgency of the problems that this sport presented made it engrossing for me. If someone banged a tennis ball past me, it was hardly the end of the world. It was just a game. When someone threw me on the floor in the dojo, it didn't seem like a game at all. I was much affected. The former reflected badly on my ability at tennis. The latter reflected badly on *me*. And if ever I threw someone it seemed somehow to be a *worthwhile* achievement, unlike scoring a goal or a point with a ball.

I enjoyed the unrelenting threat of this sport. If I came under pressure I couldn't just pass the ball to someone else. Nor could I talk my way out of it—except by saying "*maitta,*" which signifies submission. Indeed it is the virtual absence of words that so appealed. In my work, I spent my days fiddling about with words and stacking them in rows; it was good to be rid of words for a time, to follow the lead of the early circus owner, Mr. Stephen Ducrow, who coined the phrase: "Cut the cackle and come to the horses."

The utter selfishness and the excitement of fighting appealed to me. My days were filled with the endless cooperations of life on a daily newspaper, the constant demand for ambassadorial levels of tact and patience. But once in the dojo, once the *sensei* had called "*Hajime,*" I was responsible for no one and I could jettison any idea of cooperation, because everything here was about its absolute opposite. (It was only much later that I would learn just how much responsibility I had for my opponent and, curiously, just how much cooperation is involved in the business of fighting.)

I also liked the contact, the *feel* of the alien forces that had to be controlled, countered, exploited, just as I liked to feel a horse's power, to sense its mood and predict its next lunacy. I liked that moment just after a boat tacks and loses way, when there's the thump of the sail catching a gust of wind in its cupped canvas hands, that lunging lurch when the keel beneath suddenly bites and carves the strong thick sea. I enjoyed the sensation of sliding over and carving into the face of the sloping snow with its alarming repertoire of everchanging textures.

Apart from the fact that they all take place on dramatically shifting surfaces, these three activities have one other appealing quality in common with judo: They are all about maintaining a vertical configuration in circumstances that are sometimes less than helpful (or ideal). But judo offered something more: the buzz of trying to stay on one's feet while trying to knock someone else off theirs. Sometimes when one got chucked or thrown around on the floor, it was quite frightening—like being caught in the dangerous curling vortex of a breaking wave. And when I did manage to chuck someone else on the floor, it was a great sensation. I relished the extremeness of judo's movements, the totality of its action, the utter drama of its conclusions. I loved what seemed to be a licence to behave badly. Like a man with his sleeve caught in the door of an accelerating truck, I somehow had no choice but to go along with it.

My position was like a late convert to the Christian faith who discovers that the large building near his home that he has ignored all his life is in fact Westminster Abbey. And, indeed, the Budokwai is a bit like a church.

It occupies a Victorian brick building whose pointed Gothic windows suggest the ecclesiastical and a sense of higher purpose. Downstairs, the walls are hung with photographs, some of athletes dressed in brightly colored tracksuits, beaming on a rostrum and tipping their medals to the lens, and some black-and-white images of stern Oriental faces.

Upstairs is a large room with a high ceiling, exposed rafters, and a floor covered in green mats with a square contest area marked out in red. The brick walls are lined to elbow height with tongue-and-groove wainscoting bearing signs of damage inflicted where the trajectory of flying judoka has exceeded the dimensions of the dojo.

The early months of the sport took a terrible toll on my frame, which had never been subjected to so much stress. People are wrong when they talk about "aching in every bone in their body." It's not the bones that ache, but the bits of gristle that fix them all together. My ribs were crushed, my neck was crunched, my spine strained. Judo seemed to be the sport that put the harm in harmony.

Because they were bare, my feet bore the most visible signs of my suffering. They did not ask for this. They had followed me into journalism, where they played a supportive rather than a proactive role. Their one big moment came when, as a junior reporter trying to secure an interview, I actually put one of them in a door, because that's what I thought newspapermen were meant to do. But now, after a lifetime of devoted service, they were being kicked, crushed, and twisted; my toes seemed permanently bruised. They'd taken a pretty dim view of skiing, particularly during the early phase of rented boots, but this judo thing was unacceptable.

The fingers weren't much better. My hands, wracked with cramp, would suddenly contort like the raw claw of a chicken on a bonfire. In order to open a bottle of wine after a session I was forced to buy one of those fancily engineered corkscrews that I had always believed to symbolize the physical and moral decay of Western civilization. For a period my fingers were in such a distressed state that I could no longer type properly; everything I wrote looked like a page from the Central Warsaw telephone directory. This alarmed me, because a journalist is little more than a typist with attitude.

I was encouraged by the tolerance with which other members of the club accepted a newcomer. I soon learned why they were so welcoming. Among some members there was a genuine wish to welcome another worshipper to their church, but also a new sucker for target practice is always useful, and I constituted added variety in their diet, if only a meager portion. However, while the expressions of my new acquaintances might have been apparently friendly, I could not help but detect a look at the back of the eyes that seemed to say, "OK, you poor sap, let's see how long you'll last."

As a beginner, I was at first much alarmed by the prospect of training with black belts. I soon learned that they were the safest opponents of all, and that the people whom I should really steer clear of were the beginners, who were bony, clumsy, and furiously eager: people just like me.

Sometimes in the course of *randori,* the free fighting, in the early days before I became a little more robust, I felt as though I was being mugged. It was so awful that, had it been an option, I would happily have handed over my wallet, phone, and credit cards to bring this persecution to an end.

The fighting did not stop even when the session was officially over. Now came the final struggle of the day; this one was against my own sweat-soaked suit. The first struggle was about controlling the legs, which was quite easy, but dominating the arms and shoulders was more difficult. Eventually, weary but victorious, I would rise to my feet and close the door of the washing machine.

3

TO WALK THE TALK

As I tangled with the technique of this strange business, as I struggled to understand its logic and its language, my curiosity grew. How did this collection of movements, of throws and holds, get discovered or invented? Where did it all come from? I also found myself wondering about the peculiar nature of fighting, or rather, as we must learn to think of it, "the attack-and-defense form of movement."

The journey I was about to make would take me to the training grounds of a strange worldwide warrior caste whose members pledge their allegiance to rival feuding states and dedicate their lives to the pursuit of gratuitous violence. Most people will do anything they can to avoid violence, yet the business of fighting fascinates them—even those who abhor it and hold it to be uncouth, depraved, or, at best, a bit tacky. Perhaps they feel like this because they don't like to be reminded about the embarrassing propensity for violence in their society and, worse, in themselves.

Most people probably accept that any atavistic urge to fight that they might possess has been forged by the need to survive. They accept that humans still have it in varying degrees, even now that they have abandoned their caves, drained the swamps, and chosen to farm instead of hunt. And perhaps they retain an abiding curiosity as to how this function in their repertoire of responses might serve them. They cannot help wondering how they might behave if they themselves *had* to fight for their survival: perhaps in some horrible street encounter or a war. All this leads people to that uneasy feeling famously identified by Samuel Johnson when he said, "Every man thinks meanly of himself for not having been a soldier."

You might ask, "Why does man run?" and conclude that once he had to do so in order to pursue prey or escape from predators or his enemies. Today, man runs when he doesn't have to because it gives him one hell of a buzz. This is also the reason that he likes to fight. Aggression is an immutable factor and is present in everyone, although in widely varying degrees. One can, for instance, find in *The Times* newspaper a first-person account by someone who confessed to having attacked a number of men over successive weekends in outbursts of systematic violence for no other reason than that it gave pleasure.[1] The correspondent was actually singing the praises of the pleasures of her local judo club and was the wife of a Church of England vicar. If this degree of aggression is simmering in our wisteria-covered vicarages, what on earth is happening everywhere else?

If there is some chemical compound called aggression sluicing around our systems, and it is A Bad Thing, then surely we need to have some way of disposing of this hazard before it starts burning holes in the fabric of society. In fact we have a number of methods; one of them is called sport. It seems reasonable to accept that in some way or other, sports are ritualized metaphorical tests of physical speed, strength, stamina, and skill—some of the qualities of survival so vital in the hunt for food and mates and the defeat of enemies.

One of the most widely used mechanisms in sport is an ingenious device designed to reduce and cushion violence between the combatants. It separates competitors from each other while still providing a test of athleticism and skill. This device is the ball. The ball serves as the cursor in this virtual reality combat. It is an ambassador, an interlocutor, rushing around between the opposing forces, absorbing the fury of the combatants. To varying degrees it permits individuals and groups to oppose each other without attacking each other.

Fighting is what happens when people keep on playing after you've taken away the ball.

Because combat is such a dramatic event, it is a favorite metaphor for describing conflict that is not physical: whether personal, commercial, or political. The boxing ring is one of the great cartoon clichés for the political contest, and our language is peppered with the jargon of combat. We *throw our hats into the ring*. We *wrestle with our consciences*, or *come to grips* with a problem. We say he has *fallen* for her and she has a terrible *hold* on him. The awful truth suddenly *hits* us.

Someone may be *thrown* by a question or *caught off balance* and find himself *fighting for his life*. Persuasion is *arm-twisting*; quarreling feminists are *mud wrestling*; and even in the process of manufacturing laughter—about as far as you can get from fighting—we talk about delivering a *punch* line. So-and-so may be a political *heavyweight*, but another may be a literary *lightweight*. We try to gain the *upper hand* and *get on top* of the situation. We often have to *take it on the chin*.

We might be *dealt a severe blow* or deem an unkind remark to be *below the belt*. We are *on the ropes* or even *down for the count*. We are *floored* by an awkward question or *knocked out* by a piece of music. We are *brought to our knees* and forced to *throw in the towel* if we are not *saved by the bell* to emerge *bloodied but unbowed*.

Sport may be a metaphor for the fight; the fight is a metaphor for life. Combat sports have a special edge. They replicate that moment when the running has to stop. You have caught up with your enemy or the beast, or they have caught up with you. It is the moment when the realities have to be addressed. You are on your own. When things are going badly, you can't pass the ball to a teammate. There is no one there but you. If you come out to face someone whom you know to be considerably superior, it is quite understandable that you might be anxious, alarmed, or even frightened.

It's just not like that in, say, tennis. Imagine playing against the best in the world, say Pete Sampras in his heyday. It is still nothing more than king-size Ping-Pong. However worrying his presence as a tennis opponent might be, and even though the netting that divides you is low enough for him to jump over, a Sampras will always remain at a healthy distance. He won't even use the ball to attack you—indeed his aim in almost all circumstances will be to prevent the ball coming anywhere near you. Play someone like that and your physical presence is scarcely required on the court, except to serve when it is your turn. For the rest of the time you are more or less superfluous to the requirements of the game.

However, when you come out to face Sampras's equivalent on the mat—a great international champion—the situation is somewhat different. You are the very medium in which your opponent works. Your body and your discomfort are the sine qua non of his artistry. He is a painter; you are his canvas. He is a sculptor; you are his clay. He is a pianist; you are the keys. And if he is Sampras, then you are not his opponent, you are the ball.

Whaaaaaaack!

Violence is exciting and we don't have to feel guilty about celebrating it. Certainly, it is central to the joy of fighting: You can no more fight without violence than you can play poker without real money. The word does not have to be pejorative. It cannot be confined to describing soccer-stadium thuggery, or brutal robbery and murder, or the sort of horror served up by entertainers like Quentin Tarantino and William Shakespeare. It can simply mean sudden or extreme movement—and that is the essence of many sports, including golf, soccer, and table tennis. And, if you think about it, tiddlywinks.

Violent movement exhilarates us partly because it departs from the norm. It is exaggeration and caricature. Violence is larger as well as faster than life.

If we do accept, then, that much of sport is the promotion of organized, controlled, and consensual violence, perhaps combat sports offer a more interesting, edgier kind of violence than that offered by ball games.

In one you play the ball, in the other you play the man. You are not merely demolishing his skill. You are demolishing the man. It is fun kicking and throwing a ball about. It's just that judoka think that it is more fun kicking and throwing people about. Cut out the middle man.

"That ball," a frustrated player will sometimes remark, "has a mind of its own." Not true. The ball has no mind of its own. It is completely dependent on you not only for its well-being and its accommodation, but for all its travel arrangements. The ball, moreover, remains implacably obedient to the laws of physics. Pick it up, throw it up in the air, bounce it on the floor: its reaction is more or less predictable.

Now conduct the same experiment with a person. When you throw it along the ground or up into the air it doesn't roll or bounce anywhere near as well or as high or as predictably as a ball. And this is largely because, provided you do not conduct the experiment too vigorously, a human emphatically *does* have a mind of its own.

You can always take a ball by surprise. A ball never takes evasive action—it doesn't seem to mind being kicked or thrown around.

Humans dislike being treated like this. When you go to kick or throw a human, it can do all sorts of unpredictable things. When you try to pick it up, it can get out of the way. Even as you are trying to throw it, it can pick you up and throw *you*. A ball is a less challenging target than a person. Have you ever see anyone thrown by a ball?

"Martial art means honestly expressing yourself," pronounced Bruce Lee, the American-born Chinese martial arts theorist and performer, who said some wise things even if he did make some daft movies. Violence is to ordinary movement what singing is to ordinary speech. It is more expressive. The range is wider; it uses the whole of the stave and more.

In one sense, fighting *is* a sort of talking, or arguing. "War is a continuation of politics by other means" is the most quoted aphorism of Clausewitz, the German military theorist. Personal combat, which is a microcosm of war, is a continuation of dialogue by other means. It is physical argument, argument conducted in a language of the body. And there are as many different levels of fighting as there are of talking. You can fight *with* someone just as you might go for a jog *with* someone rather than run *against* them. One may engage in a collaborative combat, which is not really a fight but an exercise. The purpose is purely to practice and perfect the movement or to warm up like tennis players knocking up before a match. There, the object is to keep the ball in play and make it possible for the other person to return it—the precise opposite of the game. This movement is shorn of competitiveness as well as adversity, but it's still tennis.

Combat, like conversation, may consist of friendly discussion, lively argument, or a heated exchange that may develop into something cruel and extremely unpleasant. As it is possible to talk for pleasure, for money, or for your life (the man in the witness chair being cross-examined about a crime that carries the death sentence is talking for his life), so it is possible to fight for these reasons.

All sport is an exercise in virtual reality. Some sports are less real than others. At one end of the spectrum one might group together pheasant shooting and boxercise as pastimes which allow people to enjoy a sense of martial activity without the risk or discomfort of retaliation—the object of attack does not hit back.

However, most sports are the result of an effort to produce the excitement generated by proper violent combat, but in a safe way—virtual fighting. Martial arts are by their very definition designed for war—to inflict disabling injury or death—and so some fighting systems are so dangerous that their combatants must either pad themselves or avoid full contact—which is to say that punches have to be pulled. They are thus unrealistic. In some forms of fighting there is no contact at all. Bruce Lee described noncontact fighting as "organized despair."[2]

Competitive contact combat presents physical risk. The significance of judo as a fighting system is that it allows realistic full contact violence to be enjoyed in enormous safety. It made its appearance in a place and at a time when it was most desperately needed. It was a response to a culture of "recreational" fighting and presented itself as a sport in which any concept of safety was entirely unknown.

4

THE CRUCIBLE

My chance to go to Japan for the first time and visit the birthplace of judo came in the autumn of 2003 when Osaka was the venue for the world championships. I was staying in a hotel within a half-hour walk of the stadium. Some walk: it took me right across the city's greatest park and through the middle of Osaka Castle. This is an awe-inspiring structure built in the 1580s. Its outer perimeter wall is two miles long and includes two concentric moats; in places the giant inner wall rises more than a hundred feet above the water. The whole structure is a jigsaw of large irregularly shaped stones. The largest of them are of Inca proportions and weigh more than ten tons. All the walls slope back from the vertical so that the masonry is less likely to be dislodged by earthquake, and each corner presents a curved concave profile as elegant as a trireme's bow. This fortress, now a picture of military might in repose, was in 1614 the subject of one of Japan's bloodiest sieges, which brought to an end a long period of feudal warfare. In the ranks of both the besiegers and the besieged were men who developed an art that was to evolve into a sport. It was this sport that I was about to watch as I hurried across the wooden bridge and made my way into the stadium through the gathering crowd.

The early days of that sport were not auspicious.

> In those days contests were extremely rough and not infrequently cost the participants their lives. Thus, whenever I sallied forth to take part in one

of these affairs, I invariably bade farewell to my parents since I had not assurance that I should ever return alive. Competitions were of such a drastic nature that few tricks were barred and we did not hesitate to have recourse to the most dangerous methods in order to overcome an opponent. I have had experiences of this kind without number.[1]

That was one speaker's description of jujitsu contests in Japan in the 1880s.

Jujitsu is a very broad term used to describe a way of fighting without weapons. (The Kodokan states, "Jujitsu can . . . be defined as various armed and unarmed fighting systems that can be applied against armed or unarmed enemies.") In case of serious conflict, humans have always liked to have at hand a weapon of some kind. The possibilities are countless: a rock, or a sharp and pointy length of steel, or a thermonuclear device. But sometimes the job has to be done with bare hands. What follows concerns only this one example of the many strands of unarmed combat that were developed in the East.

Some argue that the art of jujitsu was born in Japan; others believe its origins lie in China, where unarmed monks needed to devise a way of defending themselves. Whatever the case, in Japan this art found a soil in which it took root and a climate in which it could thrive.

Although the country was notionally ruled by an emperor, its geography defied any attempt at centralized control. The land, much divided by mountains, placed real power in the hands of the *daimyos,* the leaders of the clans that inhabited each valley. The feuding of these feudal lords produced four and a half centuries of near continuous warfare until the mid 1600s. These wars were conducted by an extraordinary warrior class, the samurai. From their numbers came the armies that the valley warlords employed in their struggles for land, for control of taxes, for dominance, and, ultimately, for the position of Shogun (the chief among the *daimyos*), who, rather than the emperor, was the true ruler of the country.

As the agents of power, the samurai were inevitably a much respected class in society. Distinguished by the right to wear two swords, these men were a caste apart, inheriting their position by birth. Part landowning gentlemen, part warriors, they were the equivalent of the knights who served the warring barons in medieval England. The samurai bore striking similarities to their European counterparts in that, as well as being skilled warriors, they followed a code of honor, *bushido*, which has, as in the case of chivalry and the medieval knight, made them the focus of much retrospective romanticism and sentiment.

Many aspects of the so-called "samurai tradition" were the product of the nostalgia of subsequent generations. In fact many of the lower-caste samurai were little better than thugs, although it is true to say that the best of them were cultivated men with a strong Buddhist aesthetic, who might be poets as well as swordsmen. They had a disdain for the vulgar and a respect for gentlemanliness; they appreciated quiet restraint and despised the noisy braggart. Along with their finely tuned Confucian-inspired sense of loyalty to their lord, codes of honor, and soldierly cold-blooded ruthlessness, they pursued a monkish asceticism: a commitment to self-sacrifice and suppression of ego. Also possessing a Zen-driven zest for aesthetics, for style, they were in both the ancient and modern sense "cool."

All these qualities they brought to their martial studies. Because his job and, indeed, his life, depended on it, it was in the interest of every samurai to study well the art of fighting, and over three hundred years they developed more than twenty forms, from swordsmanship to foot and horseback archery to fighting with spear and lance. Among them was jujitsu, which they developed so that they could survive in battle if they were disarmed.

The samurai discovered and refined systems of disabling their opponents using combinations of grappling, throwing, kicking, and punching. They learned how to use the fist, elbow, heel, and kneecap, and they studied the most effective ways to chop, choke, and strangle, and how best to twist and break limb joints.

From around the 1550s—just before Elizabeth I came to the English throne—this branch of knowledge began to take a clear shape. Every warlord had specialist instructors among his army who developed and taught the techniques, each in his own way. To practice their various arts, the samurai established halls called dojos, either in their own quarters or in their lord's castle grounds. Some dojos were run by their lord, others were private family businesses.

Dojos were frequently housed in temples, because these were often the only establishments large enough to accommodate them. Temples were complexes rather than single structures and not only offered a place to pray but, like the church hall in Christendom, served as the venue for all sorts of community meetings and social events. The word *dojo* in Buddhism describes the temple's inner compound and means a place (*jo*) to follow the way (*do*). Such a location added an undercurrent of spirituality that seems to suffuse some dojos even now.

The wooden floors of the halls used for jujitsu were covered with mats made of woven rice straw and called *tatami,* the same kind as used in homes. The master of the dojo had a special authority. He was a teacher, even a preacher, and he was the ruler. All who stepped onto his tatami became his subjects. The status of the jujitsu master commanded deep respect and obedience.

Under these masters, each school of jujitsu developed its own method, which emphasized different skills and techniques—some preferred striking, others throwing or grappling. Each school kept careful and secret records and instruction manuals for all their martial arts called *densho,* which are still to be seen today.

One of the principles that recurs in many of the samurai's written teachings is contained in the phrase "In yielding is strength," a central tenet of a Chinese book on strategy regarded as the bible of Japan's feudal warriors.[2] While the *jitsu* part of the term means simply the *art* or *practice, ju* is a Chinese character meaning *pliable, gentle, harmonious,* or *yielding*.[3] So the term gives us the apparently contradictory notion of "harmonious combat," "gentle fighting," or "yielding aggression"—and it is this notion that would become the very essence of judo.

Jujitsu, meanwhile, was not confined to the samurai, but developed in parallel in other parts of society. Prison warders and policemen, for instance, also studied the art and developed it in their own way so that they could restrain people without killing them. And because commoners were forbidden to carry swords, they too needed jujitsu for their own protection, and so the art became a means of self-defense on the street as well as the battlefield. This all-in, kicking, punching, grappling style became the weaponless fighting vernacular of Japan.

Aspects of the samurai's tradition such as their Zen-ish concern with detail and style are still present today. The Japanese are a people who have turned the simple act of drawing a sword or making a cup of tea into a protracted ritual requiring years of study and practice. The idea is that the teacher's unrelenting demands for infinite precision make everything as difficult as possible for his pupil; the process crushes his pride and his ego, allowing his subconscious to take over and absorb the learning. While most jujitsu schools would have concentrated on the technical and the practical, this highly philosophical approach to their art did inform their training, even if it prevailed in only a few. And when we come to see how Japan teaches today's new generations of judo players, we will find that, after nearly half a millennium, some are still carrying on like this.

At the beginning of the seventeenth century, Japanese history took an extraordinarily dramatic turn. Centuries of almost uninterrupted warfare gave way to two hundred and fifty years of almost uninterrupted peace. The struggle between warlords ended with the victory of Ieyasu Tokugawa at the climactic siege of Ooaka in 1614. The land was united under the then-Shogun, who ruled it from Edo, now modern Tokyo, which was eventually to replace Kyoto as the capital. While the deadly alliance of salt-peter, sulphur, and charcoal had a drastic effect on the old feudal military structures in Western Europe, gunpowder had minimal bearing on events in Japan because the Shogunate accomplished the considerable feat of virtually stopping technological progress dead in its tracks.

Firearms and cannons were brought to the Japanese islands by Portuguese voyagers in 1542.[4] The weapons wrought havoc and transformed the ritualized sword and arrow warfare of the day. But, ever fearful of rebellion, successive powerful rulers placed severely enforced limits on the manufacture and distribution of cannons and firearms; they also restricted to the samurai the right to bear arms.

And almost more than rebellion they feared Christendom. Having seen the Philippines succumb to a Western conquest pre-saged by the arrival of missionaries, in 1638 the Shogun ordered the massacre of more than thirty thousand Japanese Christian converts who had rebelled, banned almost all foreigners from Japan's shores, and forbade all Japanese from leaving. Japan's retreat from the age of gunpowder, and indeed the rest of the world, was complete. And, extraordinarily, so it remained for the next two hundred and fifty years. Their feudal age continued almost without modification.

The Shogun, anxious about the threat of rebellion posed by the samurai, ordered them to decide between staying on their estates and becoming farmers, or remaining as warriors and moving into the castle towns that served as the seats of regional government. The eighteenth and nineteenth centuries were the era of the great peace of the Tokugawa dynasty: the warriors had no wars to fight. A rich tradition of sword dueling developed, but martial studies were unprompted by emergency; many of the samurai became administrators, and the lower-caste merchant class now began to prosper. It is unclear how rigorously the art of jujitsu was tested during this time, but it is reasonable to assume that, although it was a minor art in a warrior's repertoire, there would also have been contests, however informal, as schools of unarmed combat challenged one another.

While the West possesses a wealth of prints and manuals for fencing, it never achieved the sophistication of the East in unarmed combat where, notably in Japan, martial arts had been studied and developed to an extraordinary degree. By the middle of the nineteenth century, 725 jujitsu systems had been documented.[5]

In the course of a summer's day in 1853, an event occurred that was to mark the beginning of the end of the old Japan: the arrival on July 8 in Tokyo Bay of a squadron of U.S. naval ships under the command of Commodore Matthew Perry, sent by the government with instructions to forge commercial links with Japan. The ensuing decade of trade and contact had a transforming effect on the isolated nation.

The door to the West was open again and many in Japan, feeling this fresh new breeze, grew curious about the possibilities of a different kind of civilization; they became conscious of their primitivism and were now weary of it. Some of the regions rebelled against the old feudal order. The Shogun resigned and, in 1868, power reverted to the emperor, Mutsuhito.

The Meiji period, meaning "clear government," spelled the end of the influence of its warrior class who, with their families, now numbered two million out of a population of thirty-four million.

While many of the samurai class had become administrators and were part of the enlightened era, the prospects for some samurai in Meiji Japan were about as promising as those of a master of foxhounds in postmillennial Britain. Nothing symbolized their decline more than a decree issued in 1871. The final ignominy of the samurai was to be publicly neutered: they were forbidden to wear their swords. In the new era, whatever was "traditional" was decried, because it represented the bad old days, while anything "foreign" was good, because it stood for modernity

As the samurai's prestige ebbed, the great schools in the clan capitals began to close, precipitating a speedy decline in all martial arts. Many of the low-ranking samurai faced ruin. Some became _ronin_—unemployed samurai—who often lived as outlaws, terrorizing and plundering towns and villages. Many jujitsu practitioners drifted away and the art that they taught became for the most part the preserve of thugs, criminals, and the psychotically inclined.

It is not entirely clear into which category Sakujiro Yokoyama fell. He is the man whose words opened our story with his account of the dreadful jujitsu contests of the period following the Meiji restoration. His observations were recorded by an English journalist called E. J. Harrison, who arrived in Japan in 1897 and lived, worked, and practiced jujitsu there at intervals for the next twenty years.

Yokoyama told Harrison how in his youth, he and his friends from his jujitsu club used to test their skills on the toughs who would persecute innocent passersby in a rough area of Tokyo. Their favorite trick was to dislocate the jaws of these miscreants, which rendered them speechless and caused them considerable pain. The entertainment of Yokoyama's gang was prolonged because jujitsu masters, by dint of necessity, had over the years developed a sideline as bonesetters, so the injured would appear at their dojo the next day for treatment. "Often as many as half a dozen victims would require the services of our teacher," reported Yokoyama, "and we would thus have the pleasure of examining at close quarters the effect of our skill, which added to the zest of these nocturnal adventures."

Yokoyama, who went on to become one of the greatest jujitsu fighters of his time, was to play a crucial role in the development of judo. We shall meet him again. Although jujitsu reached its social nadir at this point, it continued to develop as a practical science. The police and armed forces needed it and so persevered in its study, preserving the knowledge. Meanwhile, the decline and closure of the once secretive and introverted clan schools had the effect of scattering their learning. In the absence of _daimyo_-imposed discipline, there was brawling and staged fights between rival dojos and systems. It was a brutal but instructive melting pot, a crucible for the development of ideas. Techniques could be tried and tested to destruction in a vast laboratory where the crash-test dummies were always human. A fine art had been reduced to a brutal skill. Contests, as we have seen, could be disastrous for an injured loser who, if still alive, might have to be carried off to his village to linger as a useless cripple and a burden to his family. The samurai's code of honor had faded—only the violence was left. Unemployed fighters strutted along the streets, at best searching for glory in combat in an age hell-bent on repudiating it, at worst provoking fights and bullying the weak.

Into this brutal and semicriminal milieu stepped the slight and sickly figure of a well-to-do schoolboy who, just as everyone was abandoning it, had his own desperate reason for learning jujitsu. His name was Jigoro Kano.

THE INCREDIBLE DR. KANO

Bullies can affect their victims in varying ways. Some children crumple into introversion; some can appease their tormentors by distracting them, for instance, by making them laugh; others learn to fight back. As a schoolboy, Jigoro Kano was engaged in a desperate quest to learn how to do just that.

He was born in 1860, the second son of a wealthy couple, in a seaside village that is now part of the city of Kobe. Jigoro's mother died when he was nine and his father, a businessman with interests in a shipping company and a sake brewery, moved with the two boys to Tokyo. In the new Meiji era, Kano senior was very much in the vanguard of those adopting the new outward-looking attitude, and he sent Jigoro to prestigious and modern private schools. There Jigoro studied English, which was unusual at the time. At thirteen years of age, he went to a smart boarding school staffed by European and American teachers who conducted lessons in English and German. There he was one of the first Japanese to play baseball.

Although a conscientious and successful student—or perhaps for those very reasons—the young Kano was frequently bullied. The humiliation inflicted upon him by his tormentors would frequently leave him distraught and in tears, but he derived some hope from a conversation with one of the regular visitors to the Kano household, a now-swordless samurai who had once been a member of the Shogun's guard. He told the boy about the art called jujitsu that enabled a weaker man to overcome a stronger opponent. Kano was fascinated by the techniques that he demonstrated and begged the man to become his teacher. The visitor refused, arguing that it was an art whose time had ended with the passing of the samurai and not a subject for study by a well-educated young man.

Even after he arrived at the most prestigious seat of learning in the country, Tokyo Imperial University, Kano's troubles with bullies persisted, and he became more determined to find someone who would teach him how to defend himself. When he learned that many former jujitsu teachers now earned their living as bonesetters, he began to search throughout Tokyo for their signs. Eventually he tracked down a man called Fukuda who, next to his treatment room, had a small matted area which by day served as a waiting room for his patients and by night as a dojo where he instructed a handful of students. Fukuda agreed to teach Kano.

It was a hard and painful introduction. Fukuda's method was to throw a student repeatedly until he understood the technique. The classes would have been tough for anybody, but for this little rich boy, small and weak, training alongside experienced students, it must have been a particularly gruelling experience. Nevertheless he persevered, seldom missing a session, conscientiously studying and practicing the techniques.

As he progressed, Kano found that when it came to free fighting practice, *randori,* he could cope with most of the students. But there was one, Fukushima, who was over sixty pounds heavier than Kano and whom he could never throw. Kano's approach to learning was never passive. He sought the help of a retired sumo wrestler working in the university canteen who taught him some throws, but none of them had any effect on Fukushima. Then, as he scoured the library for a solution, he found in a book about Western styles of wrestling something that he thought might work. He first practiced it on a friend in secret, then refined it on some of the other students. When he was confident, he asked Fukushima for a practice. It is recorded that the dojo shook when the big man hit the mat. In the West the throw is known colloquially as the fireman's carry; Kano named it *kata guruma* (shoulder wheel).

Then in the summer of 1879 Kano's teacher Fukuda died.[1] His widow revealed that her husband had wanted Kano to take over the running of the dojo after his death. She handed to him the secret papers containing all the techniques of the school and Kano, a mere nineteen-year-old university student, became the master of the dojo.

Although he was in charge, Kano was only too aware that he still had much to learn about his art, and the next few years were spent in finding other masters who would teach him. By now he was more familiar with Tokyo's jujitsu milieu and the task was easier than before. From new teachers he absorbed learning from the different schools of jujitsu. The more Kano learned, the more his curiosity grew. He read voraciously and practiced what he learned. He sought out books on every kind of martial art and fighting form, in the West as well as the East. He began to appreciate the ingenuity and subtlety and the devastating effectiveness of some of the techniques and schools of thought, just as he realized the inadequacies of others. He began to understand what worked and to reject what didn't. He realized that many schools had good techniques, but that these had been developed in jealously guarded isolation to maintain the purity of each school's style. There was no *general* body of knowledge.

An ambition began to form in Kano's mind. He would create his own system, a new form that combined the best from each school.

To do this he needed his own laboratory—a school of his own to which he could take all the disparate learning and develop it. In February of 1882, Kano, now twenty-two years old and newly graduated as a literature teacher, moved his jujitsu class to the Eishoji temple in the northeast of Tokyo. Temples still functioned as centers for secular activities and here he was able to rent some rooms to accommodate himself, his first intake of nine students, and a tiny dojo, which he named the Kodokan (the place for teaching the way).

Kano's independence and keenness to learn about other schools of jujitsu gradually began to impress many of his rivals, who recognized that he was committed to perpetuating their knowledge even though no one else valued it. Several jujitsu masters handed to him the scrolls that contained the secrets of their schools.

Hard though it is to believe, Kano's lifelong work in martial arts was never anything more than a part-time interest pursued alongside a full-time career as a teacher and educationalist. He was to become the headmaster of several schools and the principal of the country's main teacher training college. In the year that he founded his own dojo, he was appointed teacher of politics and economics at Gakushuin, a private school for the nobility. That year he also started two schools of his own: an English-language school and a private preparatory boarding school. With all this, young Kano was establishing himself as a modernist in the teaching profession. His schools came to place increasing emphasis on character building, for he had been much influenced by the writings of Western educationalists.

Kano's twin commitment to education and martial arts must have tested his stamina to the limit. Having spent the day teaching at one or more of his schools, the evenings were devoted to jujitsu, after which he would have to prepare for his classes for the following day, and then do English translation work to make much-needed extra money to finance his schools and his dojo. This mentally and physically exhausting regime may go some way to explaining why economy of effort became such a theme in his life and his teaching.

Week by week, Kano was putting together his ideas for his fighting system, testing and refining them. His dojo was a laboratory. The students were his guinea pigs, made to swear a blood oath not to divulge the techniques to outsiders. As a further precaution, he wrote his detailed notes in a special code, whose strange symbols were arranged not only in reverse order across the page but horizontally instead of vertically. This code was indecipherable to all but a very few: those who could read the English language.

Kano loved jujitsu. But he loved it for its excitement and for the demands it made upon him. He was all too aware of the physical transformation it had wrought upon his once weak frame: he was stronger, healthier, and had more stamina. He was equally aware of the mental change the discipline had brought in stimulating his determination and defining his attitude to life. The teacher within him could see that it was character-forming. He discerned that it was a real discipline with an application to everyday life that could bring real benefit to his pupils.

Above all that, Kano saw an aesthetic in combat. He was later to write:

> We are all aware of the pleasurable sensation given to the nerves and muscles through exercise, and we also feel pleasure at the attainment of skill, in the use of our muscles, and also through the sense of superiority over others in contest. But besides these pleasures there is that love of beauty and delight in it derivable from assuming graceful attitudes and performing graceful movements and also in seeing such in others.[2]

But this well-mannered scion of the bourgeoisie loathed the prevailing ethic of jujitsu—one of brutal kicks, strikes, joint locks that so often caused injury, and occasionally death. He hated the way the aesthetic was vanishing from this form of combat; it no longer expressed the beauty that he believed lay within it. He was also disgusted by what he regarded as the "prostitution of the art by *ju-jitsu* masters who made money from promoting prize fights between *ju-jitsu* men or between *ju-jitsu* men and professional sumo fighters."[3]

Worse still, some instructors were teaching their skills to criminals. Kano wanted his system of jujitsu to rise above all this and allow people to rejoice in physical exertion and beautiful movement. He wanted to revive a dying art, believing that it could serve as a moral and intellectual discipline as well as a physical one. But at its most basic, it had to be effective. It was designed to prevail in competition against its rivals even while the school promoted an approach to competition that was to be safe, controlled, and in a spirit of sportsmanship. Kano placed two maxims at the center of all his judo teaching: "Maximum efficiency for expended effort" and "Mutual welfare and benefit for all."

As Kano tested and refined this wisdom, he identified a number of principles that lay behind all successful techniques and that were to become the constants that informed his whole system of fighting. One of the sport's official historians once wrote that judo was not an invention, but rather a distillation of existing wisdom.

The dominating principle that Kano believed lay at the heart of the art was that an opponent's strength should be used to defeat him. If your opponent is stronger than you and pushes against you, however hard you resist, you will be pushed back or pushed over. But if you give way and keep your balance, your opponent will come forward off balance, and in that moment will be weaker than you. The art is to create and exploit that moment. Kano also argued that even if you are stronger than your opponent, it is better to give way and use this principle of breaking balance, *kuzushi*.

An essential element of the old samurai jujitsu matches was the principle of sudden death, designed to simulate the reality of battle. Although fights had a time limit, they could always be brought to an earlier conclusion if one of the combatants achieved domination by throwing or trapping on the ground—a situation which in real combat would prove fatal to the loser. There had to be a symbolic death—a rule of "one strike and you're out"—to keep a real edge in the fighting. A single mistake could be "fatal." This symbolic death was also a death to the ego, and Kano believed that overcoming this "death" developed the practitioner's character.

In combat, speed and conservation of energy are crucial, and the principle of efficiency is a recurring theme in Kano's work. Some might say it was an obsession, for he insisted on applying efficiency to every aspect of life. Seeing the maids in his house pummeling the wet soapy clothes with their fists in the traditional way, he felt the method could be improved. One day he gave them a lesson, teaching them to use the straight edge of their hand with the thumbs turned in, in a sort of karate chop. Later, when they had mastered that, he taught them how to use their whole body to increase the force of the blow. He deemed it more effective.[4]

Perhaps this obsession had its origins in the arduous schedule that he had to keep to be a schoolteacher by day and a jujitsu master by night, but he certainly made great claims for its importance. The efficient use of mind and body, he said, was the key to self-fulfillment.[5] He closed the rowing club of one school at which he taught because pupils had to travel for so long to reach a lake that he deemed it an inefficient way for them to get exercise.[6] But his concern for efficiency lay in something beyond the practical. Efficiency, as we shall see, creates an aesthetic. And for Kano the aesthete, the lover of graceful dance, flowing calligraphy, and subtle music, it was important that fighting, too, should be beautiful.

Kano's vision went beyond the mere practicality of jujitsu technique. As an educator he believed this martial art could be part of a pupil's moral and spiritual development. The idea that the well-being of the mind and body were inextricably linked had long been prevalent in the Far East, and Kano certainly subscribed to it. "A healthy body," he wrote, "is a condition not only necessary for existence but as a foundation for mental and spiritual activities." He saw education in a way that would now be called holistic: defining its purpose as enabling a pupil to gain knowledge, morality, and physical training.

One characteristic that marked out Kano's school was that his form of fighting was safer and cleaner than those of other jujitsu schools, which practiced dangerous throws and limb twists and seemed little more than places for sanctioned bullying. Kano rejected any techniques that might result in injury, which he regarded as no cause for macho pride but rather as an interruption to time spent training. What was the point of fighting to the point of an injury that prevented you from continuing to fight?

Closely allied with this is the art of "breakfall," a particular innovation of Kano's. Breakfall techniques allowed a student to be thrown without getting hurt. The trick is to tuck in the chin to protect the neck and to adjust the body in midair and smack the mat with one or both palms at the moment of landing, which has the effect of intercepting the shock and dispersing the impact over a wider area. An ability to breakfall gives a judoka the confidence and courage to risk being thrown and to cope with life after sudden death. If you were thrown, you had to get up and be prepared to be thrown again. "Seven times thrown, eight times rise."

A degree of hostility would seem to be implicit in the action of "fighting." Kano sought to strip it out. He saw fighting as merely another form of movement, one which he called "the attack-and-defense form." And these movements, while being executed with the utmost speed and effort, might be fueled by aggression, but not by antagonism. For this reason Kano wanted his jujitsu kept off the street and confined to the dojo. He punished any student who got into a fight in a public place.

Judo is generally considered a product entirely of the East, but in fact the West made a vital and sizable contribution to it. Kano was interested in Western sports including running, rowing, and gymnastics, and when he played baseball at his school he reportedly said that he "loved the spirit of the sport."[7] All these ideas helped to create the ethos he sought for judo.

Kano said he chose the name judo because what he taught was not just *jitsu,* "art" or "practice," but because he wanted to stress *do,* "way" or "principle." He wrote: "Judo is more than an art of attack and defense. It is a way of life." He chose the name of his system with all the skill and shrewdness of a successful modern marketing man. He wanted to position judo in the marketplace in such a way that it would be seen as clearly different from the other existing jujitsu schools, which were generally regarded as violent and dangerous places, where bullying was rife and injury frequent.

Judo was in tune with the prevailing mood of change in Japan. In the new era, feudal harshness was being rejected and something gentler was sought. There was a spirit of inquiry and innovation: a will to search for the efficacious, a desire to experiment, a fascination with the modern and therefore the foreign. Kano's system exploited all this. He was also careful to make sure judo was taught with the clear aim of appealing to a wide public. Realizing that the dull repetition of formal exercises as taught in the old jujitsu schools discouraged students, Kano ensured that the Kodokan taught the basics quickly and got the students fighting (which is to say sparring in *randori*) as soon as possible, because that was what they had come for and that was what always engaged and excited them.

Word of what was happening in Kano's dojo spread fast. When people from other schools came to the Kodokan to see for themselves, they were soon convinced of the efficacy of Kano's fighting form. The new adherents recognized in Kano a true master—a leader and an organizer, and also a conservationist who might preserve their arts for future generations. So they came to his dojo, bringing their knowledge and their techniques, which, if worthy, were absorbed into the repertoire of Kano's judo.

With success came jealousy. Some senseis of the old school resented the new kid on the mat. It's easy to see why. Here was Kano, who had removed the dangerous stuff from jujitsu—the blood, the guts, and the gristle—and now he was serving up his namby-pamby vegetarian version and going on like a dopey monk with his talk of perfecting oneself and contributing to the welfare of the world. All this would have been anathema to the fight-scarred, hard men of the old jujitsu schools, who just wanted to tear each other's limbs off. But, of course, what really angered Kano's rivals in the backstreet dojos was the awkward truth that the Kodokan people were a formidable bunch, and their system was superior. They knew because they had tested it often enough. Tradition dictated that anyone could walk into a school and issue a challenge; because this was a frequent occurrence at the Kodokan, Kano made sure that one of the best fighters was always on hand. It frequently fell to Sakujiro Yokoyama, whom we have already met, to carry out this duty. Yokoyama was one of Kano's four most accomplished students, who were known as the Heavenly Lords. The doughty young veteran always won, and gradually the little school overcame conservative thinking among the old jujitsu fraternity by demonstrating that *new* didn't mean *soft*.

The Tokyo Metropolitan Police Board had always valued jujitsu as an essential part of their training. In 1886, when they were wondering how to update their syllabus, they considered what contribution might be made by Kano's Kodokan judo. Although they were impressed by it, they still weren't entirely convinced that it was as effective as the best of traditional jujitsu. In the summer of 1886, they decided to put it to the test. They invited the top jujitsu school and the Kodokan each to send fifteen men to the shrine in Shiba Park to compete against each other in a tournament.

The result was an overwhelming victory for Kano's stable of fighters. They won twelve of the matches, lost two, and drew one, a victory so convincing that it established once and for all the supremacy of judo over all the jujitsu schools.

Kano now did all he could to promote and protect the Kodokan brand. He sent his representatives to every region of Japan giving lectures and demonstrations, which usually ended with a contest between the lecturer and a local challenger.[8] The judo man always won and the new system gradually took root all over the country. But Kano's ambitions were not circumscribed by the borders of Japan. As an educator, he wanted to study Western schools at first hand; besides, he had international aspirations for his beloved judo. And so, on September 13, 1889, he climbed on board the ocean liner *Caledonian,* bound for Europe.[9]

Kano's child, born in a temple and raised on a rice mat, had now grown into a healthy youth and, in the company of its proud parent, was about to begin its travels around the world.

Dr. Kano's Kodokan rules for his version of jujitsu brought a new, safer kind of fighting to Japan in the same way that the Queensberry Rules, introduced some two decades earlier in 1867, did for boxing in England. Both the Marquess of Queensberry and Dr. Kano transformed their sports, making them cleaner and safer. One man took the grappling out of boxing; the other took the boxing out of grappling. One worked with a padded fist; the other with a padded floor. In the latter years of the nineteenth century, the martial histories of Eastern and Western civilization had reached a point at which two men at opposite ends of the globe produced, within a few years of each other, the rules that were to herald unarmed combat's own age of enlightenment.

6

BEAUTY AND THE BEAST

What is judo? What is the point of it? One woman who used to train at the Budokwai told me how she had once brought her father, a former professional boxer, to watch an evening session at the club. Apparently, after he had stood there for some time staring around him at the tangle of white-clad figures spinning and tumbling around, he turned to her and, raising his hands in a gesture of deep incomprehension, said, "It's like . . . laundry!"

As it knows to its cost, judo is a bewildering spectacle for anyone who has never practiced it—and even for quite a few who have. Indeed, it *is* a bit like staring at a washing machine as it goes through the cycle—rinse, tumble dry, and spin. There is a lot of pushing and pulling, twirling and whirling, ducking and diving, and a lot of dancing around. Someone said, "They who dance are thought mad by those who do not hear the music." So what *is* the music? What is going on here?

Judo is a beauty; judo is a beast. It's like ballet in that the character of the spectacle depends on where you sit. From the back of the dress circle, you can clearly see the grand patterns of the choreographer's creation as the dancers in the corps move without effort or sound. Down in the front stalls you see the girls sweating and their rib cages heaving as their lungs fight for air. When they are still you can see their white limbs trembling under extreme pressure, and when they move you can hear, over the sound of the orchestra, those dainty little feet thundering like bison in a panic on the prairie.

Judo is similar: From the back of the stadium, a contest looks clean and crisp, the fighters sweeping and arcing through the air, creating something quite graceful and beautiful. Down here in the matside seats it's a mêlée of grazed cheekbones, bandaged feet, disheveled jackets, and sweating and gasping. But one can sense the intensity of the effort and, more important, something of the mechanics of the business.

Judo evolved from a martial arts tradition that was about fighting on a battlefield against opponents who were fully clothed, so combatants wear a *judogi*, an approximation of a traditional Japanese jacket. The use of the jacket does for grappling what the introduction of the stirrup, for instance, did for horsemanship, the keel did for sailing, and the parabolic ski did for skiing. All these devices secure extra purchase, which brings increased control, which leads to more maneuverability, which presents more choice, and therefore the opportunity of applying more skill. A jacket multiplies the possibilities for attack and transforms fighting from the narrow business of wrestling into something altogether more varied and subtle.

Imagine two suitcases placed upright in front of you, each of which you have to pick up and throw flat upon the floor. One has a handle, the other one doesn't. The difference in how you carry out this task is the essence of the difference between judo and wrestling. The collar and sleeves of the jacket and the belt provide handles for seizing an opponent and gaining the momentum needed to whip him off his feet and turn him in midair, before bringing him in to land flat on his back.

Judo acknowledges that an opponent who is on balance and rooted to the floor is very hard to throw. But he becomes vulnerable once he is on the move. The idea is to make him move in such a way that his body acquires a momentum of its own, which you can then use. Once the weight is moving, the task is to keep it moving and, suddenly, to configure one's body accordingly to make the throw. "Action; reaction" is the instructor's familiar mantra.

The judoka's pull is the boxer's punch. Just as a boxer will use smaller jabs to set up his opponent for a big punch, so a judo player will use a combination of pulls and footsweeps to get his opponent in the right position for the big pull which will evolve into the throw. In this, judo is the opposite to much conventional fighting. It is not about applying strength but about giving way to strength that is the trick: thus *ju do,* "the giving way," "the yielding way."

The European writer Lafcadio Hearn, who encountered judo in Japan at the end of the nineteenth century, contemplated its concepts with the awed tones of an explorer staring around him in an extraordinary and undiscovered land. "What Western brain could have elaborated this strange teaching, never to oppose force by force, but only direct and utilize the power of attack; to overthrow the enemy solely through his own strength, to vanquish him solely by his own efforts? Surely none! The Western mind appears to work in straight lines; the Oriental, in wonderful curves and circles."[1]

A judo contest may be dramatic, but it is not theatrical. There is a bit of bowing at the beginning and end, but it's short and businesslike. Contests have none of the preamble of sumo, none of the hunkering down, eyeballing the enemy, getting up, waddling around in a circle, scooping up the rice, throwing the rice around, flipping those weird licorice sticks, hunkering down, eyeballing the enemy, getting up . . . perhaps sumo needs this ritual partly to pad out the entertainment because the fights are so short: the eyeballing and rice-chucking last longer than the fighting.

And judo has none of the noise, the poise, or the pose of, for instance, karate, whose players hold their hands like fencers' and shriek when they launch a strike. Judoka approach each other in a looser, less stylized stance. Their movements are economical and businesslike.

While a novice spectator can roughly follow what's going on in a soccer match, even the basic plot of a judo contest is incredibly hard for most people to read. Much of the time nothing seems to be happening while, in fact, a vehement struggle for grips is taking place, the nuances of which are invisible to the untutored eye. Only a judoka can read it, let alone appreciate it.

And it all happens at the most extraordinary speed. Pete Sampras may serve the ball at 117 miles per hour or more, which means that it reaches the other end of the court quite quickly, but that is still plenty of time for at least two or three actions to occur in judo. In soccer it takes a long time for the ball to travel from the goalmouth at one end of the pitch and through the posts at the other, but in judo such a complete reversal of fortune can happen in the space of a blink—as we shall see when we come to follow the fate of Britain's greatest male champion, Neil Adams, at the Los Angeles Olympics.

In order to understand the work of Adams and the other champions whom we'll encounter, it will help to have at least an outline of a job description. Their task is to win contests governed by an extensive set of rules and measured by a peculiar scoring system, both of which have been steadily changing over the years.

A contestant secures victory in three ways: by a throw, by a hold-down, or by securing a submission from a strangle or an armlock.

THE THROW: If a throw lands the opponent clearly and firmly on his back, with the key elements of speed, force, and control, the referee awards *ippon*. That's the equivalent of a knockout, and the contest ends immediately. If he lands on his back with one of those key elements missing, the score is *waza-ari*. Those were the only scores until the mid 1960s, when two smaller scores were introduced. If player throws someone slightly on his side, that is worth only *yuko*; and if he is merely knocked onto his backside or thighs, it's a *koka*. The more valuable score always wins. So even if a contestant scores just one *waza-ari*, he will still beat his opponent who has three *yukos*.

THE HOLD-DOWN: *Ippon* is awarded if a contestant holds his opponent on his back for twenty-five seconds.

THE SUBMISSION: *Ippon* is awarded if a contestant applies an armlock or strangle and the opponent submits by tapping more than once.

Penalty points are awarded for passivity (failure to attack or being excessively defensive) and other rule infringements, such as attacking the face or threatening the spine.

It used to be the case that if the scores were level at the end of the contest, the referee and his two judges would vote and award victory to the contestant who had been the more dominant and aggressive. Now, the contest resumes for a further period and the first person to gain any score wins.

The seemingly arcane scoring system is based on the reality of a fight on a hard surface. If a person just gets knocked down five times, he would probably get up. If he gets thrown really hard and is knocked out or badly injured in the process, he would not.

TA-KA-TA. WHOOSH. SPLAT! That is the sound of judo. There may be no karate-style shouting, but judoka emit a number of involuntary gasps, grunts, screams, and that terrible yelp of someone who realizes they've been caught. But mostly it's *ta-ka-ta. Whoosh. Splat!*

The *ta-ka-ta* is the sound of the feet skeetering in for a throw—a high-speed waltz of a movement that rearranges the feet to carry the body around to face the other way and to drop low under the opponent. Next comes the *whoosh*. You can think of it in the same way as the comic-book accompaniment to the path of the hero's fist en route to the villain's chin. The *whoosh* is the noise of a judoka's flight as, very suddenly and much against his will, he is taken off his toes, forward, and up with fantastic acceleration, until he reaches the top of the arc. Then he begins to dive and turn in the air, doing a corkscrew roll.

Then it's *splat!* The body now hurtling upside down through the air smacks onto the mat. Sometimes it isn't *splat*; it is more of a *splaaaarrggh*. But when it has been done right it is like a pistol shot. Or maybe it's more like that sound you can hear all around the Mediterranean when a fisherman, to tenderize the tough, rubbery flesh of an octopus, puts his fingers inside its maw and whacks the tentacles with all his might on the stone of the quay. *Splat!*

IN ORDER TO MAKE COMBAT more humane, wise men of the world produced pages and pages of something called the Geneva Conventions. For exactly the same reason, the International Judo Federation (IJF), the governing body of the sport, has produced reams of rules. One of the essential differences between them is that the IJF document sanctions the use of torture while the Geneva Conventions emphatically do not.

In fact, judo is the only sport that not only sanctions torture but encourages it. One way in which a contestant can win is to force his opponent to submit. He does this by applying pressure to an elbow or the neck, which is to say by bending his opponent's elbow against the joint or by strangling or choking him to such an extent that he cannot stand what dentists prefer to call "discomfort," and the rest of us call pain. So when someone goes out to face a formidable opponent in a contest, his subconscious will be aware that this man not only wants to bang him on the floor, but also wants to be in a position to hurt him.

This gives judo a certain edge that is absent in other sports, but it also inclines outsiders to see it as a shade sadistic or sadomasochistic. This isn't justified. As soon as someone secures an armlock from which there is no escape, and the pain becomes unacceptable, the victim can choose immediately to tap twice in quick succession to signal his submission. This happens so fast that the pain is nothing more than a stab, and many sensibly tap even before the lock comes on properly, although it must be said that in serious competition an entirely different attitude prevails.

Judo is actually a great deal less painful than, say, long-distance running and cycling. Events such as the London Marathon or the Tour de France are long-drawn-out festivals of agony. Here competitors apply pain indirectly on each other; the harder the leading cyclist pedals, the more pain he inflicts on his rivals. We must be clear about this: it is not mere exertion they are experiencing; it is pain. And unlike judo, where any pain is momentary, these other events prolong the suffering for hours or even days. The winner is the person who can endure the most pain.

So, to set the record straight: judo permits torture, but does not insist on pain.

IF WE ACCEPT the proposition that fighting is arguing without words, then judo is one of the languages of fighting in which you may converse. It is a complete language with a vocabulary of verbs, nouns, adjectives, and adverbs. It has its own grammar and syntax. It even has its own regional variations of pronunciation.

The language is, for the most part, deployed in the form of an argument between two people. True, it is a limited argument in which each speaker asserts the proposition "I am better at judo than you are." It is not one of those polite discussions in which you take turns to speak; it is a less well-mannered one in which each tries constantly to interrupt the other to prevent them from having their say. The basic object of the language of judo is to render your opponent speechless.

Any attitude can inform the way you speak the language: you can be curt or courteous. You can argue with a lawyer's cool, a politician's passion, or the bluster of an ignoramus, but your arguments must convince. You must appeal to the other body's *reason*. If you move your opponent's weight over one of his legs and then kick that leg away from under him, he must accept the biomechanical consequences of your proposition and fall over. The judoka's task is literally to persuade his opponent that he hasn't got a leg to stand on.

Anyone who has really convincing arguments scarcely needs to raise their voice in this language—which is to say a judoka with good technique does not need to use brute force. As people may be persuaded by a combination of logic and rhetoric, so the body of an opponent is persuaded that he has no choice but to agree with you, to go along with your argument and fall flat on his back.

And as in speech, so in judo. A judoka can allow himself to lose his temper—with precisely the same unfortunate results that loss of temper in any other context usually brings. He will sound more forceful at the expense of his dignity, his control, and his ability to think clearly; his debating technique will be impaired and his argument will become less effective. He may be driven to use bad language—judo has its swear words, its oaths and obscenities—its banned words—such as attacking the face, punching, twisting fingers, and threatening the spine. Such language may frighten the opposition, but because these words have been banned from the vocabulary of the sport, they cannot be used in the argument "I am better at judo than you."

So the pupil who wants to speak judo has to learn the language just like any other. Before he can form whole sentences, he must master its vocabulary, its pronunciation, and its syntax. He must arrange his body into different shapes to form the letters of the judo alphabet and practice until he can link them in fluently executed combinations. To learn judo is to share the experience of a young child learning to read who eventually manages to utter his first sentence. It is a wonderful sentence and one that a judoka will never tire of repeating. It is "The chap sat on the mat."

7

HOW THE WEST WAS WON

In Japan, some of the jujitsu masters who were having a lean time of it in the years following the Meiji restoration had begun to think that there might be another market for their knowledge in the West. They, too, had succumbed to the changes in the country after the demise of the old feudal order. They shared the new awareness and curiosity about the rest of the world, and a willingness and freedom to visit and trade with foreign lands; they realized that they might earn a better living teaching their special skills in the West (rather in the way that late-twentieth-century British and American students saw the possibilities of teaching the English language in Japan). These men reached Europe some years before Kano and their jujitsu caused a sensation. Before long it was being practiced in sports clubs, music halls, society salons, and back-street gyms.

Because Japan had for so long been a closed country, Europeans knew about as much of this exotic and faraway land as they did about the more distant planets. So when these men from Mars strode down the gangplanks in the ports of Liverpool, San Francisco, and Vancouver, they seemed as alien as creatures alighting from a spacecraft, and they became the subject of a burgeoning curiosity in Japanese culture in general. Tales of a subtle and beautiful civilization had reached the West, capturing the imagination of many. And one of the facets of this civilization of which Westerners were also becoming aware was its martial arts. These seemed to be the source of a mystical power that lay somewhere on the continuum between supernatural powers and magic.

The man who can claim the credit for the introduction of jujitsu to Europe was Edward Barton Wright, a British engineer who had studied the art while working in Japan.[1] In 1898 he opened a martial arts school in Shaftesbury Avenue, London, and, cannibalizing a part of his own name, came up with the term "Bartitsu" to describe his method of self-defense.

Barton Wright's school failed as a business, but his shrewd and imaginative promotion of it was to popularize jujitsu in a speedy and memorably dramatic way. In the autumn of 1900, he brought over to Britain a Japanese jujitsu expert, Yukio Tani, to promote the enterprise by touring the music halls. Tani would open his act by giving jujitsu demonstrations, after which he offered to fight anyone from the audience. He made only one stipulation: that they wear a jacket. Tani, a mere nineteen years old, five feet two inches tall, and then weighing just over 112 pounds, hardly looked formidable, and so there was no shortage of challengers. Yet he took on everyone, regardless of their size—boxers, wrestlers, and street fighters. And he beat the lot of them. He soon became a national celebrity, drawing vast crowds. Someone once asked Tani if he was the champion of his homeland, but he modestly replied, "In Japan, I am only third-rate. The great champions are amateurs and they never give public shows of our art. To the masters of jujitsu our science is almost a religion."

The novelty of Tani's act began to wear thin on the music-hall circuit and he was eventually defeated, though he was grateful that his nemesis was another Japanese. Having spent most of the considerable fortune he had amassed on high living and gambling, he became chief instructor at a new martial arts club. It was the creation of a Japanese man named Gunji Koizumi, who had learned jujitsu in his native Japan and arrived in Britain in 1906 after working his passage as a ship's carpenter.

In January 1918, in the last year of World War I, Koizumi opened the Budokwai, now located in Chelsea, London. It is one of the oldest surviving martial arts clubs in Europe, and Koizumi kept it going through the precarious early days with money he earned from dealing in and repairing Oriental lacquer work (the Queen was one of his clients). The club was promoted through a series of martial arts shows at the Albert Hall, the first of which, in May 1918, included halberd fighting, sword drawing, and a bizarre demonstration of the lesser known art of *nabebuta*—the use of saucepan lids in self-defence.[2]

From Britain the craze soon spread to France. A visiting French bodybuilding pioneer, Edmond Desbonnet, met Tani at the Bartitsu Club and decided to bring to Paris what was often referred to as the "*methode Japonnaise.*"

While the public was enthralled with the exoticism of the Orient, jujitsu was attracting serious and analytical attention from the quarter where it had obvious applications: the police and the military. Europe's police forces and military academies were quick to see the possibilities, and in some the art was studied. In a strange reversal of history, three hundred years after the Europeans had brought firearms to Japan, the Japanese were now demonstrating the art of weaponless fighting to the Europeans.

While the military and police academies may have developed contests and fought hard, it seems likely that the jujitsu practiced in the upper echelons of society was probably rather more about demonstrating a series of techniques. It was considered avant garde, scientific, modern. It gave people a sense of power and so fulfilled the pleasing function of permitting a display of aggression without any risk. One suspects that this practice would have been "jujitsu-lite," with none of the joint-tearing encounters that occurred in the new Japan.

Jujitsu in Europe at this stage was really nothing more than a collection of techniques lacking any agreed-upon system for their practice. The Japanese art of grappling was entirely without any organizing structure to monitor, regulate, or promote it—until, that is, Jigoro Kano stepped off the gangplank in 1889 for what was to be the first of several visits.

With his appearance, it was now judo's turn to sweep through the world like a heady new religion. But this was the new testament. Kano's trips to Europe were ostensibly for the benefit of his work in education, but he took the opportunity to achieve the same task he was attempting in Japan, which was to supplant jujitsu as the leading unarmed fighting art, and to make judo the clear leader in this growing marketplace where the terms *jujitsu* or *the Japanese method* and *judo* were deemed entirely interchangeable. In fact, *jujitsu* was used to describe any kind of unarmed combat. Judo was Kano's refinement of jujitsu. *The Japanese method* was an undiscriminating public's way of referring to them both.

TO PROMOTE THE TEACHING of judo in Britain, Kano urgently needed an apostle. After visiting the Budokwai and meeting Koizumi during his 1920 visit, he quickly came to the conclusion that this man had the best understanding of the art of jujitsu and shared Kano's profound belief that it could be a mental and moral discipline as well as a physical one. The pair got on well and agreed that the Budokwai would adopt the principles of Kodokan judo. The link between the two men was to remain a strong one.

Jujitsu spread the word, but judo, the refined model, capitalized on it. Because of Kano's efforts, judo gradually superseded jujitsu. It succeeded because of Kano's organization and also because of what it was and how it was taught.

In Britain, judo had a particular appeal for the prosperous. They had money and possessions of which criminals were always working hard to deprive them. The well-to-do felt vulnerable to street thugs and judo was an appealing form of self-protection. Its reliance on technical complexity over brute force made it attractive to the educated class, who liked the idea that it was a science and was economical in its use of violence. To these people the practice of martial arts was exotic, and there was yet a further abstraction that attracted people: the Samurai code in which judo was rooted coincided with chivalric values. It was the gentle way for the gentle man. This activity, this mix of ancient learning and Eastern mysticism, offered an appealing cocktail of violence and good manners. The formality, the bowing, and the rituals suggested courtliness—it called for a standard of behavior to which they aspired. Judo, the gentle way, was also the *genteel* way.

However, many people then, as now, were uninterested in judo's philosophy or its spirituality. They just wanted to fight. And in judo they found a way of doing so that offered a much greater physical vocabulary than boxing, with just as much violence yet less trauma to the body.

And there was another factor that might have accounted for its popularity. The Budokwai was founded within months of the end of the bloody conflict of the First World War which accounted for nine million military deaths. Apart from the guerilla activities of the German General von Lettow-Vorbeck in East Africa and T. E. Lawrence in Arabia, it was a war of marked unsubtlety in which vast quantities of metal and men were hurled at each other. At a time when the world was sickened by the carnage, by the terrible taste of steel, along came judo, a form of fighting without weapons, an opportunity to display mettle without metal.

Judo followed jujitsu, harnessing and perpetuating the interest in this Oriental grappling through the 1920s and 1930s. Judo formalized and organized it, and became the dominant language. In the West, while Britain was the first to give judo a toehold, France was the first to refine its teaching, and Germany was to provide an infrastructure, bringing together the judo fraternity of Europe[3]—which was odd, given that that country, under Adolf Hitler's rule, was about to blow the whole continent to pieces.

By this time Kano was reaching the end of his career and his life. Having risen to high office in the education establishment, he was now a distinguished figure in the life of his country. He had been appointed head of the Tokyo Teachers' Training College, which set the syllabus and the standards of the nation. The deep knowledge of education methods and philosophy around the world that he had acquired on his frequent travels was much in demand. For thirty years Kano had been running a sort of noncommercial import-export operation, trading in abstractions. It met his own stringent demands for efficiency: every foreign trip served two purposes, to disseminate the teaching of judo and to gather information on education. Now, in his later life, he was drawing together his two worlds by introducing judo into the curriculum of Japanese schools. And he was in a position to achieve his loftier goals.

Under the leadership of Baron Pierre Coubertin, the first modern Olympics were held in Athens in 1896. They were very much a European and American affair, but Coubertin wanted the world. By 1909, Kano had already become an international figure; he had done almost as much to bring Western sports to Japan as he had in taking judo to the West. He was an obvious choice to become the first Asian representative on the International Olympic Committee (IOC). Kano, ever the internationalist, accepted and became an enthusiastic member, bringing Japan into the competition for the first time at Stockholm in 1912 and, more significantly, successfully bidding to host the 1940 Olympics.

Kano's patriotism is often misinterpreted by those who insist on associating martial arts with Japan's growing militarism. But Kano was no nationalist hawk. And he was certainly no respecter of Germany's new politics. A photograph from the 1936 Munich Olympics shows Jesse Owens, the American sprinter, standing on the victory podium. Among the surrounding officials is Dr. Kano. While many palms slope high in the Nazi salute, both of the doctor's hands remain firmly on the brim of his trilby, which he holds in front of him.

Two years later, after attending an IOC meeting in Cairo, Kano died on the long voyage home. At the end he had reason to be content that, with Japan's Olympic triumph, his once reclusive country had been brought into the community of nations through the fellowship of sport.

We are not too much the wiser about this remarkable man from what has been written since he died. There has been ample hagiography, but little in the way of biography. Indeed he receives almost the same sort of treatment as the central figure in the New Testament: the tones are pious and there are tales of the near miracles he was said to have wrought.

Little emerges of Dr. Kano as a character even later in his career. We know he insisted on efficiency in every aspect of life, from combat techniques to domestic routine, but it had to be so. He pursued a frantic schedule that entailed reshaping an entire nation's education system by day and inventing a new world-dominating fighting system by night. And we know he always insisted on taking an umbrella with him, just in case it rained. But otherwise we have no sense of the man; he is defined entirely by his achievements. Perhaps that is how it should be.

And what achievements! He rescued an art from prostitution; he rescued a whole science from decay and oblivion. Kano found meaning in combat where others saw none. He articulated—in words as well as actions—dignity, beauty, and nobility in a territory where many assume they do not exist and where articulateness is neither common nor held in high esteem.

Kano introduced to his country the notion of sportsmanship and fair play that he called "the spirit of judo." He defined the grander purpose in combat, differentiating between "small judo," which was "concerned only with techniques and the building of the body," and "large judo," which was "mindful of the purpose of life: the soul and the body used in the most effective manner for a good result."[4]

Kano was a teacher and philosopher of the technique and theory of fighting. He was a revered educationalist. And he was much more. He was an author and linguist, a calligrapher and musician, a moralist and preacher, an idealist and practical organizer, a nationalist and an internationalist. And he was a father of eight.

The small boy who was hard put to find a jujitsu teacher in Tokyo, had, before his life was done, scattered thousands of judo teachers around the globe. His great achievement was that, in the creation and promotion of judo, he offered a fighting language of such power and subtlety that it caught the imagination of people in almost every country on the planet.

WHEN KANO SECURED the agreement of the IOC to hold the 1940 Olympic Games in Tokyo, he laid the groundwork for the globalization of his creation. He did not live long enough to see the Games abandoned in the gathering storm of a terrible war, a war in which Japan would experience carnage that would make the bloody siege of Osaka Castle seem like a mere skirmish. But he had established the idea of a Tokyo Games with the Olympic Committee and with his own country.

In 1964 the Olympics did indeed come to Tokyo. As hosts, the Japanese could add one event of their choosing. Inevitably they chose judo. It was a decision that would transform Kano's creation forever. This transformation had its roots in World War II. The defeat of Japan was followed by the American occupation. In 1945, judo, along with all other martial arts, was banned in Japan.[5] The occupation authorities closed the Kodokan because it was a military establishment. They also closed the Butokukai in Kyoto, a military academy established in the 1890s that had proved to be a hotbed of right-wing extremism, with branches all over Japan and some two million members.

The ban was not entirely effective. Senator Ben Nighthorse Campbell, the Republican representative from Colorado and a competitor at openweight in the 1964 Tokyo Olympics, told me that he chose to train at Meiji University because it had such a strong reputation for judo. (Campbell, three times U.S. national judo champion, is half-Cherokee and a horse trainer and jewelry designer. Whenever he won a big competition he was given a feather for his headdress by his people.) He had learned that the reason for this reputation was that, throughout the ban, students continued to practice in a secret dojo.

Nor was the behavior of the U.S. forces of occupation always exemplary. One day in the summer of 1946, four hefty American military policemen insulted and molested the hapless Japanese civilians waiting in a line at a railway station near Kumamoto. As it happened, one of those in the queue was none other than the great Masahiko Kimura, the famous judoka who had been spared in the Pacific by his commanding officer. When the military policemen started to work on him, he resisted and, unaware of whom they were dealing with, the soldiers dragged him off to the middle of a bridge. In the ensuing fight he disposed of each of them, he records, throwing one off the bridge into the river.[6] He took the trouble to record the technique he used for the task: the shoulder throw *seoi-nage.*

Fearing serious punishment at the hands of the U.S. military, Kimura asked the witnesses not to say anything, but a few days later, some military police came to his house. He was puzzled to find them friendly and they politely escorted him to their headquarters. There he was brought before a senior officer who thanked him for dealing with the renegade military policemen, explaining that they had committed a string of abuses and deserved everything they got. He told Kimura that he knew of his reputation: Would he teach judo to some of his men? The Japanese agreed and gave a weekly hour-long lesson. The officer gained his black belt and became another U.S. serviceman who would spread the word of judo when he returned home.

In 1947 the ban on judo was lifted. But it had to be taught as a sport, not a martial art. This change of emphasis might seem minor, but before long it was to create a growing fissure that would bitterly divide the growing judo establishment.

The idea of judo as a sport was a simple enough concept. But for the Japanese, and certainly for those guardians of the faith at the Kodokan, judo was so much more than a sport. Kano had developed it as a way of life. It was irrevocably bound up with the old samurai philosophy. The *ju,* meaning "supple" or "pliable," wasn't attached to a mere *jitsu,* meaning "art" or "practice"; it was linked with *do*, meaning the "way," an altogether larger and more spiritual idea.

Certainly, contest was a vital part of judo, but only a part. Traditionalists believed that it was not enough to defeat an opponent. It had to be done with style that sought to attain the ethereal. In grading contests, candidates had to demonstrate style as well as knowledge. Furthermore, a proper approach to judo made demands on a judoka's behavior outside the dojo: the precepts of the spirit of judo should suffuse his whole life.

Speculation over Kano's precise wishes has been rife. Scholars who have studied his writings—and his devotees almost seem to treat these as religious texts—are divided in their interpretations. The modernists say that judo was born out of competition. Dr. Kano devised it to win contests and judo owed its survival and success to victory in competition against rival jujitsu schools. So, they argue, of course Dr. Kano would have favored the development of judo as a sport.

Others say that the way judo has developed as a competitive sport would have been anathema to the good doctor. Yes, he supported the Olympic movement, and drew Japan into it. But he never wanted judo to be part of the Olympic curriculum, because he believed competition would pollute the purity of judo.

Either way, judo, in the absence of the doctor, was developing a character and momentum of its own. Just as the Americans were imposing a change of emphasis on judo in Japan, so keen new converts to the creed on the other side of the world were developing the art in their own way. It was the Europeans who, keen on contest at every level, worked hard to develop international competition.

THE RENEGADE

Within Japan itself, competition had been a part of judo from its earliest days, but the first nationwide judo tournament was not held until 1931, the year of the first All Japan championship.[1] Even today it is the most important national competition, but before World War II, when serious competition was confined to Japan, it was effectively a world championship, and to win it was the ultimate goal of every judoka.

Masahiko Kimura won the tournament four times, which defined him as one of judo's greatest early champions. He entered it for the first time in October 1937 when he was a twenty-year-old student, five feet six inches tall, and weighing 189 pounds. He fought his way through to the final where he had to face the formidable twenty-seven-year-old Masayuki Nakajima, who was several inches taller and considerably heavier. It was not only the enormous size and strength of the older fighter that worried Kimura, but also Nakajima's footwork, which, in spite of his bulk, was devastatingly fast. The contest, consisting of one fifteen-minute round, would end when a major point was scored.

Kimura recounts how he was completely dominated by Nakajima for the first few minutes: "In those days, my lower body was still weak . . . whenever Nakajima pulled me around, my legs wobbled."[2] But the struggle was fast and furious enough for them both to hurtle off the raised platform several times and crash onto the press seats three or four feet below.

"Every time I fell with him, our heads and backs got slammed so hard that we became unable to breathe properly for a while." Neither managed to get a decisive score by the end of the fifteen minutes, so they were forced to continue for a second round. That too proved indecisive so, incredibly, they went to a third. They had now been fighting for thirty minutes and both were reaching the final stages of exhaustion. Kimura says he was sweating so much that his jacket was soaked and he could hardly see.

At one stage, both fighters having been ordered by the referee to stop in order to straighten their *gis* and retie their belts, Kimura found his fingers were almost powerless. But then he noticed Nakajima rubbing his calf muscles and decided he would concentrate on what was obviously a weak point. As soon as the judge called "*Hajime*" to restart the fight, Kimura attacked his opponent's legs. Nakajima crashed to the mat and, as he did so, Kimura pounced on him, trapping him in a hold from which he could not escape. Kimura was ecstatic over his victory. So ecstatic, he claims, that after he had rested briefly and eaten, he did five hundred push-ups, performed hopping squat thrusts for almost a mile, and executed five hundred karate strikes on the *makiwara* (a padded wooden post that is the karate practitioner's equivalent of a boxer's punching bag). If these figures are anything like true—and there are those who say Kimura could write a good tale—it was hardly surprising that he found himself unable to sleep because of pain and exhaustion. Whereas before the fight all he had wanted was to win the All Japan title just once, now his ambition soared with his victory: he wanted to win it again and again.

And he did.

By Kimura's own account, it was the spirit of revenge that brought him to judo. One day, during his time in fourth grade at his school in Kumamoto, his class ran amok in the absence of the teacher. Returning to find a jubilant Kimura leaping up and down on the wreckage of his desk shouting "*Banzai!*" the teacher slapped Kimura in the face and hurled him to the floor.

"I thought about how to get revenge on him for about a week, and investigated his background," recounted Kimura in a sinister tone. Having discovered that the teacher was a first dan judoka, he decided that he would get to second dan so that he could exact revenge. As a motive for studying judo, this was probably not quite what Dr. Kano had in mind. Kimura enrolled in a nearby dojo and took to the sport immediately. Although, as far as we know, he left the teacher alone; he was to defeat everyone else in Japan, becoming one of judo's greatest champions.

Born in 1917, Kimura had a competitive career that spanned World War II, his triumphs extending from victories in the aesthetically beautiful world of high-class classical Japanese judo to gruesome encounters in the bloody arena of more-or-less anything-goes prize fighting. This career first delighted and then enraged the Japanese judo establishment. Certainly, had he still been alive, Jigoro Kano would have been disgusted that such a talent should be dragged to the depths of professional entertainment for the bloodthirsty mobs of Brazil, where Kimura's most brutal encounter took place.

Aside from the extent of his achievement, the name of Kimura lives on in a way that others have not, because he was one of very few to write his autobiography. Those who fight battles in distant places and tell the story themselves, those who control the narrative, tend to come out well, as Julius Caesar and Lawrence of Arabia would vouch. Kimura, like those military commanders, has been criticized as a skillful self-publicist who is sometimes hard to believe, but no one can argue with his judo record. He won the prestigious All Japan championship four times and from the age of twenty remained undefeated for thirteen years until his retirement. It is hard to know what he might have achieved had not the war denied him those crucial peak years in the middle of his blossoming judo career. The Japanese say of him, "No one before Kimura, no one after Kimura!"[3]

IN THE WAKE OF his first victory in the 1937 All Japan, Kimura reckoned that his opponents would increase their training times in order to beat him. He had already been training six hours a day, while the others trained for three or four. If they were now going to do six hours, he was going to train for nine. He was determined to train longer and harder than anyone else.

It was not long before he began to receive reports of how his rivals were doing everything they could in their preparations to defeat him. They were studying his techniques and working on ways to counter them. It didn't do them any good. Kimura won the All Japan championship in the next two years, 1938 and 1939.

One of Kimura's great advantages was the power of his fingers. He developed this after watching karate players at his university, where he had studied different forms of that art and for a time even worked as an assistant instructor. To strengthen his fingers, wrists, and fists, he would jab his hands into a box of sand a thousand times a day. It was a time-consuming routine to accommodate within an already exhaustive training schedule. After the practice at Takushoku University he would go to the Kodokan, where he would do *randori* with the elite players from various universities, the Tokyo Police, and guards from the Imperial Palace.

Kimura's trademark throw was *osoto-gari*, which he used to practice against a tree. He would flick his right foot so that it caught his opponent behind his right leg and his whole body would come driving in as his heel swung back like the arm of a trebuchet, thumping into the back of his opponent's leg and sending him flying backward. His training partners began to beg him not to use the throw on them. No wonder. "I slammed twenty-three or twenty-four tough men one after another," he remembered. "Every day, at Tokyo Police and Kodokan, about ten men had a concussion and lost consciousness caused by my *osoto-gari*." This may have been partly because he was inclined to throw people off the mat onto the surrounding wooden floor.

WHEN I READ ABOUT KIMURA, I asked Tony Sweeney, a former British squad member who teaches at the Budokwai, what he knew about him. "Kimura?" He thought for a moment, then murmured "*Osoto-gari!*" before adding with a distant wry smile, "Yes, Trevor Leggett would go on with Kimura and told me how he would take his leg back to avoid Kimura's *osoto-gari*, but then he'd catch him anyway with a shoulder throw."

This fragment of a memory somehow made real a man who was close to mythical. I had been on the mat with Sweeney, who had been on with Leggett. And Leggett had been on with Kimura.

WHEN WAR BROKE OUT, Kimura was called up for military service, which prevented him from competing in the All Japan. It was not until 1947, when the ban on martial arts imposed by the occupying allied forces was lifted, that judo's organizers were able to re-establish the schedule of contests. In July of that year, the West Japan Championships were staged in Fukuoka. Kimura won, beating Yasuichi Matsumoto in the final. He faced him again in the spring of the following year at the Kyushu vs. Kansai championship (a major interregional tournament). Kimura records with satisfaction, "I threw him by my original *ippon-seoi,* in which both arms of the opponent are locked. His arm broke, making a snapping sound, and he flew out of the platform."

Kimura's final appearance in the All Japan championships was in 1949 when, aged thirty-two, he carved his way through to the final where he met Takahiko Ishikawa, a man so dangerous in *newaza* (fighting on the ground) that sometimes when he was training he wouldn't even bother to take off his spectacles.[4] It was such an evenly matched struggle that neither fighter could score, even though it carried on into a fourth round before the referee called a draw and gave them both the championship.

Then, as now, retiring champions could count on the judo establishment for a prestigious teaching job, and Kimura was offered the position of chief instructor for the Tokyo Metropolitan Police. He never took up the post.

Amateurism had always been an essential part of the spirit of judo. Kano had decreed this. But it was only a matter of time before a shrewd promoter realized judo's possibilities as an exciting spectacle that, given a star-studded cast of fighters, could be sold to the public. That time, as it turned out, was April 1950, when a prosperous building contractor assembled twenty-one fighters to take part in the first series of professional judo contests. Among them was Kimura, who became the first champion of the circuit. Much to the concern of the high command of the Kodokan, pay-for-view judo initially proved popular. But interest flagged after four or five months.

The promoter first reduced the wages of his fighters and then stopped paying them altogether. Kimura's position was desperate. In the years immediately after the war, the plight of Japan was pitiful. Much of the infrastructure had been destroyed and food was scarce. Kimura's wife was in a hospital with tuberculosis, which many people did not survive because of malnutrition; he had given up a well-paid and secure job in the judo establishment to join the ill-fated professional circuit, and now he didn't have the money he desperately needed to buy food and medicine. Salvation came in the form of a second-generation Japanese-American businessman from Hawaii who offered Kimura a three-month contract to take judo to the Hawaiian islands. Kimura signed up and left the pro judo circuit, which went out of business six months later.

On the tour, two other Japanese would give judo demonstrations. These were followed by the appearance of Kimura, who would take on ten local challengers in quick succession. It was a big hit. There had been judo on the islands since the first club was founded in 1909, but the Hawaiians had never seen athletes of this caliber. Kimura was pleased to note how impressed people were to see Japanese, who had been so humiliated in the war by the Americans, throwing their erstwhile conquerors around the mat. More important, he had been able to buy the expensive medicine he needed for his wife, who recovered—they were later to have a son and a daughter.

In the eyes of the Kodokan, these two ventures at least had the merit of promoting judo, although it was still resentful that its greatest champion had sullied the sport by taking money. That resentment was soon to turn into outright hostility over Kimura's decision to accept an offer from the world of fixed and phoney fights: professional wrestling. Kimura and two other Japanese judoka were offered a four-month contract by a Japanese newspaper in Brazil that was promoting pro wrestling. It proved to be a money-spinner: the fighters' pay was tripled and, in their spare time, they gave judo lessons.

One day they received a challenge from a Brazilian jujitsu fighter called Helio Gracie. The ensuing events launched a rivalry that is still being pursued in the twenty-first century. Since the early 1900s, Dr. Kano had been sending his greatest experts to destinations around the world to ensure that Kodokan judo was taught to the highest standards. The man he sent to Brazil was Mitsuyo Maeda and among his pupils was Gracie, who had since left to set up his own school, teaching what he called Gracie jujitsu, his own form of judo.[5] Gracie, keen to test his style against that of the Kodokan, was now proposing a contest that would be a combination of judo and jujitsu, in that throws or hold-downs would not count and the fight would end only when a contestant submitted—or was rendered unconscious.

One of the other judoka, Kato, accepted the challenge. Although he threw Gracie repeatedly, it had little effect because the mat was unusually soft, so he took the Brazilian to the ground and applied a strangle. But Gracie had also secured a strangle from underneath and for several minutes they desperately worked on each other's necks. Kato's face started to turn pale as he lost consciousness. Kimura leaped into the ring and threw in the towel. Gracie's students were triumphant and paraded around town with a coffin for the "dead" Japanese.

The defeat had a disastrous effect on box-office takings for the Japanese trio's pro wrestling shows; the public was now distinctly unimpressed. So when Kimura received a challenge from Gracie, he accepted it. Twenty thousand came to watch at the Maracana stadium, among them the president of Brazil; Gracie's supporters brought along another coffin, ready for the vanquished Japanese, and Kimura was bombarded with eggs as he approached the ring.

The fight began with an attempt by Gracie to throw Kimura. He didn't budge. Kimura then "blew him away up in the air" with a series of throws. He tried his notorious *osoto-gari* in an attempt to knock his opponent unconscious, but again the mat proved too soft. However, when he threw Gracie again, in around the twelfth minute of the contest, Kimura moved into a smothering hold-down which he maintained for two or three minutes; Gracie, desperate to make room to breathe, tried to push Kimura's body away. It was all that Kimura needed. He caught the Brazilian's extended limb and threaded his own arm through to form a figure-of-four or "chicken-wing" armlock. "I thought he would surrender immediately," wrote Kimura,

> But Helio would not tap the mat. I had no choice but to keep on twisting the arm. The stadium became quiet. . . . Finally, the sound of bone breaking echoed throughout the stadium. Helio still did not surrender. I had no choice but to twist the arm again. Another bone was broken. Helio still did not tap. When I tried to twist the arm once more, a white towel was thrown in. Japanese Brazilians rushed into the ring and tossed me up in the air. On the other hand, Helio let his left arm hang and looked very sad withstanding the pain.

Many years later Gracie told an interviewer that he never expected to win: "I thought that nobody in the world could defeat Kimura."[6] He said that his brother Carlos thought he would get seriously injured but that his "fear was surpassed by desire to know what . . . Kimura would do in the fight." Carlos thought that Kimura "might open the door to an unknown world for me."[7] It seems odd that Gracie would risk the loss of so much prestige by fighting publicly, when they could probably have fought privately. Kimura several times agreed to take on challengers out of the public eye, and Tani used to do the same.

Helio Gracie admitted in the same interview that when Kimura put the choke on, he actually lost consciousness. "If Kimura had continued to choke me, I would have died for sure," he said. "But since I didn't give up, Kimura let go . . . and went into the next technique. Being released from the choke and the pain from the next technique revived me and I continued to fight."

Gracie also revealed that while he was in the armlock that succeeded the choke, he could hear Kimura murmuring in his ear. Although he couldn't understand what he was saying he found himself "strangely encouraged by his voice. It gave me power." Later, when Gracie asked him what he had said, Kimura told him, "I was admiring your heart."

After that encounter, Kimura devoted most of his efforts to professional wrestling. But in 1959, when he was touring Brazil for the last time, he received a challenge to a judo contest from a fourth dan called Aldemar Santana. Kimura threw him a number of times and armlocked him into submission.

Santana, however, would not leave it at that and wanted a rematch. This time he proposed *vale tudo* (anything goes) rules. Kimura would not have accepted this lightly. These contests were hugely popular among the mob. Pretty much anything was allowed and, as we shall see later, it proved to be a grotesquely gruesome and bloody affair, an inglorious finale for a man who had begun his career as a powerful but brilliant judo player. The encounter typified the very brutality that Kano had sought to avoid.

The Kodokan, appalled at what he had done, refused to give Kimura the dan grade promotion that would normally have been his right. There was also an unseemly row about the All Japan championship flag, the trophy that was the Japanese equivalent of a cup. The Kodokan demanded its return but Kimura refused to part with it, saying that he had been told he could keep it because he had won the tournament three consecutive times. Whatever. In the eyes of the Kodokan, Kimura, with his antics in the professional wrestling ring and his participation in prize fights, had committed the sin of apostasy—he had abandoned his faith.

In the end he did return to the fold, this time as a preacher. In 1960, during his retirement, Kimura went to teach judo at Takushoku University. The champion terrified everyone around him. "His training regime was so severe that [his own students] feared every practice session," wrote Canadian judoka Paul Nurse. "The only thing they were more afraid of was not showing up for practice. He was known to go to your house and tear the place apart demanding to know why you were absent without leave."[8]

In 1993, aged seventy-five, Kimura was admitted to the hospital to undergo an operation for the lung cancer that would soon kill him. Shortly after surgery he climbed out of bed and started doing push-ups.

THE END OF SUPREMACY

Kano's wish for Japan to host the Olympics had finally been realized when the international organizing committee chose Tokyo as the site for the 1964 Games. To show off the national sport at its best, a special new arena was commissioned. Workmen fenced off several acres in the corner of the gardens of the Imperial Palace in Tokyo's Kitanomaru Park and construction began on the Nippon Budokan, a vast octagonal building seating fifteen thousand people. With a design based on ancient Japanese architectural principles, the Budokan was to be a temple to the martial arts.

Japan wanted judo in the Games partly to showcase their own contribution to sporting endeavor, but also because this was the one way they could be sure of winning a medal. Japanese athletes were beginning to make inroads into many unfamiliar new areas of Western athleticism, but they were by no means near the front rank. It would be humiliating for Japan as host nation to win nothing. They had had more than their share of humiliation in the last twenty years with defeat and occupation, but in judo they believed they were supreme. Meanwhile, the sport was gaining in popularity in Europe, where judo had made great progress; international contests on the continent were beginning to thrive. But they couldn't beat the Japanese. Unknown to the Japanese, however, in one small European country scarcely above sea level there was emerging a Great White Hope.

IN UTRECHT IN 1948, a fourteen-year-old Dutch boy called Anton Geesink went along to a soccer match in his home town at which the organizers put on a judo demonstration as halftime entertainment. He was immediately gripped by what he described as "the judo fever." He gave up soccer and swimming and started learning the sport. He said he was so taken with it that he saw a career for himself as a judo instructor. He and a group of friends started their own club, teaching themselves from books.[1] Geesink came from a working-class family and life was particularly tough in those hard postwar years. His father believed that the boy would be more useful if he was put to work on a building site than sitting on a school bench. During the day young Geesink earned his living as a construction worker; he spent his evenings and weekends either training at judo or studying to complete his education.

A high-grade Japanese judoka called Haku Michigami who had been sent to Europe by the Kodokan encountered the teenage Geesink in 1953. Michigami said this tall creature with a long face, neck, and legs "looked like a beer bottle," but he could certainly see his potential.[2] And Geesink began winning a number of competitions. He was extremely athletic and fantastically determined. When the crushing of the Hungarian insurrection of 1956 by the Soviets forced the cancellation of that year's European championships, Geesink, now twenty-two years old, in order to keep up his training, abandoned his *gi*, took up Greco-Roman wrestling, and won the Dutch national championship that year and on two successive occasions.

The European theater of the judo war was one thing, but Geesink had set his sights on winning in Japan. Although he was far from ready for that task, the young man was sent to Tokyo to compete in the first world championships in 1956, not in the expectation that he might win (in fact he gained a bronze in the openweight), but simply to experience competition judo at its highest level. His intention was to prepare himself for his first real goal, the third world championships that were to be held in Paris in 1961.

The venue for those 1961 world championships was the Stade Pierre de Coubertin in the west of the city. The layout of this little arena—it has only five thousand seats—brings the spectators close to the contestants, creating an extraordinary intimacy and excitement. On December 2, 1961, the stadium was packed with a capacity crowd from which rose dense clouds of cigarette smoke. There was a single raised mat area. When the two Japanese referees, both former world champions wearing judo outfits, entered the arena for the first time there was spontaneous applause.

Geesink made a striking impact on everyone from his very first contest against Sudjono of Indonesia, whom he felled in nine seconds. Among the spectators was a writer for *Sports Illustrated* magazine, who wrote, "In that fleeting time Geesink proved himself perfectly coordinated, with miraculous reflexes, a straight and proper judo stance, and an ability to blend strength and technique in the best judo manner." He recorded that "Geesink's long torso and relatively short and powerful legs were an ideal build for a judoka, because the center of gravity is low, allowing rocklike balance against attacks."

The Dutchman was to come up against three of Japan's finest fighters that day. For the captain of the British team at the event, George Kerr, Geesink's most exciting fight was against Akio Kaminaga. Kerr recalled, "Kaminaga was probably better technically but Geesink was a superb athlete. There were a few shouts from the crowd at the Coubertin Stadium—people were much more reserved in those days, but it was a knowledgeable crowd. It was a great contest; Geesink got only a small score but it was clear, unanimous, and uncontroversial." It was not the last these two would see of each other.

In the semifinals Geesink met Koga. To at least one young Brit in the stadium, Geesink's opponent "seemed very nervous and he never really opened up. He obviously did not want to go to the ground and at one point, to avoid doing so, he scuttled out of the area on all fours, looking rather comic. Eventually Geesink came in with *uchimata* [inner thigh throw], Koga blocked successfully but Geesink persisted and Koga eventually went over for a big *ippon*. The Japanese among the crowd had grown increasingly apprehensive as the evening progressed. Their finest fighters were being defeated by this Dutchman.

Because the organizers had had little practice in running a major competition, everything ran overtime, and it was nearly midnight when the time came for the final, the last test of East versus West: Geesink against Koji Sone, the reigning world champion. This Japanese fared no better than the rest; he tried a couple of desperate *osoto-gari* ("major outside reaps") but Geesink did not budge and then threw Sone twice, though not decisively. When the Japanese went down for the second time, Geesink held him with *mune-gatame*. The klaxon sounded to mark the end of the thirty seconds, the end of the contest, and the end of Japan's supremacy.

To the horror of the Japanese, some Dutch supporters immediately rushed onto the mat with their shoes on and tried to raise Geesink onto their shoulders. The referee had not yet declared the result of the contest and Sone was still flat on his back. It was an extraordinary moment, but there was little noise from the crowd in those times of deep restraint. One Briton described what he regarded as the extraordinarily effusive behavior of his fellow countryman, Trevor Leggett. "Leggett never normally went to contests and he was very reserved, but he got out of his chair and went to shake Geesink's hand as he came off the mat."[3] Geesink had become the first Caucasian to defeat the Japanese; such were the actions that passed for wild abandon in 1961.

One of the many far-reaching consequences of this victory was that the Japanese, who had so long opposed European efforts to modernize their sport, quickly changed their minds. The Westerners were pressing to break up tournaments into weight categories to make it fairer for a wider range of athletes. In Paris, on the day after the event, the International Judo Federation voted to introduce four separate weight classes in future world championships. The Tokyo Olympic Games were now three years away. The truth was that the Japanese were appalled at the idea of having an Olympic judo event with only one category—which a foreigner might win. More categories would increase their chances.

The new world champion still lacked confidence in his judo technique; Geesink said that he felt he was not yet "mature." He was particularly worried about his groundwork, which he sensed he had to improve if he was to consolidate his supremacy. To this end he started to work on *sangaku-waza* that he found promising. In these techniques the attacker hooks one foot behind his knee to create a triangle with which he can hold down, armlock, or choke his opponent by crushing his neck and one of his arms. Then Geesink returned to Japan for three months to train at Tenri University, where the regime was notoriously hard and the groundwork teaching highly regarded.[4] All this and a grueling program of European contests helped him prepare for the supreme challenge: the Tokyo Olympics.

IN SPITE OF their defeat in Paris, the Japanese were expected to win the Olympic judo contest. Many of their coaches still could not accept that a non-Japanese might be really good at judo; Geesink's victory, they believed, had been a mere hiccup in the natural order of things.

Japanese fighters were technically superior and therefore in the end they would triumph. Eight months before the Tokyo Olympics, one of their number took the trouble to suggest otherwise. As one who had become aware of the "beer-bottle" Dutchman's capabilities from an early stage and had seen him develop over the years, Michigami was convinced that Geesink would triumph in Tokyo. He wrote as much in an article for a Japanese martial arts magazine which was billed as a "Bombshell for the Kodokan."[5] The article excited some comment, but many regarded Michigami as a mere maverick who had "gone native" after spending so much time in Europe, while some cursed him as a traitor to his nation. But other, less vociferous members of the Japanese judo hierarchy were also beset by the nagging possibility that the stadium now being constructed in the corner of the imperial gardens might turn out to be a giant tombstone, rather than a monument to Japan's supremacy.

The approaching Olympics galvanized not only the competitors, but the very sport itself. This was the first time judo would be seen in the Olympics, and these were to be the first television Olympics. (Parts of the prewar Berlin Olympics were televised, but the coverage was seen only within the city.) Judo would be exposed to a worldwide public in a way that it never had been before. This was the sport's big chance. The officials of the IJF fully realized that they would have to do a lot of work to present their sport in a new way—a way that an ignorant general public, both the spectators in the stadium and television viewers around the world, would find appealing and comprehensible. As we will see, they would still be struggling in vain with this challenge nearly half a century later.

The Olympics were a crucial part of the restoration of the Japanese nation's pride. Nearly twenty years after a war that saw the attack on Pearl Harbor and the dropping of the first atomic bomb on Hiroshima, the Tokyo Games were to be not only a gesture of reconciliation but a showcase for the recovery, industrial efficiency, and growing prosperity of the new Japan. But the event was also to show something of the country's heritage, such as the science of the martial arts that had existed centuries before the discovery of nuclear fission, or even of gunpowder. So in the period before the judo contests, the public in the Nippon Budokan was presented with demonstrations that included kendo, archery, and sumo.

In the first three days of competition, the visiting judoka went down like ninepins in the face of the Japanese onslaught. The host nation made a clean sweep of the gold medals, winning the light-, middle-, and heavyweight categories. Spectators unfamiliar with the possibilities of the sport were astonished to see—among many, many strange things—Isao Okano, the great Japanese middleweight, courteously revive the opponent whom he had just strangled unconscious.

All this was regarded as a mere overture for the real event, the one category that really mattered: the openweight. Here, contests would retain one of the greatest and most revered original values of judo, the chance for the small to defeat the large; technique over brute strength. And it was in this category that Anton Geesink would fight on October 23, the very last day of the Games.

Geesink had his own plan for the preliminaries, which was to try and bring all his opponents down with one of his favorite throws. This was *sasae tsuri komi ashi,* in which he would trap his opponent's instep and whirl him in a sweeping circle until he lost balance and somersaulted to the floor. He would then try to end it by attacking his opponent on the ground. He was anxious to win as quickly as possible so that he would not be forced to reveal other techniques to those he had yet to fight. And this was more or less what happened.

Japan was quite happy to have given judo to the world, but it wanted to keep the medals for itself. They thought long and hard about who should be their contender for the openweight class; it was either going to be Isao Inokuma, who had won gold in the heavyweight category, or Kaminaga. "Inokuma, a little lighter, a little more mobile, a little more fanatic," as Geesink saw it, "but yet for me less dangerous than the somewhat older, somewhat quieter and more experienced Kaminaga."[6] He later wrote, "Every day the judo of these two Japanese giants was in my mind," so for months the Dutchman had been working with training partners who had a similar build and fighting style. Now, at last, the announcement came, and it was not what he wanted to hear: it would be Kaminaga. (He wasn't the only one who was unhappy. Inokuma was said to have wept when he heard he was denied the chance of fighting this crucial battle for his country.)

Geesink weighed 279 pounds and was six feet six inches. Kaminaga weighed 220 pounds and was five feet eleven inches. They had met in the preliminary rounds. The contest had lasted the full duration, Geesink winning by only a small margin, but that did not in any way make the encounter in the final anticlimactic. Kaminaga was a formidable fighter and a brilliant technician; in one of his earlier rounds he had thrown an opponent in four seconds. The Japanese fans understood that it was inevitable that their champion would face the giant Dutchman again in the final and therefore, until then, that Kaminaga would want to maintain an element of surprise and refrain from using his most devastating techniques.

The people who crowded into the martial arts hall had come to see "Kaminaga put the crown on Japan's Olympic Games." Wrote one European historian:

> In every Japanese city, town, and village people gathered around shop windows to follow the events on TV. This was something that nobody wanted to miss. Millions came out to support Kaminaga, on whose broad shoulders Japanese pride now rested. There would be no parliamentary business that day. Patriotic bosses made sure that their companies had at least one television on each floor. People sent verses in praise of Kaminaga to the newspapers.[7]

At the stadium itself, however, there was one notable—and ominous—absence: the emperor. He had come to watch the third day of the tournament in which the Japanese had again been victorious, but his advisers had now made their own calculations of the risk and concluded that the loss of face for their emperor would have been too great had Japan been defeated in his presence in the most important competition of them all.[8] To those in the know, his absence was a clear signal of doubt in imperial quarters.

The agreed protocol was that both athletes would step onto the mat at the same time. But Geesink ignored the formality. He later admitted that what he did next was with the sole intention of demoralizing his opponent. His giant frame brushing past the hapless official who tried to prevent him, Geesink launched a preemptive occupation of the mat. He stepped up onto the platform and stood there. He knew that this would impress the Japanese and demoralize the unfortunate Kaminaga, who would have to see his opponent, a giant in any terms, from below the dais, a viewpoint that made Geesink look even larger. Then, when Kaminaga himself tried to get up on to the dais, he was prevented from doing so by officials. By the time he did eventually climb onto the raised platform, Geesink had taken the psychological high ground; he *owned* the mat.

Fifteen thousand people were packed into the Budokan. As if Kaminaga wasn't already aware of the daunting pressure upon him, in the silence that followed, when the two men were called forward to face each other, a lone Japanese voice from somewhere high in the stadium shouted out, exhorting him to win for the honor of Japan.

The contestants came out, bowed, and then, as they advanced, both threw up their outstretched arms as if greeting each other like long lost brothers. The struggle lasted eight minutes, during which the physically stronger Geesink wore down his opponent and then caught him with the *sasai* he'd used in earlier fights. He followed Kaminaga down to the ground and held him in a *kesa-gatame*, a scarf hold, which wrapped up the smaller man's shoulders and brought a terrible crushing force against his ribs. The Japanese was helpless. A photograph of the final seconds of the contest shows Kaminaga on his back clamped in Geesink's arms. Behind are the faces of the spectators, mostly Westerners, smiling at the impending triumph. One Japanese face is transfixed with frowning concern as the seconds tick by and Kaminaga shows no sign of being able even to attempt to escape. This was Haku Michigami.

As the referee raised his hand high and called *ippon,* one Dutch supporter, a member of the boxing team, ran jubilantly onto the mat. Geesink angrily waved the Dutchman away: "A gesture," as one commentator observed, "that endeared Geesink to the Japanese forever afterwards." James Bregman, a member of the U.S. judo team, praised Geesink's action in gesturing his supporters off the mat. "He was extraordinarily dignified. What was at stake was the decorum and demeanor of the entire venue. It could have turned into a Brazilian soccer game. There was no security as we know it today, but there was a heavy mantle of tradition."[9]

Now Geesink rose slowly to give Kaminaga time to recover himself after being crushed for half a minute in *osekomi*. They both went back to their marks in the middle of the mat and knelt down, as custom in those days dictated, to straighten their *gis*. They stood and, as the referee formally declared the result, they bowed to each other. Then they rose, shook hands, and embraced each other. They bowed to the officials and walked off.

Isao Inokuma, whose own heavyweight gold medal victory could not inure him to the grief that now overwhelmed him, was one of many Japanese in the stadium who were visibly crying. And the tears were not confined to the stadium.

The whole nation wept. Grown men clustered around the television sets in shop windows collapsed in tears. For Japan, this defeat on their home ground—hallowed ground in the corner of the emperor's gardens—was a national disaster, a cause for national mourning. True, their supremacy had already been toppled at the world championships three years earlier, but that was in faraway Paris where few had witnessed it; it had been confined to the world of judo. This new defeat had occurred in Japan's own capital city in the full view of a global television audience.

That night Japan's head coach, Yasuichi Matsumoto, and Koji Sone, the man whom Geesink had defeated for the world title in Paris, went to a bar to drown their grief. Sone pronounced what every Japanese then felt: "We won three gold medals and one silver, but we were defeated. . . ." Soon after that, Matsumoto, in a traditional gesture, shaved his head in penance at his failure. It would not be surprising if his reaction to the final contest was a little confused, for it is arguable that his greatest role in the affair was not as the trainer of Kaminaga and the Japanese team, but as the man who had coached Geesink when he trained at Tenri University. Matsumoto was the one coach whom Geesink would always single out for acknowledgment.[10]

Meanwhile, some feared for Kaminaga's state of mind. Quite apart from the private shame he would have felt at being responsible for this historic and very public defeat, he faced open insult and vilification by some of his fellow countrymen for what they saw as the dishonor he had brought on their country. Two other Japanese athletes, a marathon runner and a woman hurdler, later committed suicide after they failed to come up to expectations.[11] Kaminaga's friends were concerned that he might do the same. In fact, he went back to work and rode out the storm, but after the ordeal he was to say that he was now able to bear anything that might happen to him because of what he'd gone through in "that extreme situation."[12]

"Overconfidence, fanaticism, a shrill sense of inferiority, and a sometimes obsessive preoccupation with national status—these have all played their parts in the modern history of Japan," wrote one commentator. "But one quality has stood out to serve Japan better than any other: the grace to make the best of defeat.

"Geesink would be treated as a hero in Japan for ever after."[13]

ANTON GEESINK was a giant and a giant killer. This six-feet-six-inch Dutchman had slain the behemoth that was Japanese judo superiority. By the time he retired three years later, he had become Dutch champion twenty-one times in different weight categories, European champion twenty times, and world champion three times. But nothing he did would surpass his achievement at the Tokyo Olympics.

Great victories and those who won them are commemorated in the names of streets and squares and railways stations in cities around the world. This one was no exception. In one residential quarter of Utrecht you will find Anton Geesinkstraat and in the center of the city is a large bronze statue, making him the only judoka to be thus commemorated. He was showered with honors by other nations, not least by Japan, where he received the Order of the Sacred Treasure, Gold Rays, from His Majesty the Emperor of Japan himself. More important than any of these things is perhaps that he became one of the handful of tenth dan judoka in the world.

THE SHATTERING OF Japan's invincibility on the mat had a significance that transcended national and East-West rivalry. Geesink's victory secured judo's future as an international sport. If the Japanese had won every single category, judo would probably have been taken out of the Olympics. But Geesink had proved that you didn't have to be Japanese to win. Judo now belonged, not just to Japan, but to everyone. When Geesink conquered Japan, judo conquered the world.

THE CLUB

While Japan's champions are nurtured in its schools and universities, in the West the breeding ground of great players is the judo club. Wherever the dojo, newcomers will find roughly the same training routine. There is a period of warming up, and then in varying order there will be some *uchikomi*—a form of repetitive practice, some teaching of techniques, and a period devoted to *randori*, free fighting or sparring—standing work (*tachiwaza*) and groundwork (*newaza*). *Randori* is the most taxing and the most exciting part—the highlight of any session. This is what it's all about—"the soul of judo," Geesink calls it. It may be divided into bouts lasting, say, three or four minutes with a minute's interval between each to allow people to recover their breath, retie their belts, and find their next partner. And the joy of judo, as opposed to many of the striking martial arts like karate and taekwondo, is that beginners are able to have a bit of a fight in their very first class.

A session may also include some fitness training—push-ups, rope climbing, shuttle running, and stretching. It ends with the class kneeling in a line and bowing to the *sensei* in an echo of the formalities of centuries past conducted in the dojos within the castle grounds of the samurai lords.

Dr. Kano did everything he could to make judo safe and the unspoken understanding is that everybody has got to be able to get to work the next day. But to go onto the mat with someone for the first time is to enter potentially hazardous territory. The most common danger usually comes from a clumsy or incompetent opponent. Sometimes it can come from people who are used to a looser interpretation of the rules.

For judoka from the former Soviet Union who came to live in or visit London after the fall of the Berlin Wall and were in search of a hard practice, Wandsworth Lightning Club in South London became a favorite destination. Their appearance at the club could turn an already vigorous practice into mayhem. "You knew what it was going to be like as soon as you saw them coming through the door," remembers Simon Hicks, who helped found the club and instructed there. "You could see it was going to be blood and sweat and know that the last half hour was going to be hell. They were going to hand out a real pasting and our boys knew that too. These people would do really rough and illegal techniques that weren't judo—spinelocks and so on—and I'd have to walk round and keep an eye on what was going on and say, 'No, you can't do that.'"

There's also always the rare possibility that you might find yourself opposite someone with a screw loose—a bit of a nutcase. They're like those apparently domesticated animals that without warning suddenly revert to the feral, like a dog whose bewildered owners are left saying apologetically, "But he's never done anything like this before!"

Of course, it is extremely unlikely that you will come across someone like that, but there are always one or two and appearances can be deceptive. Paul Ajala, a former British squad member and Budokwai instructor, told me of an encounter with a pupil at a well-known private school. The boy, a brilliant classicist, was a serious academic type. He viewed his two worlds, the ancient and the modern, with a thoughtful gaze from behind small spectacles. He was fastidiously courteous and deferential, always calling his sensei "Sir." And when Ajala called him out to do a free fighting practice with him, the student politely accepted. With prissy precision he folded his spectacles and placed them on the windowsill before stepping onto the mat. Blinking nearsightedly, this student of the great Greek texts advanced, bowed with a careful formality, and then suddenly leaped at his instructor, seizing his collar in an iron grip and launching a series of attacks of such unrestrained violence that, for the few minutes of their encounter, the *sensei* was convinced that he was in the hands of a psychopath. As Ajala put it, "Basically he went completely and utterly mad!"

What you see is not always what you get.

Judo, like any sport, is an expression of personality as well as a test of it. Some like brute force, some high art, some lurk with low cunning. Some are straightforward and honest and some are deceptive. There are the nippy and the plodding, the consistent and predictable, the wayward and inspired. Stoics and whiners; stickers and quitters. Some are neat and tidy and some fight like cabbages. Those who come to the door of the club dojo do so for very different reasons. Some are parents who want their children to be less fat, others who want them to be more fit. Some come to do judo because they are no good at ball games. Some come because of their parents, some in spite of their parents. Fathers may be lured to the mat by watching their sons, sisters by watching their brothers. There are the misguided who show up under the impression that this Eastern art is a slightly more energetic form of yoga.

Some exasperated mothers arrive in the belief that this sport will control the aggressive; others hope it will embolden the nervous. Schoolchildren come along, inspired by the victories of the stars of competition. There are boys brought by fathers who are twitchy about what they see as the increasing feminization of society and who want to instill some masculine values. In the United Kingdom at least, not a few children are brought by parents who harbor some half-focused belief that they may be better prepared to defend themselves in the streets and playgrounds of a newly violent realm.

PERHAPS THE MOST STRIKING aspect of any club is the floor, which is to say that's the part that strikes you. Good dojos have proper tatami laid on sprung wooden floors. You might encounter canvas stretched over compacted sawdust; but the worst combination, they say, is a very soft surface laid to compensate for a really hard floor beneath: concrete, for instance. This is the equivalent of putting a horseshoe inside a boxing glove. Lucky clubs have their own premises with a permanent mat area, but that's rare. Many members who train in halls and recreation centers have to lug the heavy tatami in and out before and after each session.

It is the frequent and violent contact with the floor that is largely to blame for judo's greatest problem—its high dropout rate. People give many reasons for abandoning judo. Their friends are all doing other sports and they'd prefer to be with them. Judo demands too much: it is not enough to do judo to get fit, people have to get fit to do judo. That means more time spent in training in the gym or running. Nor is it a sport that can be done occasionally. Learning is a painfully slow process and one class a week is just not enough. All in all, it requires more commitment than most people can afford.

Commitment aside, for many people the sport is just too unpleasant. The white suits and the bowing are fine. But not only is there repeated and sudden contact with the mat, there is also the frequency of unpleasant contact with your partner. For instance, just to be on the receiving end of *uchikomi,* which involves no fighting at all, is uncomfortable; with certain people this drill can feel like skiing into a tree a hundred times. *Randori* is extremely tiring and sometimes painful. People come to the conclusion that being repeatedly smacked onto the floor is not how they really want to spend their precious spare time.

As the judoka progresses, he will learn to handle extreme physical exertion and suffering, but there is one thing that will push his endurance to its very limits. This occurs in social encounters with friends from the world outside the dojo who will, during a lull in the conversation, suddenly flatten their palms and do some weird movements while asking, "Are you still doing the old . . . karate?"

JUDO BRINGS YOU down to earth. It is in every sense a great leveler. There is no expensive equipment; a judo player brings only himself, his skill, and his strength. A small man can throw a big man. Those past their prime can beat those who are still in it. The poor may flatten the rich. And by using this language devised by Dr. Kano, a Mongolian can talk to a Cherokee, men can converse with women, adults can talk to children, and a beginner is allowed to argue with a world champion. Moreover, as soon as they start to speak this language, the verbally silent may suddenly become loquacious, the inarticulate may become lucid, and the talkative may be rendered speechless.

A dojo has a curious quality—the whiff of a sports hall mixed with the tingle of a temple. The faithful are drawn from miles around to worship and feel guilty if they fail to attend. Here, where priest and congregation all dress in white, they bow but there's no altar; they kneel but there's no prayer.

There is another quality, too, here in the tatami-filled room. The dojo is a place where men can behave like children and children can behave like men.

WHILE THE SNOBBERIES of class and wealth count for nothing, that is not to say judo is not extremely status-conscious. In what other sport are you made to declare the level of your competence by tying it round your waist? It was in Britain, at the Budokwai, that colored belts, judo's own class system, were first introduced. (They have only recently begun to be introduced in Japan, where traditionally belts have been white, brown, or black.) The novice starts as a *kyu* grade with a white belt before moving through yellow, orange, green, blue, and brown.

Only one obstacle lies between a judo player and a belt of a different color: grading. In order to be promoted through the ranks of these colors, he has to pass an exam divided into theory and practice. The theory part of the grading tests his knowledge of a few Japanese terms and his ability to demonstrate some throws and groundwork techniques. For the practical part the player is given an empty mat and a partner of roughly his own weight and ability and instructed to throw him or armlock him, or use any other winning technique, within the space of, usually, three minutes. There is one snag: the other person has been told to do exactly the same thing. The winner goes up a grade.

This, then, is not *randori,* which is just sparring for practice; this is full contest, *shiai,* a match.

Nothing can prepare anyone for it. Completely different from *randori,* it is much more vehement. Most candidates are racked with nerves and openly admit they dread the occasion. One of the things that makes it a great deal tougher than even a hard training session is that they have the mat to themselves, so there is a lot of room to move around and there are no interruptions, unless you go outside the area. It is physically more stressful. Also, it *really* matters to everyone, because they badly want the promotion. Those waiting to fight are watching in an audience swollen by friends and relatives. As if all this weren't bad enough, the contests are conducted in an eerie silence because spectators may not cheer for either combatant—they may applaud only at the end.

Some are less bothered than others, and maybe being older made it worse for me, but the routine of grading was a terror that I came to dread. I would start to feel anxious about six days before and it got worse and worse as the week wore on.

In order to reduce this anxiety I tried to deconstruct it. What exactly was I scared of? Partly I was scared of fighting in public and making a complete fool of myself—which is to say, scared that someone would make a complete fool of me. The possibilities for personal humiliation in judo are particularly rich. Being quickly and comprehensively defeated by someone much smaller, lighter, and younger loomed large in my mind, as did being seen to be timid. Being injured so badly that I would have to be carried off on a stretcher also had me sweating and wakeful in the small hours. Silly, of course, because it is an extremely rare occurrence.

These ridiculous anxieties led me to understand the expression, "Does he have the stomach for the fight?" I also discovered a new medical condition. At the philosophical end of martial arts there is much talk of getting the mind and body working in perfect harmony. I did manage to achieve this state, but not in quite the way I had planned. On a number of occasions I experienced a spasm of pain in my knee or ankle. There was no obvious explanation for it, but it would occur in the days before a grading. It was so intense that I would immediately find myself thinking, "I'm injured in some way; I can't possibly do a grading." Within a moment of my thinking this, the pain would vanish. Try as I might, by manipulating and flexing the joint, I could not make it come back. As my excuse departed, my anguish returned. It seemed perfectly clear that mind and body had collaborated to provide an excuse for me to withdraw from my contests. I have named this condition "holistic cowardice." It is my small contribution to medical science.

THE SCENE IS a Sunday morning at Syd Hoare's London Judo Society (LJS), a dojo in a large church hall in Stockwell. Even now I still feel slightly ill when I have to drive through this part of town, so vivid are the memories. On the way from the subway station, I have fallen in with someone else on his way to the grading. He is a student of Austrian history and as we make our way through the streets lined with towering concrete council blocks we have a faintly fatuous conversation about the Hapsburg Empire just to try to keep our minds off the certain death that awaits us, but my throat is so constricted by nervous tension I can scarcely talk.

I don't feel any better when we get to the LJS because loitering outside there are, as usual, a gang of thuggish-looking shaven-heads who are here for the same reason that I am. Normally, I would cross the road to avoid a gathering of people like this for fear of confrontation but today, ridiculously, I have come here specifically for a confrontation: Any one of them could be an opponent I may have to face. It doesn't matter that they offer a friendly greeting.

When I enter the hall all the candidates are pale and clearly nervous beneath outward displays of good humor and bravado. I see someone I know from the Budokwai, a big, tough Irish building contractor. His normally healthy complexion is the color of the finest cement dust. One part of me says, "I really don't need to be here." The other part isn't quite sure what to say.

I get changed and feel even worse. The coarse cotton of my newly laundered and bone-dry jacket feels harsh on my skin. I'm trying to look cool but I'm just feeling cold. My morale is like a sycamore seed spinning in a downward spiral. I think about making a run for it. Would anyone notice? Yes, the people that I know here would. The news would get back to my club. And I've paid and my name is on a list. I once saw a brown belt who was due to grade come into the changing room, apparently looking for something. He left and I never saw him for the rest of the day, or indeed ever again. I can only guess that when he'd taken a look at what he might encounter he decided against it. I thought none the worse of him for it. I wish I had the guts to do what he did, instead of sitting here waiting to be slaughtered.

Enough. I have to get a grip. I start doing breathing exercises and changing my demeanor. If I look confident, I'll feel confident. I compose my face into an expression of quiet, sinister nonchalance. Now I'm sending out the signal: Don't even think about it! Look at me: I am a lantern-jawed, cold-eyed killing machine!

I am congratulating myself on the way I have rallied my morale and transformed my appearance when a man in the spectator seats leans forward and says in a kindly, cajoling tone, "Don't look so worried, mate: it's not *that* bad."

Aaaaaaggh! My hard-man stuff hasn't fooled anyone. It is a miracle I don't just cut and run. I scrabble for a hold as my morale slithers down the rock face. My brain is bursting with two contradictory propositions: "I'm here because I want to be here" and "I just want to go home." I find myself searching for some magic fast-forward button. I don't care what happens next, I just want to be on the far side of it—quickly.

Now, if you say to me, "Wait a minute, all you have to do is go out there and stagger around until one or the other falls over?" I cannot argue with you. I only answer: This is the way it is for many people. Sturdier souls than I have been reduced by the experience.

It doesn't get any better when I start looking at the opposition, most of whom have now emerged from the changing room and are quietly stretching and warming up. Good grief, look at the size of them! They've been reared on steak. They're all fit and strong and young. And there's me. When I was a child, horses dragged wooden carts around the streets laden with milk in glass containers; health clubs hadn't been invented. I was born at the end of a mighty conflict that tore the world asunder. Displaced populations and the ragged remnants of half-starved armies scavenged for food in the rubble of this war-ravaged continent. It's a miracle I survived. But I'm not up to this; I'm going to be torn to bits out there!

Now the contests have begun. Lots of *ta-ka-ta-whoosh-splat!* Some end with unpleasant speed. There is some skill, but an awful lot of brute force and clumsiness. Sometimes one can wait up to an hour to fight. Eventually I hear my name called. I cannot believe it belongs to me. And then my opponent's name. It strikes a terrible chill. What kind of name is that? Oh no! Don't tell me. *I've got to fight a Mongolian!*

My imagination is now sliding in all directions like stilts on an ice rink. I've been put up against some newly arrived escapee from the steppes where the kids fight with their brothers day-in and day-out and live on a diet of lichen and camel gristle. Moreover, this man is a malevolent delinquent, brought up by a vicious drunken father who maltreated him for once forgetting to feed his cousin's yaks. Now I'm going to have to face the wrath of this son of Genghis who wants only to assuage the devils that plague him by offering them my corpse. What is he doing in this country? Who let him in anyway? This immigration thing is getting completely out of hand.

My opponent, emerging from the crowd on the other side of the mat, turns out to be just one more hopeful contestant, outwardly white and inwardly shaking, who has probably come up for the morning from some leafy suburb. He has a Huguenot name from his long-settled family and is even now thinking that I look like a lantern-jawed killing machine what with my composure, my cold eyes, and everything.

Compared with the waiting, the contests were the easy bit. The fighting was exciting, interesting, and, when I won a new-colored belt, very rewarding. Colored belts are one of judo's most addictive ingredients. Because your white belt is like a sign announcing to the world that you are a mere novice, you want to get a color, any color, so long as it's not white. As soon as I earned my orange belt, I wanted the next one, and so it went on until I'd got to brown, when I vowed that I would never go into a grading competition again. I'd done my part. Brown was more than acceptable. But it didn't take long for the satisfaction to fade. I'd come all this way; why stop now? Surely black was not such a remote possibility?

How wrong I was.

To become a black belt (or dan grade) you have to win at least ten contests against other brown belts over a period. But the preferred way is to do it by winning five contests on a single day. If you win the first two, you gain entitlement to a lineup in which you have to beat three opponents, one immediately after the other. Only the first five grades of black belt have to be fought for. Sixth to tenth dan are honorary and awarded to very distinguished figures for their contribution to judo.

The pursuit of these belts obsessed me. Gradings began to take on a terrible significance in my life. A craving for progression constantly clawed at my gut. The experience made me think about those at my club who pursued competition judo at the highest level. They had to face the best in the world. I had the diversion of an absorbing full-time job and any sporting failure was a mere sideshow. But for a career judoka, every result was crucial. What were they going through before a tournament when the course of their whole lives depended on how they fought?

I would never suggest that I could begin fully to appreciate the extraordinary pressures of serious sporting competition. But the ordeal of grading gave me an inkling of it and a new and abiding respect for any competitor.

In the minds of many who come to the sport, there persists a vague notion that judo is character-building. It is a nice-sounding idea, but what exactly does it mean? Surely sitting in front of the television eating chips all day is character-building, but what kind of a character does it build? Should the question we are asking be, Is judo character-*improving*? Does the study and practice of throwing people onto the floor really make someone a better person?

Kano made great claims for judo: it was a training for the mind as well as the body; it was a training for life. One can probably go along with this. We have seen how judo can be regarded as a metaphor for and a microcosm of life, so we can accept that some benefit must flow from the intensity of the sport, its sudden and extreme variations in fortune, the manner in which it rewards study and effort. Surely one can assert that the vicissitudes of judo must induce resilience, its individual nature must nurture self-reliance, exhaustion and discomfort must breed stoicism, speed and complexity must teach concentration. And equally, as a fighting sport it must stimulate fighting spirit—a determination to persevere in the face of adversity—as well as teaching restraint and self-control.

We can solemnly continue with this pious litany to the stirring mental accompaniment of the theme from *Chariots of Fire*. We can declaim that self-discipline, initiative, confidence, and courage are all fostered by judo, while we neglect to remind ourselves that these are also the very qualities required to be a successful bank robber. They are merely muscle groups of the mind; the important question is, What *instructs* them? Can judo bring any influence to bear on the moral steering wheel that directs us?

Kano thought it could. But if Kano was right, how come judo has had its share of failed drug tests, cheating, bad sportsmanship, and gratuitous brutality? The sport is fraught with skulduggery both on and off the mat. Maybe the answer is the same as the response to criticism of appalling behavior by those who are apparently religious: "Think how much worse they'd be if they *didn't* go to church!"

And maybe there's also a catch here. Maybe the research sample that judo provides is fundamentally flawed and unrepresentative. There is evidence to suggest that those who are keen on the sport are more likely to get into trouble.[1] Certainly I have been constantly surprised to learn from some judoka about the number of scraps that they get into. A Russian acquaintance who worked in construction told me that he got involved in barroom fights, not by choice, "about once every six weeks." This was no macho boast but the weary resignation of someone talking about a tedious and inevitable inconvenience of daily life, like parking fines.

Perhaps judo by its very nature attracts some of those most prone to get into trouble. Perhaps there is a wider truth in the half-joking assertion made by Mike Callan, director of Judo at the University of Bath (one of British judo's high-performance training centers), that the best way to find promising judo competitors is to start by picking out those schoolchildren who have got into trouble for fighting. Indeed many parents take their sons to a judo class *because* they are always getting into fights, because they are "a bit of a handful."

ANYONE WHO STRUGGLES to believe that judo builds character might find it easier to accept that judo certainly reveals it. The act of fighting uncovers truths about people. You cannot predict how someone will behave on the mat. One might seek a connection between the way they do judo and the way they live life, but surely this is just an endearing human desire to see patterns and connections where none exist. One has only to consider how some horrible people possess beautiful taste in music—and vice versa.

Those who exhibit the qualities of civility and courtesy can become quite savage on the mat; some who have the appearance of callous thugs behave like true gentlemen. I remember one man with whom I used to train who was a liar, a bum, and probably a thief, but who on the mat exhibited a courage, decency, and generosity of spirit that I found hard to reconcile with the rest of his behavior.

Some claim that judo can imbue its adherents with new qualities, but Geof Gleeson, a former British coach and one of the sport's philosophers, dismisses such claims as exaggerated. The confidence imbued by judo, he argues, is often mere brashness concealing timidity. A tendency to bully is exacerbated as often as it is suppressed. Judo, he argues, tends to emphasize what's there already.[2]

Similarly, Syd Hoare, who represented Britain at the Tokyo Olympics and who is a European silver medalist and an experienced instructor, has encountered myriad personalities. He maintains that "a first-class competitor can be a second-rate person and a second-class competitor can be a first-rate person. Judo ability is just judo ability—it does not necessarily tell you much about the man or woman."[3]

Again, we should beware of false connections. Physical courage doesn't only reside in heroic beings. It can happily share the same premises as moral cowardice.

THE SOVIET MENACE

The Soviet Union came to international competitive judo in its own unique and oblique way and, in the two years preceding the Tokyo Olympics of 1964, suddenly emerged as a serious judo force.

When the USSR met Japan in a match held in Kyoto in 1963, the year before the Games, the awesome Isao Okano, reigning champion of Japan, was sent on against another middleweight called Boris Mishchenko. The black-and-white film footage of the event is still today repeatedly shown to all Russian competitors. It doesn't last long; they see an aggressively confident Okano skip and bound forward as soon as _hajime_ is called, while the Russian retreats, his arms extended defensively and his palms raised almost in supplication. Okano presses forward and punctures the defense. Then the trap springs shut. Suddenly those supplicatory hands clamp the Japanese's collar and sleeve in a powerful grip, and the Russian, dropping onto his back and blocking Okano's stomach with his foot, drags him forward to the floor. As he does so, Mishchenko flicks his leg over the extended limb to trap him in a textbook _juji-gatame_ (straight armlock). Now in full control of the vulnerable elbow, Mishchenko has merely to stretch and arch his back to bend the joint in the wrong direction. Okano is helpless. In intense pain and finding no way to escape, he is forced to tap in surrender. The whole contest lasts just twenty-seven seconds.

The Japanese had never seen an armlock like this before and Okano had been taken by complete surprise. He felt so deeply humiliated by this defeat, it is said, that he refused to leave his house for six months.[1] Some of the Japanese old guard were furious with him for bringing shame on his nation by submitting before his arm was broken.[2] They felt that he had acted selfishly in preserving his limb because he wanted to be fit to fight in the Tokyo Olympics. The contest highlighted a new phase in the struggle between the nations. Western Europe in the person of Anton Geesink had launched a successful attack on Japan's preeminence at judo. But now, from another quarter, came an assault, not only against the Japanese, but against judo itself.

HIDDEN FROM THE REST of the world behind the Iron Curtain that it had drawn around the borders of its vast empire, the Soviet Union had been developing and exhaustively testing new secret weapons in its armory of unarmed combat techniques. These were now unleashed on an unsuspecting world. Those who saw them were dazzled; those who had to face them were frankly fearful.

The art of jujitsu had reached Russia at more or less the same time as the rest of Europe, early in the twentieth century.[3] Within a few years judo followed. It didn't have far to travel: Vladivostok is within 550 miles of Japan and it was here, in Russia's great Pacific seaport, that the founder of Russian judo was born.

At the age of fourteen, an orphan boy called Vasili Oshchepkov was funded by a charity to attend the city's Tokyo Christian school, which served as a training ground for Russian priests destined to work in Japan. While there, he learned judo, twice making the journey to Japan to grade. Kodokan records show that he gained his black belt in 1914 when he was twenty-one. He was an enthusiastic student and started his own judo club in his home town in the following year. In 1917—the year of the Russian Revolution—he arranged for a team from Japan to come over for a match against his own pupils. This, the first judo tournament between two countries, marked the birth of international competition.

In the years following the Revolution, Oshchepkov worked in Tokyo, ostensibly as a military interpreter but more probably as an intelligence agent.[4] Certainly, orphans with their lack of ties and loyalties were a popular target for recruitment by the secret services. Oshchepkov's fluency in Japanese and his practical knowledge of unarmed combat would have made him a promising candidate.

Throughout Oshchepkov's Tokyo posting he continued his study of judo at the Kodokan and on his return to his homeland he was commissioned to devise a self-defense system for the Red Army.[5] He collaborated with a jujitsu expert named Viktor Spiridonov to produce a series of hand-to-hand combat manuals.

The citizens of the Soviet Union were a receptive audience. For centuries, each of the peoples of the territories that now constituted the fifteen Soviet republics had developed their own highly individual wrestling styles. These were their national sports; fighting was what they did. All that was needed was a cotton jacket and the determination to throw an opponent on the floor. Oshchepkov's task was to use Kodokan judo as a framework on which he could fuse these indigenous styles of fighting.

In a program of "creative sessions" at four main sports centers in Moscow, including the Red Army Central Club, Oshchepkov brought together people from all over the USSR to meet in a succession of exploratory confrontations. The techniques of the Tajiks were assessed against those of the Khazaks; Georgians, who never fought on the ground, were pitted against Turkmen; Uzbek throws were tested against the pick-ups and leg-grabs of the Azerbaijanis. The system which evolved from all this was initially confined to the armed forces, notably the Soviet special forces troops of the Spetsnaz and the security services.

Later Oshchepkov and Spiridonov were ordered to develop judo as a sport that could be disseminated among the civilian population. In the face of an imminent war with Germany, the high command wanted citizens to have some knowledge of unarmed self-defense that would provide the basis for military combat training. The art of self-defense was to be forged into a weapon of civil defense.

It would have been an extraordinary time for those who took part—designing and creating a new system in this living laboratory—but in the dark and feverish world outside the dojos of Moscow, a terrible political situation was worsening. Every citizen of the Soviet Union lived at the mercy of the murderous and demented Joseph Stalin. Paranoid about the possible presence of enemy spies, Stalin was pathologically fearful that his subjects might have been contaminated by contact with foreigners. The security forces responded with their usual blind obedience and, in consequence, anything that provoked the merest suspicion could cost a man his life. Oshchepkov, whose dossier showed long-standing links with Japan and probably some sort of murky role in intelligence, was doomed. In the great political purges of 1937, like many others who had traveled abroad or consorted with foreigners, he was arrested by the NKVD, the state security police, and declared a spy. Within ten days of his imprisonment he was dead. It is assumed that he was interrogated under torture to force a confession of guilt and betray the "accomplices" he never had. He was forty-four.[6]

Oshchepkov's very name now became anathema and had to be obliterated. The word judo was also to meet the same fate. In 1938 the government of the USSR banned its use and, on November 16 of that year, it decreed that the term "judo" was to be replaced by the term "sambo" (an acronym for the Russian words meaning "self-defense without weapons"). By the dogma of the day, the Soviet authorities could neither acknowledge that any kind of foreign influence—and most certainly not an imperial one—could be benign, nor admit that anything worthwhile could have come about through the talent and leadership of a mere individual. Only the state could possibly be responsible for the creation of its system of self-defense; the records had to be falsified to conceal the fact that sambo was fathered by judo and to demonstrate that, through a sort of immaculate conception, it was born of Mother Russia.

In truth, most of the sambo syllabus consisted of techniques from Kodokan judo. There were some differences: sambo fighters wore tighter jackets, making for a more strength-based contest; in contrast, it is the looseness of the Japanese *gi* that gives judo its whippy speed. The rules of sambo contests closely resemble those of judo in the 1920s, with some differences. Judo forbids leg locks and allows strangles, while sambo has it the other way around. Prolonged belt holding, barred in judo because it is seen as passive, is legal in sambo, in which it functions as the basis for attack. And, unlike in judo, in which thrower and thrown often both go over, a sambo contestant has to remain on his feet to score from a throw.

WHEN THE OLYMPIC COMMITTEE announced that judo was to be added to the 1964 Games in Tokyo, the commissars of Soviet sport quickly spotted the opportunity to harvest a rich crop of medals that might bring them the worldwide prestige they so desperately sought in their Cold War struggle with the West. There was, of course, one snag: they didn't have any judo players because they had abolished them, along with the sport. So they scoured the ranks of their sambo fighters for the most likely candidates and retrained them to fight by the rules of judo. The consequences were to astonish both Japan and the West.

The finest products of the Soviet training halls were now suddenly unleashed on the international judo tournament scene, with devastating results. Their lethal armlocks were only part of an array of new weapons to be launched against a world that had hitherto confined itself to the armory of the Gokyo, the list of techniques drawn up by the Kodokan.

The creed of the Kodokan was being challenged by the heretical tenets of the Russian unorthodox church. This new idea of judo, this furious flurry of leg grabs and pick-ups, was a far cry from the stylish spectacle of classical *tachiwaza*. The freeness of its style elicited the same sort of reaction provoked by the first French Impressionist painters: Yes, it was dazzling, different, and spectacular; but was it art?

The Soviets didn't give a damn about the "art"; they were solely concerned with the "martial." They carried no sentimental baggage packed with "the philosophy of mutual benefit" or ideas about the sport being "a training for life"; this was a competition event seen through totalitarian eyes, fought with weapons that were not only devastating because they were unfamiliar—but were legal. The Gokyo was merely the set menu for judo—a list of recommended techniques—but anyone could always choose à la carte. There was nothing in the rules of contest judo that forbade anyone trying any technique outside the Gokyo—as long as it complied with the rules: no leg locks, no punching, no eye-gouging, and so on.

Confronted by this completely new style of fighting, judo men couldn't understand what was going on. The whole approach was unorthodox. The Soviets didn't grip or even move around the mat in the normal way. Their opponents often found themselves utterly defenseless in the face of the unpredictable. The very word "sambo" began to take on a menacing significance for judo men. One day judo would have its own sweet revenge, but that was a decade or so away; meanwhile the samboists wrought their terrible havoc.

Like Genghis Khan's Mongol hordes at the city gates of Jin Dynasty in China, the Soviet warriors appeared at stadiums around the world to effect their own kind of pitiless destruction. For those who had to go out and face them on the tatami, the new techniques were perplexing enough in themselves; moreover, they were executed by unnervingly fit, highly trained athletes possessed by a desperate hunger to win.

In 1957 these sambo-trained fighters made their first appearance in judo competition outside the USSR when they were unleashed on two of the Soviet Union's satellites, Hungary and the German Democratic Republic, beating them easily. But it was not until the European championships in Essen, West Germany, in 1962 that the Soviets finally emerged from behind their Iron Curtain to take on the wider world. In the spirit of judo, the European countries accepted the outstretched hand of friendship, which promptly grabbed them by their jackets and gave them the pounding of their lives. The Soviets beat everyone, including the French, who were three-time European champions.

When the Japanese heard about this massacre of Europe's finest they realized they needed to find out what was happening. In the following year they arranged to send a squad to the USSR for a series of tournaments in Moscow, Kiev, and Leningrad (now St. Petersburg). To their horror, in this, the first confrontation between the two countries, the Soviet Union won all three matches. In addition to a ferocious desire to win, these men seemed quite uninhibited by the awed respect for the Japanese that permeated the ranks of Western judoka.[7]

The Japanese were now in something of a panic. The Olympics were drawing closer. Were they going to be routed on their home ground by these ancient enemies of their nation? Were their champion judoka going to be humiliated in front of their own countrymen—in front of their emperor? The Japanese authorities needed to understand more clearly what they were up against; they needed more detailed intelligence about the enemy. So, at the end of 1963, they invited the Soviets to Japan for a further series of tournaments in three different cities. The Soviets accepted the invitation; some say this was their big mistake. When they arrived an army of Japanese experts was waiting to scrutinize and analyze their every movement. This time, although the result was uncomfortably close,[8] the Japanese won two out of the three tournaments, demonstrating that they had already learned lessons from their earlier defeat. More important, by the end of the tour (during which Okano fell victim to that surprise armlock), the Japanese had found ample opportunity to learn about the enemy in greater detail than ever before.

One facet of the new judo confronting them—indeed, confronting anyone engaged in fighting the Soviet menace—was a doctrine introduced by Oshchepkov known as the Concept of Permanent Combat. Oshchepkov had given much thought to those many moments of neutrality in a fight when combatants prepare for or recover from attacks. Convinced that these gaps in the action could be exploited, he taught his pupils to close the space between themselves and their opponents so that they were always in a threatening position, always ready to strike. This increased the workload and demanded a fantastic level of fitness but its effect was twofold: first, it drastically accelerated the pace of a contest; second, these infighting tactics made for a less elegant style of combat.

When the Olympics in Tokyo finally came about, the judo event was completely dominated by Geesink's celebrated triumph over Kaminaga. But some Japanese were as concerned by the overall performance of the Soviet team as they were by the achievement of the lone Dutchman. The Soviets represented much more of a menace, for theirs was a menace in depth: the USSR had entered their full quota of four contestants and every one of them won a bronze medal.

In the decade that followed Geesink's victory, it was the Soviets who led the assault on Japanese hegemony. Judo was dropped from the 1968 Olympics in Mexico, and when it reappeared at the 1972 Munich Olympic Games (by now reorganized into six different weight categories), a mere reserve light heavyweight on the Soviet team, Shota Chochoshvili, defeated world champion Fumio Sasahara with a devastatingly decisive shoulder throw in the second round and then went on to take the gold. The result stunned the Japanese, who had to accept other defeats. In the 1964 Olympics they had won three of the four gold medals; this time they came away with only three out of six. They were now truly embattled and desperately needed a champion of their own to rally their forces.

They were to find one.

THE EMPEROR

"If they could see on my face what I feel in my heart, no one would ever fight me." These were the words of a jovial giant named Yasuhiro Yamashita when asked why he smiled so much. So just what *did* he feel in his heart, his fans would wonder; the opponents brought before him for ritual slaughter might have questioned whether he even had one.

Anyway, he wasn't smiling now. Not now, not on this Olympic afternoon in Los Angeles in July 1984 as he stood staring blankly across the mat toward his opponent, waiting for the final to begin. He had sacrificed his whole life to this sport—hours of superhuman training, years of endless combat, a trail of unbroken victories. He hadn't lost a contest since he was nineteen years old in 1977. It is not just that he won some great tournaments—three world championships and nine All Japans—it is that he won *everything*.

Everything except the one that mattered most to him, the most important trophy of them all: Olympic gold. This was Yamashita's first chance to get it. And his last. He wanted it more than anything. He had dreamed of it since seeing the Tokyo Olympics on television when he was in his first year at primary school. And as if the challenge wasn't hard enough, now that he'd finally got his opportunity, now that he was having to face the best that the world could send against him, right at the end of his career when his whole frame was battered and weary from a life of incessant competition, the gods of war had cruelly saddled him with a fearful handicap. He was about to fight for a gold medal in one of the most athletically demanding of sports with a badly torn calf muscle. The final chapter of a sportsman's life doesn't get more dramatic than this.

IN 1966, MRS. YAMASHITA arrived at the dojo of Mr. Seiki Fujitsubo with a large, plump, badly behaved nine-year-old boy. She explained that she wanted her son to do judo because he was overweight and cantankerous at school. He would push his way to the front of the food line[1] and was inclined to get into fights with anyone of any size. He had little understanding of the effect of his bulk and strength and even in good-natured play he would unwittingly hurt other pupils. Some children were so frightened by him that they actually stopped coming to school. His parents wanted him to do judo so he would learn some discipline. What follows is the story of a fat brat who fashioned himself into a sporting god.

Young Yasuhiro fell in love with judo straight away. One of the qualities in it that he once said he found most appealing was "its violence."[2] And he has since said that someone once told him when he was young: "Imagine that the man you are facing has just killed your father."[3] Whatever part these notions might have played in his motivation, his sheer skill and fighting spirit were impressive enough to catch the eye of a high school judo supervisor on a talent-scouting expedition for his establishment at Kumamoto on Kyushu Island. He realized that he was watching a *kaido*, a gifted child, and immediately sought to recruit the boy.

The Yamashita family accepted the offer of a high school education for Yasuhiro and sent him to live in Kumamoto accompanied by his grandfather, who agreed to live with him and take care of him. As an infant, Yasuhiro's grandfather used to massage him with ice and dip him alternately in hot and cold water to toughen him. When he was a year old, Yasuhiro won a local contest for the healthiest baby. Now the old man had become a great influence and supporter, appearing at the school each day to watch his grandson practice. Later, he was to accompany young Yasuhiro to competitions around Japan and abroad, looking after him and cooking all their meals himself.[4] Yasuhiro's schoolmates nicknamed him Ojiichanko, grandpa's boy.[5]

The school took judo extremely seriously; the practice was demanding and the boy grew so tired that he often went to sleep on the bus and missed his stop. Yamashita's new teacher seemed free of any doubt about the potential of his gifted pupil and gave him two simple targets: to be high school champion at age fifteen and Japanese champion at age eighteen.

All went according to plan: He became high school champion. But both his family and the school realized that if he were to stand a chance of winning the national title, he would have to go to Tokyo for more advanced teaching. Accordingly, he was enrolled in the high school attached to Tokai University, then as now one of the preeminent training academies for future talent. The establishment was certainly glad to have him. There were others who had spotted his talent: scouts from a sumo wrestling stable had tried hard to recruit him while he was at high school. But Yamashita said he didn't like sumo and wanted to do judo so he could win a gold medal in the Olympics.

It was Yamashita's great fortune that at Tokai he came under the wing of a brilliant coach, twice world champion Nobuyuki Sato, who ran the university judo club. Yamashita had arrived with the declared intention of being champion of the world and Sato thought he could do it. And so in the summer of 1974, as the great coach wrote, "our three-legged race began."[6]

Yamashita went to live with Sato's family, which proved to be an invaluable experience for the seventeen-year-old boy. Sato was a sensei in the traditional sense, a wise and experienced man who saw judo as a means to broader fulfillment—for him it was indeed *do,* the "way." Yamashita records: "The evenings after dinner became very precious. While we enjoyed tea prepared by his wife, we discussed sportsmanship, education, and life in general."

But it was not all dainty cups of tea and earnest philosophical discourse, even by Sato's own account. "When Yamashita came to Tokyo in his second year at high school I was worried about the media treating him like a genius at that time and there has been virtually no one who has succeeded after such treatment," the coach recalls. "I warned him straight away: 'If you become arrogant I will break your nose, OK?'" The greatest part of Yamashita's character, Sato would maintain, was that he was always willing to listen even after he had become a champion. "The successful players are the obedient ones. But I didn't want Yamashita to become just a machine in order to win or to be a robot player who only moved as I ordered. I always wanted him to be someone who thinks, decides, and fights for himself."

By January 1976, the time had come for Yamashita to get a taste of foreign flesh. He was selected to go to the Tournoi de Paris, an invitational tournament that the French use to try out their squad at the beginning of the season.

For the Japanese, the first trip to a Western competition is something of an ordeal, and it was particularly so for Yamashita, then only eighteen years old. His high school teacher had made it clear to him from the early days that when he fought outside Japan his opponents would be heavier than he was. To make matters worse, his Japanese rivals took relish in trying to scare him with tales of giant European judo players with chests covered in thick hair and arms like tree trunks. His confidence returned when he actually saw them and found that they were not much bigger than he was, which is to say 279 pounds and five feet eleven inches tall. He buried them all and walked off with the gold.

"Yamashita is blessed with a rhino's torso and a cat's feet; the combination makes it virtually impossible to flip him onto his back," was how one commentator described the champion's ideal heavyweight build with its very low center of gravity.[7] As the coach of one of his rivals observed, "It is like fighting a refrigerator."[8] His training regimen consisted of at least four hours a day of running, weightlifting, and mat work with just two Sundays a month off. But he always believed that mental strength, concentration, and effort were more important than physical condition.

The spirit of Yamashita as expressed in his judo struck a chord with all who watched him. As well as being admired as a competitor, he became adored as a character. His brilliant technique was only part of his appeal; people loved the way that technique was an expression of his personality. A writer who went to visit him in Japan said, "Ordinary Japanese recognize him instantly, as they would the sunrise, and approach him from all sides to talk to him and touch him. The etiquette and formality that keep them a respectful distance from their other heroes somehow melt away under the glow of Yamashita."

With the approach of a major competition, Yamashita followed the samurai tradition of scrubbing his apartment and his body so both were spotless should he die in competition. Then he hung the name of his greatest rival upon the wall to stare at. "It was often said to me, 'Losing doesn't occur to you, does it?' It is not true." He was endearingly frank about his nerves. After his retirement, untypically of the guarded Japanese, he talked openly of the exhaustion, doubts, and despair that plagued him as year after year he faced the pressure of maintaining his place at the top.

He wrote about the psychological tricks and excuses he would adopt to help himself. Before the 1977 world championships in Spain, he was uncertain about facing the Montreal Olympic medalist, Sergei Novikov from the USSR. "I convinced myself that it would not be my fault if I lost since he was the best in the world and I would blame the Japanese Judo Association for sending a mere twenty-year-old to this championship."

Yamashita developed little strategies for overcoming the precompetition nerves that might make him tense and depressed. "I would pick up wastepaper to clean up the road. If I bumped into a beautiful lady or if it was a fine day, I would interpret these as good omens." This is the touching irrationalism of the superstitious sportsman; presumably his opponents, who were unlikely to be more than a few hundred yards away, were enjoying pretty much the same sort of weather. But for the true star making an appearance on the world stage, the sun is merely his personal spotlight.

"If I find myself yawning before a contest," Yamashita wrote, "I take a deep breath to refresh my body. When you are nervous you always feel like going to the toilet. Do not resist this feeling. By going to the toilet you can get the poisons out of your system."

While most of the squad would stay in their rooms and read, Yamashita found this too nerve-wracking, so he would go out for a walk with a teammate. They would sing popular songs or just sit on a bench and watch passersby. Occasionally he would do some deep breathing. He said all this refreshed him and helped him to sleep well.

When he was at home, he would often climb a small hill called Mount Kobo. "I felt I could gain vital energy by taking in the fresh air and listening to the birds." When he reached the top those birds also got a chance to listen to him: he liked to sing "My Way" in Japanese.

Sometimes when he wasn't worried about a contest, he would worry about not being worried. About to face the European champion, Wojciech Reszko of Poland, in the openweight final of the world championships in Maastricht in 1981, he said that he had never felt so confident, but that confidence made him uneasy—it might make him careless. However, he won the contest on the ground, exactly as he expected to, with *okuri-eri-jime*, his favorite strangle.

Never one to rely on technique and strength alone, Yamashita had a profound belief in the value of intelligence about the opposition and was assiduous in gathering it. "Some people despised me, saying, 'Yamashita is surprisingly small minded.' But I didn't care what other people thought about my preparations. My belief was that I could fight best when I knew both about the opponent and my own condition." At training camps, where he had a chance to see his rivals in action at close quarters, he made a point of familiarizing himself with their techniques. He knew that he himself was often being scrutinized, so he would try to move out of sight, particularly when a serious rival was present. Nor did he stop observing when practice ended. "Even off the mat there are opportunities to gain useful information," he observed. "Whatever you are doing, whether watching television, reading newspapers or having a chat with your friends at the bar, you should not lose any opportunity.

"I believe that I analyze my opponents more than any other player does. I used to play video tapes over and over again in order to memorize my opponents' techniques, movements and habits. In order to build up the analysis, I would listen to everyone's opinion. Before the fight I imagined how the fight would be conducted."

Yamashita was never just an athletic powerhouse of technique and brawn. He always had a good brain. At school he may have been a playground menace, but he was one of the cleverer pupils. Although Japanese universities, like their American counterparts, admit some students whose academic efforts are a mere token, Yamashita was not one of those. In spite of all his success in competition, he felt under constant pressure to study and would complain to his coach about the pressure of writing his thesis for his finals. Academically, he ranked in the top ten of the 350 students who graduated in his year at Tokai.

He would surprise those who met him with his cultivation. "Interviews with Japanese athletes tend to consist mainly of series of terse, unrevealing utterances," wrote one interviewer. "Yamashita is very different. His replies are discursive, informed, and playful, covering a wide range of subjects."[9]

FROM HIS EARLY DAYS, Yamashita set himself on the road to glory, determined that he would leave "an indelible footprint on judo history." He wanted two Olympic gold medals—one in

Moscow and one in Los Angeles. The first was to be denied to him because Japan observed the boycott that followed the Soviet invasion of Afghanistan in 1980. Angry and disappointed, he confined himself to his room for a few days—to avoid "sympathetic remarks"—before emerging to go to a bar with his best friend and get fantastically drunk. As it turned out, he would never have been able to take part anyway. In a qualifying contest another great rival, Sumio Endo, attacked him with *kanibasami*—a technique whereby the legs make a flying scissors movement, chopping down those of the opponent. Yamashita countered, but in doing so broke a bone just above his left ankle. The following year, however, brought some consolation.

The world championships of 1981 were held in the Dutch city of Maastricht. Yamashita, now twenty-four years old, was at the peak of his condition and the Japanese selectors, confident of his powers, entered him in two categories, the heavyweight (over 209 pounds) and the openweight. Their confidence proved entirely justified. In the first event, he won all five contests by *ippon* in a total of nine minutes four seconds. When he weighed himself the next day, he had lost eleven pounds. This couldn't have been due to physical effort, he said, because he never felt he was in trouble on the mat. He was convinced it was entirely due to mental pressure.

These victories came as a great relief to the beleaguered Japanese, doing much to restore their ailing fortunes. Yet, although Yamashita was feted when he returned home, the double triumph was curiously to herald a terrible downturn in his morale. "I felt all my enthusiasm ebb away, and I did not know why. I had lost the desire to win." He asked his sensei why he seemed to have lost his energy and his fighting spirit. Sato's analysis was succinct: "You have got too big for your boots."

Sato, his coach, was one of two men who helped drive Yamashita to ever greater efforts. The other, just a vowel away, was his greatest rival, Hitoshi Saito. One did everything he could to help him and the other everything he could to hinder him. For most of his life, Saito was doomed to fight in Yamashita's shadow.

Although by no means as well known as his great rival, he too was a giant of judo and won two Olympic medals—a gold and a silver. Yamashita maintained how important it was to have rivals and admitted that he had been galvanized by the fact that Saito had by this time become a serious threat to his supremacy. The most celebrated encounters between the two men took place at the annual All Japan Judo Championship. To the Westerner this may seem like an unimportant local affair, but the presence of so many world-class players in Japan makes it an incredibly tough competition. Indeed, many Japanese have regarded it as tougher than the world championships or the Olympics. It was only after his great rival's retirement that Saito was able to win the All Japan. Yamashita won it nine times.

"WHEN YOU HAVE REACHED your peak physically and technically, your mental stability is the vital factor." By 1983 Yamashita had passed that peak. "I began to feel a gradual waning of my physical power," he wrote. "You have to make up for your decline in power not by overtraining but by your high spirits. In my latter period as a player, I had to struggle relentlessly to gain power and spirit."

The grim realization that his physique and his fitness were now in inexorable decline formed in Yamashita's mind just as his greatest and most important battle loomed. Since childhood his great ambition had been to win the Olympic gold medal and the Los Angeles Olympics, to be held in the summer of 1984, would be his last chance. He would be thirty-one years old by the time of the next Olympics in Seoul. "No one has remained as a champion until thirty," he said, "and I don't think I can do it either." His strength was beginning to ebb and he found he was feeling increasingly tired after his matches.

For a man who had enjoyed an unbroken run of victories since he was nineteen, each successive contest added a little more pressure. He could never relax for a moment. Every opponent that he faced, from no-hoper to serious contender, wanted to go down in the record books as The Man Who Stopped Yamashita. The champion was now suffering seriously from the pressures of age and expectation. Word went round: "The full moon is waning."

The phrase "Olympic village" suggests some calm and cozy idyll. The truth is very different. It's Tension Town, a place of athlete's apartments filled with bundles of raw and jagged nerve ends bagged up in shellsuits. Among those in Los Angeles in the summer of 1984 was Yamashita, waiting for the fight of his life. He no longer had the reassuring presence of his grandfather. The old man, bedridden at home in Japan, would only see the event on television and Yamashita's confidence was uncertain. "Two images of myself came across my mind when I was alone," he wrote. "One had me waving to a large crowd of spectators with a gold medal, and the other had me hiding in the changing room after being defeated." He had never felt like this before.

Now he found that he would talk to himself in the mirror, reassuring and exhorting himself. In the course of these mind games he observed a shift in his attitude. This time he wasn't so bothered about winning for his country. "I wanted to win for my-self," he later said. In order to help him relax, he was given special permission to take a day off. He set off to the Japanese quarter in Los Angeles, where he did some shopping, visited a sauna, had a swim, and enjoyed a Japanese meal. He found that the excursion dispelled "the heavy atmosphere of stress in the village."

The judo event was held out on the campus of California State University and the crowd was buzzing in anticipation of seeing the great Yamashita in action. His first opponent, Lansana Coly from Senegal, lasted just twenty-eight seconds. Next came Arthur Schnabel of West Germany. The German didn't—couldn't—do much, but when Yamashita turned in for a throw, he felt a terrible pain in his pivoting foot. He moved as normally as he could so as to conceal the injury from his opponent, but a stirring among the crowd made it clear that they had noticed him limping. Yamashita had badly torn a muscle in his right ankle. "I had to tell myself, 'Do not show any pain. Fix your eyes on your opponent.'" Yamashita caught his opponent when he went down on the ground and strangled him into submission.

When he went up to the platform for his contest against the next opponent, Laurent del Colombo of France, he was clearly hobbling badly and the situation was made even worse when he was attacked on his injured leg. Unable to move it out of the way in time, he went down for a *koka*—the first time he had conceded any score for many years. But he recovered enough to throw his opponent with a footsweep and then hold him down.

Meanwhile, throughout the day, the man he was to meet in the final was making his way through the preliminaries: the Egyptian, Mohammed Rashwan.

It was in the tense period before the final that Sato, the man who had worked with Yamashita for the last twenty years, chose to tell his charge that after the coming contest was over he wanted to end their long-standing master–pupil relationship. The precise nature of Sato's psychological calculation is not clear, but the redrafting of this very Japanese contract between them, formal yet unwritten, had the desired effect. Yamashita was tired and injured and supremely nervous yet, as he says, he went to the competition arena with "renewed determination."

Just before the contest began Yamashita was sitting beside the mat with his eyes closed. He said he could feel Rashwan's arrival. As he opened his eyes he caught those of the Egyptian and found himself smiling unconsciously. Rashwan returned the smile. At that moment Yamashita was convinced he would win. "His smile eased his antipathy towards me." Yamashita realized that Rashwan's smile was genuine—an acknowledgment of their parallel situations. Yamashita's was not. It was nothing more than a brief facial expression. "Of course," he was later to say, "I could not smile in the back of my mind."

When Yamashita came onto the mat, the crowd could see that the favorite was limping very badly and feared the worst for him. But once *hajime* was called all signs of the injury disappeared. It was not a spectacular contest given what was at stake, but Yamashita seemed to have overcome the pain and was able to counter one of Rashwan's attacks with a footsweep that threw him, allowing Yamashita once more to move into a hold-down from which the Egyptian could not escape.

"The referee's call of *ippon* seemed to come from far away," he said. "I stood in the middle of the loud cheers and felt I was the happiest man in the world. I threw myself at Mr. Sato, just like when I became Japanese champion at nineteen. My childhood dream had come true."[10] When it came to the medal presentations, Rashwan had to help Yamashita up onto the podium.

That was his last international competition but not quite the end of his competitive career. There was still one remaining task for him: to win the All Japan just once more. He said that he never suffered so much as he did while training for this final effort. Although recovered from his Los Angeles injury, his morale was low, for he was grieving the loss of his beloved grandfather, Taizo, the old man who had bathed him as a baby, had cooked for him, had looked after him in his youth, and had been beside the mat at all his important contests. Nothing could lift his spirits. His training lacked vigor. He kept getting beaten by his own students at the Tokai University dojo. He knew they were worried about him, that they were thinking he would lose at the All Japan.

Yamashita said that what lifted him from his depression was the sudden realization of how much he had derived from practicing with the students over the years, how much they had helped and encouraged him. Indeed, he faced one of his own students in the semifinal. But the man whom he would eventually face in the final was his greatest rival, Saito.

"Saito was showing his fighting spirit but it did not bother me. For me it was more important that I should dominate the contest. During the fight I lost a point by falling while attempting a *sasae-tsuri-komiashi* [a foot technique]. In order not to be defeated I had to continually attack with my favorite techniques. I was aware that throwing Saito was very difficult, if not impossible." When Saito was penalized for passivity the scores were leveled and the ten-minute contest ended with the decision going to Yamashita, who much regretted that he didn't get a more decisive win. He also conceded that there were those who thought that Saito had won, and he was big-hearted enough to say so in print. But now his work was done. At the end of the contest he bowed to his old adversary and stepped off the battlefield for the last time.

By the time he retired, Yamashita had inspired and entranced hundreds of thousands of judoka across the globe. He represented the very finest aspect of the sport and the extent of his victories has never been equaled. As one correspondent wrote, "Yamashita had transformed judo, restoring to his country the dominance of the sport they invented. When he retired, Japan's supremacy crumbled."[11] Another who encountered the champion preparing for his final battle noted that his significance in Japan was much wider than the mere sport itself and wrote, "In a blinking, beeping, robot-ridden country, Yamashita is a great chunk of spirited matter waddling among the people, calling them back to elemental truths."[12]

13

THE ARMS RACE

"Westerners are stronger than Japanese," Mr. Hirotaka Okada told me, sipping tea at a café in London before our encounter on the mat. While he was instructing at the Budokwai and learning English, he functioned like a member of any nation's judo hierarchy, fulfilling the role of military attaché: overtly gathering intelligence on fighting techniques and training methods. He would later bring Japanese competitors to experience and learn from European training camps. Yamashita had done the same sort of thing when he retired from competition and came to the Budokwai in 1986. During his time there he studied and reported on European strength training methods, for which the Japanese have a great deal of curiosity and respect.[1]

As the success of Western competitors steadily grew in the 1960s, alarm bells started to ring in the minds of the Japanese squad managers. Part of the problem was that Westerners were bigger. Disparity in size can in most circumstances be overcome by technique, but, as Geesink's victory over Kaminaga demonstrated, if the West could produce a fighter who was bigger and stronger *and* equal in technique, then the Japanese were in trouble. At this stage the Japanese still remained technically superior, but the newcomers were gaining ground fast and their strength was changing the game. "The techniques of Japanese judoists today are more varied and on a higher level than those of their foreign counterparts," Isao Inokuma, the Tokyo Olympic heavyweight champion noted in 1979, while observing that "Japanese judo-ists are inferior to foreign counterparts in basic physical powers and, as a result, lose their bouts without being able to apply their techniques to the fullest."[2]

It was the upper-body strength of the Westerners that really worried the Japanese. At the core of the problem faced by the Japanese was a fundamental difference between the Eastern and Western physique. The essential design characteristic of the Japanese chassis is that the engine is housed between the hips; judo evolved around this configuration. Westerners, however, are designed quite differently: the engine is sited in the chest and shoulders, which gives them much stronger upper bodies. The coaches of the Japanese national squad realized that they would have to radically change their approach to physical training, a subject that in any case they had a lot to learn about from the West. The Orient tended to rely on tradition; the Occident preferred science.

It was in the West that the advanced principles of scientific weight training were developed. They were introduced to the Japanese by visiting judoka, notably Donn Draeger, an American author studying judo and training at the Kodokan, who collaborated with Takahiko Ishikawa, one of Kimura's great adversaries, on a book called *Judo Training Methods,* published in 1961. A number of high-level Japanese competitors came to Draeger for advice; among the first of them was Inokuma, who enlisted his help in 1957. Inokuma said that as a child he "was rather sickly and did not have much of a physique."[3] He had, of course, always used weights as part of his contest preparation, but Draeger taught him to train with them in a planned and systematic progression. As a result of this, Inokuma became markedly larger and stronger—increasing his weight from 160 pounds to 191 pounds by the time of the 1964 Olympics.[4] Reeling from Kaminaga's defeat at the hands of Geesink, his fellow countrymen were resentful of the way in which Inokuma generously acknowledged Draeger's contribution to his Olympic success.

Word about the Western approach to weight training began to spread. As more and more coaches got the message, the weight room began to become almost as important as the mat. In dojos across Japan, thousands of tons of iron were being lifted every day in a bid to strengthen their forces against encroachment from the West. The grinding repetition of bench presses, reverse curls, and bent-arm pull-overs began increasingly to intrude on the judoka's training day. In a determined effort to match the firepower achieved by Europeans, they started to beef up their shoulders and strengthen their forearms, biceps, and triceps. Japan had joined what was, literally, an international arms race.

QUITE A FEW OF the people who train at the Budokwai do a number of other sports. I used to be surprised how often the rugby players among them would complain about being unfit when they returned to the mat after being away playing the game. The consensus is, "If you're fit for judo, then you're fit for rugby; being fit for rugby doesn't make you fit for judo."

"Mat fitness" is a peculiar quality. Judo makes drastic demands on competitors' physiques in a way that most other sports do not, and once a promising competitor has been selected for the national squad, he will embark on a training regime the intensity of which he is unlikely ever to have experienced. He will learn the difference between what the Japanese call "hobby judo" and "serious judo." At one stage he is doing judo for fun, then suddenly it becomes his life. One former competitor told me that at the end of his first week with the junior national squad he was in a state of exhausted despair. They were doing judo every day, three times a day and the training was so hard that by the end of the first week he was saying to himself, "I wish I had never started this."

Of course, many a sport demands extremes of physical effort, but these demands tend to be quite narrow. At the heart of the challenge facing judo coaches and competitors lies the fact that a contest can pass through the entire spectrum of physical exertion.

Judo uses the physical effort of sprinting, gymnastics, weight lifting—and more; it requires strength, speed, agility, suppleness, and stamina. A judoka has to have the suppleness to enable him still to be operationally effective even if he has been folded and half-crushed on the floor. Lightweight judoka are high-speed contortionists. And even some of the heavyweights such as Yamashita and the Frenchman David Douillet were remarkably supple, having the ability to execute high-kicking *uchimata*—in which the attacker spins round and swings his leg back to catch his opponent's leg, lifting him over onto the floor.

A competitive judoka may take part in eight or more contests over a twelve-hour period. The interval between each may be as little as five minutes or as long as three or four hours. This requires a combination of two completely different kinds of fitness: those of the marathon runner and the sprinter. Each time he goes out onto the mat, he has to go from zero to ninety in seconds.

The movement in a judo contest requires intensive effort. Even when standing the body may be bent over, constricting the function of the lungs; in groundwork the constriction is even worse. All this makes the sport almost completely anaerobic, which is to say that the action in a competition is too intense to allow oxygen to be replenished at the rate it is being used. Fighting may tire the legs, but a judoka is less likely to be "on his last legs" than "on his last arms." The strain on the forearms from maintaining a grip on his opponent's jacket even as it is constantly torn from his grasp is severe. In a long hard contest, competitors can find that an excess of lactic acid prevents their fingers and forearms from functioning.

STRENGTH, UNLIKE TECHNIQUE, is something that anyone can buy. You go to a place where they will exchange your money for large steel coins which you then push towards the heavens in repeated offerings to the gods. In acknowledgment of these tokens, the gods will grant you extra portions of strength. But strength is much more than lifting heavy weights with one's arms. Consider the proposition that a ballerina is stronger than a weightlifter.

We say a man is strong if he can lift a heavy weight and push it above his head. We do not describe him as weak if he cannot do the same thing with his foot. If you were to ask a competitive weightlifter to raise one foot above his head, he would probably find himself in some difficulty. A ballerina, however, could do it and so, by this measure at least, she is stronger than the weight-lifter. You may say this is just because she is more flexible, which she undoubtedly is, but the ballerina's flexibility merely *allows* the movement, she still has to have the necessary muscular strength to *achieve* it.

Judo, like dance, calls on unusual strengths in every part of the body, from the toes to the tips of the fingers. Grip fighting in judo is horribly punishing to the fingers and forearms. It is hard to retain a grip on a stiff cotton jacket while its owner is trying to tear it out of your fist. A professional judoka's fingers function like pliers. Probably only rock climbing makes greater demands on the fingers, which is why rock climbing is sometimes built into a judoka's training. The feet have to be extraordinarily powerful in order not only to deliver athletic movement, but to help generate the powerful spring that lifts an opponent off the ground. It is not enough to have a good sense of balance unless one has the muscular control in the feet to maintain it. There are judoka who have developed a surprising simian-like strength and dexterity in their feet so that they function almost as a second pair of hands. When one encounters this, it feels disturbingly like grappling with a monkey.

Necks are vulnerable to strangles and chokes unless strengthened to resist. They also have to be strong enough to protect the spine when piling headfirst into the mat. In an advanced exercise designed to strengthen the neck, the judoka lies on his back and then forms a bridge, supporting himself on his feet and head. He then turns his body through 180 degrees so that he is face-down. He moves between these positions as many times as he can without anything other than his head and feet touching the floor. I see that you are itching to have a go. Do, if you must, but it is perhaps best attempted under supervision. Core strength is also essential to support the weight of an opponent and drive the throw, and arms must be strong and effective enough to function when behind the back or high above the head, at angles and extremities not normally reached by the arcs of conventional weightlifting routines.

Strength must not be built at the cost of speed, so players have to be careful in their weight training. They need long, quick-twitch, whippy muscles and must avoid gaining bulk, which may push them up a weight category and make them slow and cumbersome. It is said that the essence of the breeding of English thoroughbred horses has been to produce the most powerful engine on the lightest possible chassis, and this is pretty much what top judo coaches are trying to do.

The engine which has to drive all the machinery in a contest will produce a pulse rate of over two hundred beats per minute, a rate unusual in most sports. There will be immense demands on a competitor's stamina. Contests may be as short as five minutes or less, but they are extraordinarily demanding and a competitor may have to face as many as seven opponents in the course of the day. Practices are even worse, with contestants often fighting for over an hour with only very short breaks in between opponents. In Japan *randori* can last much, much longer.

As running is the basis of all training, a typical day's training includes a middle-distance run of approximately three miles, either on road, track, or machine. This is in addition to shuttle runs and interval sprints.

Some players have developed their own personal training and fitness techniques. Dave Starbrook, the formidable British light heavyweight of the 1970s, used to carry around a tray of bricks, which gave him a massively strong hold-down in ground-work. I came across one player who, during lectures at college in the United States, would roll up sheets of paper and crunch them as tightly as he could to build up power in his hands and fingers. A British squad member told me that when watching television, he would sit on the floor on his heels to stretch his hamstrings. There are judoka who feel unable to use the "up" escalator, and instead find themselves obliged to run up the "down" one.

When raw strength is harnessed to ever-improving technique, overall effectiveness is multiplied drastically. In strong judo countries where the science of sports medicine is well advanced, fitness training has become such an intensively studied area that its supervision has been devolved to specialists so that the coaches can be freed to concentrate on technique and tactics. Athletes are forever subject to a barrage of tests that are becoming increasingly sophisticated. The combined needs of technique and fitness demand a terrible level of sacrifice. It means a life of rising at dawn for a three-mile run, followed by hours of weight training and sprinting and stretching; of technique practice and fighting; of fasting to the point of desiccation to lose weight; of foregoing drinking, smoking, and parties; of trying to keep a relationship from fracturing under the strain of it all. And all the time having to endure the aching psychological anxiety stoked by looming contests.

Small wonder that, by the time their first big competition draws near, some can be an alarming sight. Pared to the ribs, their skulls shaven, limbs bandaged, with the darting eyes of the hyperanxious, wired to monitors as they scuttle on treadmills, they have been pushed to the boundaries of physical and mental exhaustion. As they carry out the mad tasks that their trainers and sports scientists demand, they look like half-starved, maltreated lab rats. There are moments when a compassionate observer might wonder if they shouldn't just open the door of the cage and set these wretched creatures free.

14

ZEN AND THE ART
OF *UCHIMATA* MAINTENANCE

The origin of Dr. Kano's development of judo lay in his obsessive interest in the idea of enabling a weaker person to overcome a stronger person—he needed such a method to defend himself against bullies. Judo, then, has been designed not around strength but around technique. A competitor may be strong, but he'll be flattened as soon as he comes up against an opponent who has superior technique. Judo is a highly technical sport, which is why a large proportion of its athletes' time has to be spent on technique training.

There is an awful lot to learn. In the modern Kodokan repertoire—the Gokyo—there are sixty-seven throws;[1] because they can be performed left and right, this effectively means there are 134. This compares with the four techniques (jab, cross, hook, and uppercut) available to a boxer. Of course, even an experienced competition player will only be able to do a fraction of these, but he must be aware of many of them so that he can defend against them. Each throw has one or more counters to it. He has to develop an appropriate grip for each throw and there are a dozen or so of those, as well as numerous ways of breaking each of those grips. And then he must learn to use the throws in combinations, just as a boxer does, eliding them into groups of two, three, four, or more.

That is just the standing work. On the ground a contestant has a choice of seven ways of holding down his opponent, ten armlocks, and twelve strangles or chokes, and there are endless variations of executing those techniques and escaping from them. Because of this complexity the judoka is forever resolving the relationship between two lines on the graph paper of his life: one marks the steady rise of his technical ability; the other the rise and inexorable decline of his physical powers.

When Neil Adams came along to the Budokwai one evening to teach at a class, he told us how judo technique was constantly changing and how new ways of executing throws would suddenly become popular. They could often be seen for the first time at the Tournoi de Paris, the first big tournament on the calendar. He made it sound like the Paris couture collections at which the latest designs are unveiled by their creators: this is the place where everyone comes to see who is throwing whom with what this year.

To develop any throw takes time; none are easy to execute. In judo, to score *ippon* you have to throw someone so that they land flat on their back *with force and with control*. The art of positioning your body correctly to kick a ball or hit it with a racket or bat is tricky enough, but it is a great deal more difficult to whisk an opponent of the same weight into the air. Every part of one's body has to be correctly configured to shift its portion of the load and get the whole person airborne. It doesn't end there. Using the sleeve and collar controls, this flying mammal has to be forced to turn in the air and brought down to land on its back. Throughout this process the target will do everything in its power to resist.

The basic method of mastering a technique is *uchikomi*, meaning literally "to go in." The attacker *(tori)*, working with a stationary and compliant partner, the defender (*uke*), comes in for the throw, begins the technique without actually carrying through the throw, and then moves out again. And he does this repeatedly, in and out, in and out, sometimes in sets of ten or twenty or sometimes even one hundred or more. This interminable repetition allows the technique to be grooved into the muscle memory, etching the chip that programs every part of the body. Each day he must make his technique a little faster, sharper, and stronger—until he can catapult his opponent through the air without thinking.

Uchikomi is the equivalent of the boxer working at his punch bag, a bowler in the nets, a golfer on a driving range. It is also a little like a concert musician doing his scales. No pianist would take on a formidable concerto, bare-knuckle, full-contact, for the whole three movements in front of a large crowd in an arena without practicing his scales every day in the weeks before the encounter.

The repetitive search for perfection in a throw is the same as that required for a stroke with a club or a racket, or an arm or an oar in the water. It gives the pursuit of judo a Zen-like quality that appeals to many and that may explain why so many judoka are avid golfers.

Serious competitors devote hours to the exhaustive refinement of their technique, some even practicing without a partner. This is known as shadow *uchikomi*, a description that was literally true in the case of the great Kimura, who would get up in the middle of the night and practice his dreaded *osoto-gari* against a tree. This endlessly repetitive rehearsal of technique with thousands of *uchikomi* requires enormous concentration and discipline to sustain it. Such dedication, with equal parts of power and fighting spirit, is the hallmark of truly great champions.

Once the player is reasonably proficient at the technique, he can begin to introduce it when he is sparring lightly in *randori*. At first he will practice on quite low-grade partners. Kimura, who had nothing to fear from anyone, would make a point of training at a dojo where the opposition was weak just so that he could perfect a throw on people who could not even begin to counter it. And one would have to feel sorry for them.

As a player becomes more confident in a technique, he can work with better opponents, until he is able to throw good people with speed and precision in hard *randori*. Until he can do that he will not dare to risk using it in the heat of serious contest, for fear that the mechanism might still have a few rough edges. It can take two years before a new throw or combination is ready for top-level competition, which is to say the technique can be done without thinking. It has to be like this because, in contest, the judoka will never have the time to think. The movement has to be instinctive, triggered by a momentary opportunity when the target is perfectly configured. "The best judo," as Neil Adams put it, "is usually when instinct is allowed to take over. The best victories are when you are looking down at someone who is lying on their back and you have no idea how they got there."[2]

Before the throw can be executed, Kano decreed, the opportunity has to be created. This requires the application of *kuzushi*—the breaking of balance. I received a lesson in the art of *kuzushi* in the unlikely surroundings of a Paris restaurant.

I MET KATSUHIKO KASHIWAZAKI for the first time while I was in Paris for the world championships in February 1997. He is the world lightweight champion who threw everyone all over the place at Maastricht in 1981. After he retired from competition in the following year, he came to London to teach at the Budokwai, where he met and became close friends with the celebrated photographer Terence Donovan, who trained at the club. Now, a year after Donovan's death, the former champion was chief professor of judo at the International Budo University in Japan and had come over to Europe for the world championships. While in Paris he had arranged to meet Donovan's widow, Diana, through their mutual friend Nicolas Soames, who was covering the tournament for several newspapers. As someone who had known Donovan, if only briefly—he had given me an enormous amount of encouragement during my early days at the Budokwai—I was invited to join them at Restaurant Balthazar near the Place des Ternes.

In an interlude between reminiscences about Donovan, Kashiwazaki talks about life at the Budo University and shows us an aerial photograph of the campus on the back of his phone card—which he gives me. Then, as if reminded of his duties as a teacher, he says in an aside to me, "In judo, if you want to throw someone one way, you must first move them the other way." He takes a menu, holding it upright, and tips it one way and then the other. It is an easy idea to express, although more difficult to effect on living opponents. But it is fundamental to judo, which is presumably why Kashiwazaki, a committed teacher, took the trouble to emphasize it. (It is so important that I took the liberty of demonstrating it on you, not in the language of judo, but in the language of words, in the opening paragraph of this book. Whether it worked on you or not, it was an attempt to unbalance you by taking you in one direction and then suddenly whisking you in another.) In judo a moving target is an easier prospect than a static one. A judoka on the move may be harder to catch but he's easier to throw; it's nearly impossible when he is rooted to the floor. So the trick is to get your opponent moving around. As soon as he moves, little opportunities present themselves, one foot becomes exposed, there is a momentary transition of balance, his very movement provides some momentum which you, the attacker, can steal and exploit for your own purpose. (It is, of course, true that while you are doing this, you are also creating lots of opportunities for your opponent.)

The essence is action and reaction. The point that Kashiwazaki was making in the Balthazar is that you must move your opponent in one direction so that he immediately resists by moving in the opposite direction—the direction you really want him to move. Once you have provoked that reaction, you have some movement to use as the basis for the throw. You have ignition. Now you have to do everything you can to keep this small movement going, magnify it, and achieve liftoff.

IT TOOK ME much longer than it should have to understand that, however closely they might become entangled, "fighting" and "technique" are very, very separate. One Sunday at the London Judo Society I had just come off the mat after a grading contest that had irritatingly ended in a draw—I felt I had dominated it but I just couldn't get a decisive throw. I passed Larry Stevenson, an instructor who trains at the Budokwai. He was smiling ruefully and shaking his head. "Oh Mark, it's no good. You've just got to get some technique!"

As a brown belt I went through the ordeal of grading every couple of months, but I wasn't getting the decisive throws to earn the points I needed. I became exasperated because I had made steady progress through the *kyu* grades—white to brown belt. In the lower grades you can get by on brute force and a smattering of technical ability, but at brown belt the only way you are going to throw someone is if you have reasonable technical ability. You have to be able to get a dominant grip, move your opponent around, and execute your throw. Do it right and you are David Beckham; do it wrong and you are Tom after Jerry has given him the exploding cigar.

It is vital to develop technique, but it requires application in quantities I have never possessed. And standing on the side practicing throws isn't nearly as much fun as going out and sparring. I diagnosed my problem and tried to do something about it. But I didn't have what it takes. Once I even tried to give up *randori* for Lent, vowing to do only *uchikomi*. But when I saw everyone else having such a good time throwing each other around, I cracked within fifteen minutes of the next session and joined in.

IT IS POSSIBLE FOR a judo contest to be utterly devoid of technique. I went to one grading where I saw two white belts, both probably in their mid-twenties, face each other. A smallish man who had some knowledge of the basic techniques was up against a very tall, quite powerful man. The latter appeared to have no knowledge of judo at all, but that did not stop him attacking almost continuously with a bizarre series of throws and holds, none of which had a prayer of working.

The contest was like watching a piano recital by an orangutan. The unfortunate smaller man was picked up and hurled to the floor several times, but he always landed on his front—or on his head—or was flung out of the area. It was vintage Tom and Jerry but for the absence of the right sound effects: swanee whistle, creaking ropes, and a trombone with a wah-wah mute. The victim was pushed and pulled and thrown all over the place; he was sat upon, stretched, twisted, and jumped on, but all to no avail: the giant had no idea what to do. He would pin his hapless opponent to the mat, but always the wrong way up; he would throw him into the floor but only to land face first.

The referee kept standing them up, perhaps in the vain hope that one or the other would happen to fall on his back and let him conclude the wretched business. The giant's instructor was cowering with embarrassment at the side of the mat. He began to call out instructions at his charge, but as this is against the rules he was silenced by the referee, after which he confined himself to a groan emitted at intervals as he covered his eyes in despair. The encounter went its distance and, because there was no score, it was declared *hiki-wake*—a draw. The event was funny and terrible, but not uninteresting in that it was a rare chance to see a judo contest from which judo was entirely absent.

I saw the smaller man in the changing room at the end of the day. He seemed none the worse for the encounter and when someone asked him about it, he vouchsafed cheerfully that it had been "quite an interesting experience."

THERE ARE THOSE WHO, when they read poetry out loud, affect a special poetry voice. I noticed that fighting can have a similarly transforming effect. People suddenly feel obliged to imitate a gorilla and seize their opponent in a crunching grip to crush them with their power. This they regard as their "fighting voice." It doesn't work, at least on an opponent who has a bit of technique. This physical and mental attitude literally cramps your style. Rounded shoulders reduce the body's flexibility. Stiffness makes you vulnerable to attack and stifles the speed that you need to make an attack; it also increases the quantity of information traveling down your arms so that any movement is telegraphed well in advance and kills all surprise. A judoka is much more dangerous when he "talks" in a natural, unaffected voice. Although techniques have been put in writing since the early days of jujitsu, the most valuable knowledge resides in the minds of the senseis. Nothing in print can adequately take the place of teaching by demonstration on the mat by the wise and experienced instructor, a sensei who is a veteran of a thousand encounters—someone who knows what really works. Someone like Tony Sweeney at the Budokwai, ninth dan, a three-time European bronze medalist who took part in the Tokyo Olympics of 1964. Now he is an instructor and undiscriminating purveyor of judo to anyone who feels he can help them, from stars to wannabes and to the humblest orange belt. He stands at the edge of the mat of the Budokwai most days of the week dispensing priceless biomechanical wisdom.

An extraordinary repository of vital experience and knowledge, he is the archetypal sensei, a high priest guarding a tradition and passing it on to new generations. In his youth he fought among the best in the world and now he is devoted to the cause of pure classical upright Japanese judo. He knows a mass of techniques and a myriad of refinements and alternative methods for each one. He knows how a particular player can make his judo more effective, and how to suggest combinations of attacks that will suit an individual's physique and physical ability.

Always watching, analyzing, and constructing, he is a biomechanic in white overalls, checking the power steering, tuning the performance. If there's a technical problem, there is a technical solution. When he first started to learn judo, Sweeney found that every time he tried to do a certain forward throw, he'd lose control and collapse on his knees. His solution was to devise a special exercise that he did every day. You can try it yourself. Rest your fingers on a ledge or shelf that is about chest height and stand so that your arms are almost straight. Next, keeping your back vertical and looking straight ahead, slowly push your knees forward and sink down until they touch the floor without resting on it. All the time keep your hips over your knees and use your fingers for only minimal support. Now bring yourself back to the standing position. Sweeney's repetitions of this exercise not only built up the strength where he needed it, but gave him the *feel* of what he should be doing—the feeling that if someone was clamped to your back, it would take only a smallish movement to send them whistling past your ear. It was later explained to him that the Japanese could execute judo techniques more easily because of a vital difference between Eastern and Western bodies, which lay in the fact that Westerners sit on chairs and Japanese do not.

When a Westerner sits, he bends his knees and pushes his backside out to rendezvous with the chair. When a Japanese sits, he bends his ankles, which sends his knees forward and down until he is kneeling on the floor, and then sits back on his heels. These entirely different and much repeated actions give the two physiques completely different properties. The quad muscles of the Japanese, which have to support this movement, are much stronger; dropping down to the floor by pushing the hips and knees forward, the key to so many throws, is a completely natural movement to him. For the Westerner, it is an alien movement (although it is part of skiing technique) and difficult for many.

Sweeney has a thousand metaphors and similes to help describe the movement a judoka needs to make. He'll talk about how to emulate ice-skaters spinning in their own space—inside an invisible cylinder—or greyhounds "not bouncing along the track but running *into* the ground in order to take energy from it," or how the art of quickly dropping low to make a throw is not to think of pushing yourself down, but of suddenly taking both your feet off the ground. (Try it. It works.)

Sweeney deplores brute force. He works to take the strength out of people's judo and refine it to grace and technique. In his earnest concern for the precise position of the hands, he will adjust the angle of a half-turned wrist with the obsessive fastidiousness of a choreographer creating a work. He explains how to maintain the tension on an opponent's collar as you reconfigure your hand from a lifting claw into the shape needed for "throwing a javelin." And all the time he urges, "Yes, like that, that's right. No, that's too much effort. *Just enjoy the movement.*" And while you are in the thick of some *randori* mayhem in the middle of the room, you can hear Sweeney's voice from his usual corner saying to someone on the matside, "And if I do this and you do that, then you're strapping yourself onto a disaster area. Yes?" And next, in his unlimited stream of knowledge, comes "progressive loading," "scapula glide," and a welter of other concepts.

Just when you begin to think all this ethereal theory, all these dainty refinements, aren't going to help you bang anyone onto the floor in *randori*—which is all you want to do—Sweeney will, very occasionally, ignoring his artificial hip and his frozen shoulder, demonstrate the efficacy of some fearful technique. It might be his *hizagaruma,* which wreaked such havoc in his day (that's the one where you suddenly block the other guy's right knee with the sole of your extended left foot and wheel him over it). With a few gentle movements, and a vehement running commentary, he starts to zigzag you around the mat faster and faster. And suddenly the whole dojo is spinning and it's as if you're trapped on one of those rides at an amusement park when you really just want to get off. Then, for just a moment, as the walls of the dojo whirl by, you get a terrible vision—some blurry black-and-white flashback footage showing what it would have been like to face him in the days when he was in his prime, a monster of the mat.

And when you come in to land some distance away and you pick yourself up off the floor and taxi back across the tatami to where he is standing, he is still elaborating upon some technical subtlety about how the speed and trajectory of your flight have been determined by some slight adjustment of the angle of his elbow. As you see him gesture and hear him talk, you realize not only how much he and all those who were before him have experienced, but how deeply they have thought about everything. And how delicate and precious this knowledge is.

For all the books that have been written about judo technique, whole volumes devoted to a single throw, it is the senseis like Sweeney who are the custodians of this learning, and it is they who pass it on. The written word is better than nothing, but nothing can convey the *feel* as clearly as this combination of words and demonstration. What you see is not what you feel.

So the techniques are passed on in this way, by word of hand, which is subject to all the fragility and distortion that such a method possesses. It is no more than waves of sound and fragments of feeling which are being carried down through the generations. How odd it is that the creation and mastery of this incredible force depends for its perpetuity on such a fragile link.

MY FATHER, who had in his youth worked as an animator, once explained to me when I was a child how cartoon films were made. He drew a series of stick figures, each one very slightly different, in the corner of successive pages of his notebook; then, thumbing back the corners, he allowed the pages to flick over. Entranced by this tiny flickering movie of a dancing man, I began to draw such figures myself—just three or four lines and a blob for a head, looking a bit like musical notes escaped from their staff.

I was struck by how much they could convey about the nature of a movement. Conversely, I learned that, if you take the trouble to look, you can see these lines in the movement of people all about you, in the street, in the office. In order to do so you have to take away not merely the clothes, but the flesh and even the bones. Beneath all these lies a stick figure, an abstraction notating the essence of the movement.

These are the lines that many judoka see, whether they are conscious of it or not. Their eyes penetrate the flurry of the cloth, the flesh, and the bone to sense the pattern of the power, the trajectory of fire, the arc of delivery. Judo is a language: You are speaking it when you practice it, you are reading it when you watch it. These lines are its alphabet, which is written in the air.

The perfection of technique requires constant practice and testing. A throw has to work against lots of different players—left-handers, right-handers, the short, and the tall. Anyone who is contemplating a career as a serious competitor must practice their art on lots of different bodies—skillful bodies, awkward bodies. The best place to find an infinite supply is Japan.

15

HELL ON A VERY HOT MAT

The day when a young hopeful is told he's going to Japan is a crucial one in his career. His elation at the prospect will be tinged with a little anxiety. Our tyro will have been warned by those who have gone before him that the training in Japan is both wonderful and terrible. They will have told him tales of what happens in the dojos on the far side of the world, in the land that gave birth to his sport. They will have told him of *randori* sessions that go on for hours, of the Spartan life and the training regimes, of the ambivalent attitude to foreign students, of the bullying culture at some of the university judo clubs, and the tyrannical nature of some of the senseis who rule over them.

A foreign judoka's experience in Japan will depend largely on where he is sent. His destination will probably be one of the great judo universities. These are the apex of judo in Japan and the source of Japan's international competitors. Preeminent among these is the formidable Tokai, a private establishment founded in 1969 by Isao Inokuma, who brought in Nobuyuki Sato as chief judo instructor. It was there that Sato nurtured Yamashita and he still runs judo there today.

Tokai scours the high schools in its search for talent and tends to get the pick of the crop. As a private university with various business interests, it can afford to give promising judoka financial help as an inducement to come to the university, where they usually study in the physical education or sports science departments. Judo is a subject in its own right, one that is respected by employers and can help a student secure a job in business, education, or the police.

Top competition judo players are effectively funded, in that their academic workload is reduced so that they can train hard full time. Japan does less to pamper the egos of its top players than other nations, but it does offer them more security. After university, top players can get jobs as coaches for company and university teams who are similarly indulgent about giving them all the time they need to train. John Bowen, a British squad member, once taught English at the Nippon Steel Corporation. "You could see well-known judoka sitting at their desks, scratching their cauliflower ears and staring glumly at the papers on their desks," he said.

Mike Callan, who is the director of judo at the University of Bath, recalls his arrival as a student for the first time. "We'd just got off the plane after seventeen hours of flying with a five-hour wait in Moscow and we went straight to the dojo at Tokai, changed and went on the mat—because that's what we'd gone there to do. We were thrown all over the place. In fact, we spent the next three weeks just doing breakfalls until we could work out what was happening."

Instead of the British clubs' hour or so of *randori*, in Japan it is not uncommon to have three or even four hours of free fighting with a break of a mere minute or two every six minutes to change partners. The idea is that by training to the point of exhaustion, a student will have no strength left and will be forced to use technique instead. Anyone unlucky enough to have a teacher of the old school gets really hard training, because that's all those teachers know. But they are beginning to learn from the West that this may be counterproductive and that there are other ways.

The Japanese certainly enjoy the arrival of new foreign blood—and the chance to taste it. Neil Adams recounts how, when he and some teammates were training at the Kokushikan, a particularly tough university club, in 1984 before the Los Angeles Olympics,

"They kept firing new opponents at you all the time. Inevitably, it did sometimes get out of hand, they would try and throw you against the wall and things like that, and you had to retaliate. That's just human nature."[1]

Jimmy Bregman, an American who trained in Japan before the 1964 Olympics, in which he won a bronze medal, recounted the routine at the Kodokan. "Every day you came to practice in drab surroundings, the air almost astringent with sweat. You . . . winced as you tried to get into your limpid heavy judogi, which never completely dried out from the exertions of the day before. You walked toward the mat and there, first up for some rousing *randori*, was the monster you were happy not to see the day before."[2]

During his first trip to Japan in the 1960s, Roy Inman, who was then in the British squad and was later to become the highly successful coach to the women's team, remembers how he and his fellow British visitors would be taken around other university dojos for judo practice and were always made to stand out in front. "I was sick three times after practicing in my first week. After about an hour my legs simply gave out. But the Japanese would keep coming at you one after another."

In his first few days there, Inman remembers how he was caught in a choke during groundwork practice. Although he tapped in submission his training partner refused to stop and carried on strangling him until he was unconscious. "If the Japanese think you have given in too early instead of struggling they feel they have the right to put you out," says Inman. "When I came round, the chap was just sitting there smirking. I complained that I'd tapped, but he just shrugged and smiled. I'd never been strangled out in my life before. I was angry and frightened, so I punched him in the face and he went crashing back against the wall. The next day I thought I was going to have some real hassle, but nothing happened. The Japanese say you can do something like that to each other but you don't do it to a foreigner."

Once over the novelty of giving foreigners a hard time, the Japanese are universally recognized to be excellent training partners. One aspect that every visitor notices is that their hosts, who we assume to be so much concerned with "saving face," are in fact particularly relaxed about being thrown. As part of their early training they spend a lot of time practicing breakfalls, which gives them enormous confidence and enables them to train in the proper spirit of judo—going for big techniques and accepting the risk of being thrown. (Certainly the beautifully sprung cedar-wood floors that lie under the tatami in a proper Japanese dojo make for a much more pleasant landing than is possible in most British clubs.) In consequence, they do not resort to pokey, cautious, defensive judo just to stay on their feet. British players tend to feel, quite wrongly, that being thrown diminishes their reputation. Neil Adams complained that when a squad member was thrown he would "get up hurriedly and glance around to see if anyone had witnessed the 'disgrace.'"[3]

Those interminable hours spent doing *randori* give every Japanese an immensely powerful grip. Once they take hold, you feel that your collar and sleeve have somehow gotten caught in the steel door of a bank vault. Japanese strength has been described as not big strength but "inner strength." Adams says that the Japanese just "feel" different—he describes European judo as "more angular"—and maintains that even if he was blindfolded he would be able to tell if he was fighting a Japanese.[4] Others describe the Japanese as being more subtle and more explosive in their judo than Westerners.

The Japanese ethos is always to go for the full *ippon* rather than fight for the little points; they like the big throw that brings affairs to a dramatic and decisive end. And the Japanese adore style. If judo is a language spoken with the body, then the Japanese use a language that is clear, classy, neat, economic, authoritative, and confident.

The rigor of the technique training is matched by the toughness of the physical conditioning. The long steep flights of stone steps leading to some hilltop pagodas offer special opportunities for cardiovascular training and building up the quad muscles;

this in itself presents an arduous challenge, but it becomes something else when judoka have to run up and down carrying someone on their back.

Seikijuku is a private dojo founded by Isao Okano (a gold medalist in the 1964 Olympics and later coach to the Japanese team) to bring serious judo men from Japan and abroad to train and live together. He wanted to revive the "right spirit" (*Sei Ki*) of judo's pioneers, which he felt had been lost. The routine at Seikijuku began at 5:30 A.M. with the playing of the Japanese national anthem and a four-mile run. Halfway around the circuit was a temple on high ground reached by a flight of three hundred steps. The students would first run up them, then bunny-hop up, and then carry someone up on their shoulders. They had to do that three times before running two miles back to their college. On alternate days they ran to the park and did *uchikomi* on the trees.[5]

To increase upper-body strength, students are made to climb a rope using only their arms. A popular refinement is to tie them into a chair with judo belts around the waist and legs and then make them climb. It stops them from using their legs. Fear of an incredibly unpleasant landing if they fall helps them to hang on.

While, elsewhere in the world, dojo discipline is likely to be as relaxed as that in any other kind of sports club, in much of Japan the samurai tradition prevails. A drum on a dais in the dojo is beaten to signal the beginning and end of each *randori*. White belts or junior students are expected to clean the tatami after every session. Yamashita was in his first year when he won the All Japan championship, but although he was now one of the greatest contestants in the whole of Japan, he still went around collecting everyone's judo outfits at the end of a practice at the Kodokan to launder them, because he was a junior.

The Japanese insist that the dojo be treated with great respect, while the sensei exerts the same authority that he had when he was training warriors in the grounds of his lord's castle. He continues to command a degree of status and obedience among his pupils that is hard for Westerners to comprehend. Pupils are at best in awe of their sensei, at worst in terror of him, and they pay him enormous respect, for which they tend to be rewarded with complete disdain. The deference some students show to their sensei can make visiting Westerners cringe.

Colin Savage told me about Japanese national squad training at Tokai under the fearsome Hidetoshi Nakanishi, who had defeated Neil Adams's nemesis, Ezio Gamba, to become world champion in Moscow in 1983. (Nakanishi was the visiting instructor at the Budokwai just as I was starting, and I remember how he corrected my collar grip in the beginners' class.) Like many Japanese, he was a mellow figure away from home, but in Japan he was very different. Savage recalled, "When the great man was looking for a *randori* partner, some two hundred judoka would suddenly become fantastically engrossed in retying their belts, so he would just come over and grab someone. He was nicknamed Tetsu jin—iron man—and would throw people extremely hard; when they couldn't get up anymore or were slow about it, he'd go over and drag someone else off the wall." But, as Savage pointed out, Nakanishi only expected the same degree of commitment from his students that he demonstrated in his time. This was the man who, on the morning after winning the world championships, reported to his sensei for training as if it was any other normal day.

Roy Inman's sensei, the revered Isao Okano, also had a notorious reputation as a fierce disciplinarian. When some Japanese showed up after their 10 P.M. curfew, the sensei made them change into track suits and harangued them about the honor of Japanese judo and Seikijuku. He sent them for a fifteen-mile run—it was about 11:15 P.M.—and they did not return until 1 A.M. They weren't allowed to bathe afterwards and had to be up for their routine run at 5:30 A.M.[6]

Inman saw one minor example of Okano's robust attitude. The great sensei was leaning on his stick beside the mat at his dojo when a student came up to him and asked him for some advice on how to correct a problem. Okano listened impassively and then instructed the boy simply to spend the whole practice throwing only on the left and not doing any other technique at all. When the boy, a right-hander, returned to the mat, he inevitably kept getting thrown all over the place but was unable to do the same to his opponents. Finally, just before the practice ended, in exasperation the student performed one right-handed throw, with which he flattened his partner. "Okano shouted out for the student to come over," Inman remembers. "When the boy presented himself, Okano stood up and punched him very hard on the nose! As far as Okano was concerned that was quite acceptable behavior. The sensei has told you to do something and you haven't done it: repercussions! I'm not sure it would work over here, but it works in that culture."

Nevertheless Okano was, according to Inman, capable of real kindness. Homesickness, the rigors of training, and the spartan nature of life in dormitory accommodation under Okano's roof occasionally proved to be a morale-sapping experience for Inman. Observing this, the great teacher asked his pupil what the matter was. Inman spoke longingly of the things he missed: a chair to sit on, toast instead of rice for breakfast. A few days later, when he returned after a weekend away, he was astonished to find a big armchair and a toaster. "He'd been out and bought them. They were just for me. No one else was allowed to use them!"

Partly because Inman was a foreigner, but also because the twenty-two-year-old Londoner had a wife and two children back in England, Okano accorded him a sort of *senpai* status (a senior, as opposed to a *kohai*, a junior). There was something else that endeared Inman to Okano. When entertaining Inman to drinks in his home, he opened his giant cocktail cabinet. Half of it was decorated with patriotic regalia, the other half was filled with Cliff Richard records. As it happened, Inman's wife was a devotee of Cliff and so Inman was familiar with Richard's libretti. To the delight of his sensei, the two of them were able to sing and discuss the songs together.

THE AUTHORITY OF the sensei is rooted in their role as founts of knowledge. They are respected as gurus rather than mere sports coaches. Bound up with respect for the sensei is a great veneration for age. Trevor Leggett, a trainer at Budokwai, told of an old sensei who continued to practice after he had suffered a stroke.[7] He could only make quite small movements, but whenever he did so much as blink, the chosen student would pretend to be thrown, hurling himself into a huge somersault and landing flat on his back with a noisy *splat!*

Disciplinary standards are not imposed by the sensei alone. The students are quite good at enforcing discipline themselves. The Japanese take their hobbies seriously, and if you fail to turn up for training they will often come and get you.[8] Indeed, much of the discipline of a dojo is enforced by its students, and sometimes the tough discipline can turn into something more sinister.

Roy Inman observed "a bit of a bully culture between the senpei and the kohai. And there are some loonies out there. But the senpai is responsible for the kohai and the kohai accepts it because one day he is going to be a senpai. In fact, some of the worst were foreigners—the ones who had been at a university for a long time and had taken on senpai status."

Japanese culture is informed by the tenets of Buddhism, which holds that the ego is the cause of stress and dissatisfaction in life and a potential obstacle to learning. Therefore part of the teaching process is devoted to grinding down pupils' ego; the means to achieve this is humiliation.

Some judo clubs in Japan indulge in the sort of initiation process practiced by such tight social groupings as American college fraternity students, African tribes, and the fire services and armed forces of the United States and the United Kingdom. Initiates are subjected to a variety of humiliating and unpleasant treatments to test their loyalty to the group and their resilience under pressure. Sometimes the process, often referred to as "hazing," goes too far: accounts appear periodically in the Japanese media of the death of the victim. This is reportedly most prevalent among baseball, karate, and judo clubs.

A number of Britons have witnessed quite severe bullying at some universities. One Budokwai member who trained at a notoriously tough dojo recalls that bullying was rife and that it was quite common for students to strangle their juniors unconscious. Some couldn't cope with the brutality of the regime, and the university had a reputation for students running away.

Although this mutual testing among groups of men is a worldwide phenomenon, there is something peculiarly profound about the nature of Japanese cruelty. As Robert Twigger, poet and author of *Angry White Pyjamas,* watched the crutches of an injured man being kicked away from him by a gang of able-bodied middle-class youths, he concluded that "no one distances themselves from the vanquished underdog more than the Japanese."[9]

QUITE APART FROM the sensei and his colleagues, because of the enormous variations in the Japanese climate, a visitor's experience can depend much on the time of year and the place where he trains. When Paul Ajala, formerly a British squad member and now a Budokwai instructor, did his stint in Japan, he was sent to Katsuura, a fishing village on Tokyo Bay. He arrived in the height of the summer and the mat was so hot that it felt as though his feet were being burned; he had to keep standing on one leg and then the other to cool the soles of his feet on his sweat-soaked trousers. The humidity in Japan is so great that the skin tends to come off the softened fingers, which is why Japanese players are fastidious about taping up their fingers.

In contrast, the winters can be extremely cold in some places. In Hokkaido, for instance, they always start the training session with groundwork, a safer way to warm up than standing work.[10] And Roy Inman remembers winter training at the Tenri Institute in the west of Japan. "It was bitterly cold outside, but the dojo was quite warm—until the sensei called for the huge doors to be opened and in came a bitter howling draught. In judo you should be warm and loose but everyone just stiffened and froze. They just wanted to be tough. It was mad."

THE NUMBER OF practicing judoka is declining as people are presented with a wider and gentler choice of sports. But judo does still thrive outside the schools and universities where international competitors are sought out, trained, and nurtured. Although there are very few independent clubs, large corporations have their own dojos and their teams compete in a league. Inevitably, the armed forces encourage the sport. The other main source of judo talent is the police, as it has been since that historic day in Shiba Park when the Tokyo police department pitted the traditionalist jujitsu against Dr. Kano's new system to determine which they should adopt.

Every major police station has its own dojo with an instructor who is at least a fourth dan. And it is the police who provide judo's most notorious school of hard knocks at Keishicho, the main police dojo in Tokyo. "Before going to one of the universities in the afternoon, we would be taken to Keishicho in the morning," recalls Inman. "It was hard *randori* but it didn't last longer than an hour because the police had to fit it in with their duties. Sometimes you'd turn up and if there was a riot on there'd be no one there. All the Japanese police were ex-university judo players, so they knew what to do! It was good. They weren't quite as sharp because they were older, but they were sneakier." Many of the denizens of Keishicho have that trademark of a serious judoka, a cauliflower ear—known as *gyoza*, the name of the small fried dumplings that are served all over Japan.

"There was an old boy there bald as a billiard ball. He wouldn't do standing work, but he liked his groundwork. He used to tie me up time and again. This went on for a month. I couldn't do anything with him at all. I used to hate it. Once I sent someone in ahead of me to see if he was there and he said he wasn't, but when

I went in the old boy jumped out from behind a pillar shouting, 'Newaza, Newaza!' He wasn't a bully; he just did good judo."

When Neil Adams followed in Roy Inman's footsteps a few years later, the Keishicho routine and its character were little changed. The training session was from ten until eleven every morning and the main police dojo was still, as Adams recounts, "a horrible practice." He says, "The judoka were stiff and strong and extremely tough and it always ended up a bit of a battle." They would make a point of trying to strangle him out. Once, because he was throwing them around, they waited until he grew tired, when five of them lined up and started throwing him off the mat onto the surrounding wooden floor. Adams was sixteen years old at the time.

Most remember Keishicho with some alarm. Nobody ever bothered with a warm-up. The minimum weight for police is 154 pounds (70 kilograms), so there were no light players. They could be arrogant and would simply refuse to practice with some visitors. Others remember training with the police at the Imperial Palace, practicing every morning in their beautiful traditional building inside the palace grounds with its highly polished floors, a judo dojo on one side and one for kendo on the other. Dickie Bowen recalled how police instructors from all over the city would come to this dojo to train with each other once a day.

Other dojos are less prepossessing. Christopher Holmes recalls of his time in Japan in the 1980s: "Police stations have a dojo attached. I trained in one about fifteen minutes from the Kodokan. It was pretty basic. When I asked where the changing rooms were, they just laughed. There were no showers. Just a tap and a couple of buckets."

Earlier generations of visitors to Japan left the twentieth-century West to visit a land that appeared medieval. Even in the 1960s foreigners were surprised to see the wagons that collected the sewage from homes: the ever-present threat of earthquakes made a piped sewer system impossible at that stage. Neil Adams records his surprise at what he found on his first visit to what he thought was a clean and well-ordered country. His Kodokan hostel was falling apart and the place was infested with cockroaches so large "you could have put saddles on them."[11]

One student in his early twenties was sent out from England to one of the best-known universities. "There were eight of us to a room," he recalled. "You unrolled your bed at night. They were all complete slobs and the place was filthy. The food was terrible. It was cooked by junior students who had never cooked before: it was basically slops. There was a dog and some of the students used to kick it. It was very suspicious and nervy and sometimes it would bite the students. I used to feed it but it got me once. The place was as bad as a prison. The sensei had been a great competitor and he couldn't understand why some people just weren't able to do some techniques; he used to get furious. He had a drinking problem, which made things worse. But he was a good man."

While life for the visiting judoka is sometimes a daunting prospect, it has its compensations. They have had the excitement of seeing a faraway country up close, of enjoying its extraordinary society, and of encountering every day the most beautiful classical judo.

The school and university clubs ruled by the All Japan Judo Federation and the Kodokan form a powerhouse generating a steady supply of world-class judo talent. The regimes they impose have nurtured superlative spirit, dedication, and technical brilliance. And this is what any competitor from the rest of the world has to contend with when he sees a Japanese judoka bow and make his way toward him across the mat.

HOW THE WOMEN FOUGHT TO FIGHT

The dawn of the Meiji dynasty heralded an era which would bring change to many aspects of life in Japan, notably to the lives of women, for whom it marked the beginning of a liberation. A new kind of woman was emerging, more willful and independent and less fettered by tradition; to her the possibilities of jujitsu, in which skill could triumph over strength, exercised an unyielding fascination.

As a "new man," the good Dr. Kano saw no objection to females practicing the art of attack and defense. He believed that they could derive the same benefits as men from the study and practice of judo and set about organizing classes for his wife and her friends. The first woman was enrolled in the Kodokan in 1893; in 1926 the women's section of the Kodokan opened and was run by Kano's eldest daughter.[1]

When jujitsu took the West by storm, interest was not confined to men. The women of Europe and America were embarking on their own struggle for independence and self-sufficiency. High society was at the forefront of that struggle, as it was in the study of the "Japanese Method." *The Fine Art of Jiu-Jitsu*, written in 1906 by Emily Watts, carried a preface by the Duchess of York.[2] In 1912 the Countess of Abzac begged modern women to acquire strength and freedom in a preface to a book called *Defendez-vous Mesdames*. In Britain, the suffragettes began to see the advantages of studying the "Japanese Method"—it would help women tackle policemen.

As judo superseded jujitsu in the 1940s and 1950s, more women were encouraged to take it up. However, while it was possible for women to practice judo, it was quite another matter for them to compete at the sport—to fight. Women had been allowed to compete in grading contests, but were not permitted to take part in normal competition until 1950, when the first women's competition was held in France.

When the first official women's competition in the United Kingdom, a team championships, was held at Liverpool University in 1966, the organizers felt that the sight of two women struggling on a mat would be an inappropriate spectacle for a general public that had yet to feel the full liberating force of the sixties, and insisted that the contests were conducted behind closed doors in front of an invitation-only audience. In 1969 the event, which was growing in popularity among contestants, was held at Crystal Palace, but a curtain was drawn to hide the contest area from general view.[3] The United Kingdom can claim to have hosted the first international women's tournament, the British Open championship held at Bracknell in 1971, in which a German team took part. The event marked the beginning of a rapid expansion in European and American women's contests. Japan left the West to pioneer female competition, but when the Japanese realized how well the European women were doing, they knew they had no choice but to follow if they were not to be left behind. In the late 1970s women started to appear in the main dojo at the Kodokan.

RUSTY KANOKOGI WAS LIVID. They had cheated her. They should have let her keep that medal and they wouldn't—just because she was a woman. It was ridiculous: women did do judo, but they weren't allowed to compete. But she was damn well going to change things.

The year was 1958, the scene the New York State YMCA championships. Someone had dropped out of the Brooklyn Central men's team and Kanokogi, who trained with them regularly, had been asked to take his place. After all, they knew Rusty would be all right—she was 180 pounds and five feet nine inches tall, and a very tough cookie.

Raised on the streets of Brooklyn, she lived the life of a wild child. Her parents were poor. "They didn't have any special skill," she says, "they just worked to survive and take care of their bad habits." Her aunt was Lee Krasner, the hell-raising artist wife of the painter Jackson Pollock. "When I was growing up, all my heroes were sportsmen. These were the people I wanted to emulate," she says. "I was a tough street kid, a fighter. When I took up judo I was the only woman in a class of forty at the YMCA and I thrived on the *randoris* and hard training. My physical condition was good: I always stayed fit and strong. I was considered an exceptional woman, a woman who played judo like a man."

As women weren't allowed to compete, she cut her hair and taped her breasts and entered the New York State YMCA championships as a man. She won her weight category, but when the officials were told that she was a woman they made her give back her medal. From then on, "male" was specified on all entry forms to prevent her competing again.

So much for the Judo-Christian tradition. As an example of male prejudice, it doesn't get much better than this. Kanokogi's victory at that New York tournament was all the more devastating because it was incontestable. There was no possible suggestion that because she was a woman she had been given an easy opponent or that her opponent had gone easy on her—they didn't know she was a girl. Kanokogi just showed up, took her chance, and beat her man. That, of course, does no discredit to the man, to his virility, his manhood, his sexuality, or whatever else anyone in their ignorance might rush to impugn; it merely demonstrated that his opponent was better at judo.

Kanokogi was certainly a tough and skillful player. Later, when she went to Japan to study at the Kodokan, she complained that the judo in the women's section was too restricted and tame. She did manage to find a few women who were really competitive: "We got together before and after class to go at it when the *senseis* weren't in the dojo." She became the first woman to practice with the men when they invited her to join them in the main dojo. She was later to marry a Japanese judoka.

THE DECISION TAKEN by those YMCA officials may now seem ridiculous; it certainly made them look small-minded, ungracious, and weak. And it wasn't in the spirit of judo. However, you have to feel a shred of sympathy for their plight. The prevailing wisdom of the day was that women didn't fight, couldn't fight, and shouldn't fight. The issue went to the heart of male attitudes toward females fighting. Such attitudes have long been beset by a tangle of confusions over the nature of femininity, both physical and psychological, accompanied by a generous portion of sexual tension, but perhaps most significant of all is the challenge that a fighting female presents to male supremacy. Many men—and indeed women—have a visceral objection to the idea of women fighting. At its mildest, it is an unease. The sexual revolution is very much a work in progress.

Male authority over women is said to originate in the advantage of men's greater strength (by some measures, men are on average 50 percent stronger). Fighting has almost always and almost everywhere been a male preserve; when women fight it is seen as an aberration, an act of trespass. There are men who fear it as a challenge to their masculinity; there are men and women who see it as a travesty of femininity. As they scrabble around for rational objections, they reach for medical causes: They argue that fighting and the excessive training it entails can jeopardize a female's ability to bear children, although these objections are equally applicable to much of sport and, of course, dance. Moreover, mothers have appeared in the ranks of top-level judo competitors.

Whether through nurture or nature, or both, some females are now incredibly strong. As Cuba's chief women's coach, Ronaldo Valdivie, said of his squad, "No one had ever imagined that a woman could climb a rope using only her arms; today all of them do it as a regular part of their daily physical training."[4]

As for other characteristics, it is accepted that women have higher endurance and a higher pain barrier than men, while International Judo Federation records show that fewer passivity warnings are issued in women's judo than in men's, which suggests that women are more aggressive.[5] The simple truth is that some women want to fight, just as some men don't want to fight. Women are from Venus, but some come from Mars.

IN JUDO IT IS QUITE common for women and men to train, if not compete, with each other. This is partly out of necessity: there are too few females in most clubs to provide enough training partners. But it is also because the special nature of judo permits it and makes it worthwhile.

Once I saw a 198-pound man doing *randori* with a 105-pound bantamweight woman. It was a remarkable mismatch, but most instructive to watch. The small woman had to use all her speed, strength, and skill to move a much larger opponent who was nearly twice her weight. The man's task was to eliminate almost all his strength and rely on speed and technique to attack a small and very fast-moving target. It was an intriguing challenge to them both and demonstrated that, with the right approach, even two people with such an extreme weight disparity could profit from the experience.

Usually the balance is much more even: for example, when a female who is strong, experienced, and skillful is training with a male who has less skill and experience. In these circumstances the female can beat the male. When a man is beaten by a woman it can come as something of a psychological as well as a physical shock—particularly on the first occasion it happens. The world as the man knows it is turned literally and metaphorically upside down. Whisked into the air and dumped on the floor like a sack of laundry, he instinctively feels that the natural order of things has gone wildly awry. He needs to summon every ounce of "the spirit of judo" to cope with this disturbing damage to his male ego.

Believe me.

THE MONDAY NIGHT CLASS I attended at the Budokwai was quite different from the other training sessions, which consisted of a quick warm-up, a few minutes of *uchikomi*, and lots of hard *randori*. This class was equally energetic, but it focused much more on teaching competition techniques and competition fitness. It was particularly popular with girls, and the class almost always included several of the national senior or junior women's squad. This was because the Monday night instructor was Roy Inman, a legendary figure in the world of women's judo. Inman, an eighth dan, coached members of the British women's judo squad who, from 1988 to 2000, won six Olympic medals.

I never really had a chance to talk to him until meeting him at the Tournoi de Paris, where I listened to his thoughtful comments on the action taking place in front of us and about coaching judo in general. Because I was desperate to get my dan grade and he had always been patiently encouraging, I asked him if he would give me a couple of private lessons. So, one spring Monday morning, I found myself making my way through the overgrown patch of Fairholme's garden and into the old wooden building, along a corridor to the dojo. There was something vaguely familiar about the offcuts of carpet that had been laid haphazardly everywhere: then I recognized the livery that adorned the aisle of every aircraft in the British Airways fleet. The place looked pretty decrepit. There was a punch bag in the corner and Ultimate Fight posters on the walls (some of the circuit's fighters used the gym to train). The various items of old weightlifting equipment that were scattered around would have been refused admission to any modern-day health club.

In the dojo itself, I found a blonde woman hurling Inman repeatedly against a crash mat propped up against the wall. This was Kate Howey, whom I had interviewed in Paris for the *Daily*

Telegraph when she won the world championship in 1997. Now she was getting ready for the Sydney Olympics. After Howey had finished, Inman gave me the first of a series of valuable lessons, and over time I learned something of his story.

Inman had two careers in judo. One started just as the other was ending. He had been in the British squad for eleven years and was twice British open champion at under 205 pounds (93 kilograms). In 1975, as he was coming to the end of his competitive career, he was asked to coach the British women's team for a session. "They were a nice bunch of girls and they really paid attention," he remembers. "I did some more sessions and I started to get quite enthusiastic.

"In the early days I just taught what I did, but after a year I knew that something was not quite right, because 60 percent of the squad still couldn't use the techniques in competition. I decided to rethink my approach." He realized that he was making the mistake of training women as if they were men. "Everything I taught was geared to a physical ability that *I* had."

In the following months, Inman focused on trying to find the techniques women could and couldn't do. He found that if they attacked when their posture and timing were not absolutely right, they simply collapsed—they didn't have the power to throw with sheer strength or to compensate for the slightest error.

"I spent the next two years learning about lightweight judo," says Inman. "I searched for the techniques where speed, movement, and surprise were the essential elements, rather than setting up the opponent and exploding into a throw with full power." He discovered that the solution lay in compensating for the lack of power with greater precision, better timing, and greater fitness, thus permitting more movement.

Consequently, Inman had to demand a level of fitness that the women had never before contemplated. "The women were not very strong. The majority of their resistance work came from judo, very few did running or weights seriously—they might run to lose weight." He instituted a demanding training regime, structured around their competitions, which rivaled that of the men's squad. Once, when a broadcaster asked Nicky Fairbrother, who had just won a major competition, what she was training for next, she replied, "Squad training." She found it hard to convince the confused reporter that the demands of working with the British women's national judo squad were so hard that they had to train for the training.

One of the greatest problems confronting Inman was to find people for his squad to spar with in a sport where there were few female players of any caliber available. "Most men hated to be seen being thrown by a woman, so they would become very defensive and spoil the possibilities of useful *randori*." But he discovered that the ideal partners for his girls were sixteen-year-old male brown belts. "They were skilled, fast, fairly strong, but without a mature man's strength. They were healthily competitive and, realizing they were up against world-class adult women, didn't mind being thrown by them and felt pretty good if they managed to catch someone. They made the *randori* lively and inventive."

The endless repetition of movements in technique training can become monotonous and boring, so to relieve the tedium Inman turned to music; he found it made for a more relaxed atmosphere. He assembled tapes with music from Queen and Jerry Lee Lewis. Howey says she always remembered "Crazy Horses" by the Osmonds. In the early days they couldn't afford a movie camera, so he used to cut photographs out of old judo magazines and put them on epidiascope (a device for projecting still images on a screen that was a sort of PowerPoint of its day). When times got better and video technology became available, Inman was one of the first to use the new tool and carried out more video analysis than most other coaches.[6]

"What I taught them was completely new stuff for their bodies. The great satisfaction was seeing that it actually worked in a fight—that was good for the ego!" Inman says, smiling at the memory. "And to this day I still get that feeling of enthusiasm and satisfaction. I never quite achieved the level I could have done as a player, but I did manage to achieve it as a coach. I produced eight world champions."

Gradually, over the months and years, Inman developed his own theories of competition training for women, and their effects became abundantly apparent: the women returned from competitions with an ever-increasing tally of trophies. His ideas and his teaching were to prove so effective that he coached Britain's women to the top place in the world for the next fourteen years. The O.B.E. (Order of the British Empire) that he was awarded in 1992 was certainly well deserved. Overall he coached the winners of six Olympic medals, thirteen world championship medals, and twenty-one European championship medals. He admits that the best of the coaches supplied him promising material.[7] "They were good when I got them; I made them better."

In fact, he made them the best. Two of them were the best in the world.

JANE BRIDGE at 105 pounds (48 kilograms) was a bantamweight fighter who appeared from the North with the most beautiful classical judo. Inman found that this skill came quite naturally to her and realized that his task was not to teach her to be good at judo, but to be good at fighting. In 1980 he took her to represent Britain in the biggest women's judo event yet to be organized—the first women's world championships. Held in New York, it was the result of the lobbying, fundraising, and organizational efforts of an unceasing campaigner for the promotion of women's judo: Rusty Kanokogi.

Bridge won her weight category. Given that there was no such thing as women's judo in the Olympics at the time, this was the greatest goal that a woman could possibly achieve. As her country's first-ever judo world champion, she is one of Britain's greatest unsung sporting heroines. Her victory marked the beginning of a long period of British superiority in women's lightweight competition.

A few months before Bridge's world title triumph, a new face appeared at Fairholme. It belonged to another bantamweight, a small, fair, scrawny, seventeen-year-old girl from Hull. Socially she was mousy, grotesquely shy, and uncertain; on the mat she was a little terror. Her name was Karen Briggs.

Briggs was always going to be a champion. Aside from her stringy but whippy physique, she was not only brimming with a frenetic energy and application, but was also possessed of an intelligent skill which she brought to anything she did. Her frame seemed to house a small but extremely powerful engine, constantly revving and waiting to engage. The sport she chose to harness to this energy was judo. Aged twelve, she read something in the local paper about classes at the Hull Dock Labour Board Club, asked to be taken, and realized immediately how much she liked combat. She says she preferred competing with boys rather than girls because she would get a better fight.

At fifteen she graduated to the Hull Prison Officers' Judo Club and would run the six miles from her home to the dojo, her father following patiently in the car. After a series of successes in northern competitions, she was spotted by Roy Inman and invited to train with the British national squad at Fairholme. She later described how embarrassed she had been by her clumsiness, her lack of technique, and not least by the little blue suitcase she arrived with, instead of a sports bag like everyone else. She was also mortified by her complete inability to look Roy Inman in the eye.[8]

Inman was insistent on proper squad training and brought the women together at intervals. This was expensive: they were constantly short of funds and he was forever having to wheedle money from wherever he could to pay for transport, training sessions, and equipment. Paying for the girls' accommodation was out of the question. The best he could do was make Fairholme available to anyone who needed to be on hand for squad sessions. Before she took part in her first world championships, Briggs needed to move down to London. She and Diane Bell (who later went on to win Britain's only Olympic judo gold medal, at Seoul in 1988 when women's judo was a demonstration event) would sleep in the hallway. It was hardly ideal. Briggs remembered how, exhausted by their training, they would have to wait until everyone had left at night before they could turn in. In the morning they would wake up in the same place where they'd be working all day. "But," she said, "it did concentrate our minds."

Briggs admitted to having "an obsessive desire to train." Just before a judo session she would do an eight-mile road run, sometimes with weights strapped to her ankles (she later concluded that this had caused her knee injuries). Even while recovering from a bad injury to her foot, each day she would swim two miles and cycle the twenty-five miles to and from the physiotherapist to maintain her cardiovascular fitness. Inman often had to tell her not to train but to rest.

In 1982, within a couple of years of arriving at Fairholme, Briggs became world champion in Paris. Three of her fights were won with her newly acquired _tomoe-nage_, a "sacrifice throw"—so called because in order to execute the technique you sacrifice your normal stance for an apparent disadvantage. To execute the throw the attacker suddenly drops onto his back and, using his outstretched leg like a pitchfork, impales his opponent's stomach on the sole of the foot, lifts him into the air and flips him into a somersault onto his back.

But she also learned to become extremely formidable on the ground, and it was with the power and skill of her _newaza_ that she won her second world championship. By 1986, when the tournament was held in Maastricht, she was so cool and assured that she actually prolonged one of her preliminary contests deliberately in order to feel more settled. She went on to take the title.

Having won three world championships in a row, she looked likely to take a fourth at Essen in 1987. But luck was against her: as she turned in for a throw her opponent's foot came down on her outstretched leg and she fell down in agony. Thinking it was a dislocation, she tried "to put it back." Ken Kingsbury, the British team doctor, hurried onto the mat. He could see the injury was serious but could only question her and instruct her how to test it; had he touched it, Briggs would have been disqualified. In the event it wouldn't have made any difference. "I tried to straighten it out," recalled Briggs, "and then I tried to stand on it. I collapsed." Understandably. Both her tibia and fibia had been snapped clean in two and her ankle dislocated; they had to carry her off on a stretcher. The operation required fifty stitches and a long recuperation.

The leg recovered, but her right shoulder was to present a greater problem. It popped out of its socket while she was in the act of retaining her title yet again with a hold-down in the final of the world championships in Belgrade in 1989. Indeed, it was to be a recurring problem. It was only when parts of her body got broken or ceased to function that Briggs was stopped in her tracks. Otherwise her determination could usually overcome any obstacle in her path.

When training back in Hull, her day would begin with a run, sometimes augmented by swimming fifty lengths of the pool. Then she returned home, where she had turned a spare room into a gym with weights, an exercise bike in one corner, a sit-up board in the other, a mat in the middle of the room, a special bar fixed to the wall to strengthen her wrists and fingers, and straps and a belt for shadow *uchikomi*. The walls were covered in charts and programs recording her tasks for the week and her progress. Like many other committed athletes, Briggs made a point of taking frequent and detailed notes about her opponents and her own performance in training and competition.

Her records show for instance that, at age nineteen, she weighed 101 pounds (46 kilograms) and had a resting pulse of fifty-two. She could do fifty-six situps in one minute, eighty-three push-ups without a break, forty-three squat thrusts alternating with star jumps in one minute, and could run one-and-a-half miles in nine minutes two seconds.

While the effort of maintaining the highest physical fitness was a terrible strain, it was not the worst pressure that Briggs faced. She was later to write that when a world championship tournament appeared, her anxiety was not whether or not she would have the satisfaction of winning it, but rather living up to everyone's expectations. "This," she said, "is the hardest burden to bear."

Briggs's career ended before Kanokogi and the sisterhood had secured women's judo as a fully fledged Olympic event but what, apart from four world titles, marked Briggs as one of the greatest of the great was her repeated triumphs in Japan's most celebrated women's tournament, the Fukuoka Cup. The event attracts the best in the world and is one of the toughest competitions a woman can enter. Briggs won it five times and became a darling of the Japanese crowd.

In the United Kingdom, Briggs did receive some publicity. but she was certainly not a national celebrity. The Fukuoka experience gave her a taste of the star treatment that the Japanese mete out to judo players in a way that the British never can—reception committees at the airport, TV cameras dancing constant attendance, and a stadium packed with adoring and knowledgeable fans. It was something that one of her successors would enjoy to a degree as yet undreamed of.

Sitting among the spectators watching one of Karen Briggs's Fukuoka victories was a teenage schoolgirl who had been taken along by her parents. Her name was Ryoko Tamura. She idolized the English girl, who became her inspiration. Tamura practiced and studied and trained so hard that she worked her way to the front rank of her contemporaries. And so it happened that in 1990, tiny Tamura, now fifteen years old, stepped onto the tatami in the semifinal of the same tournament, and came face-to-face with her idol.

Four-time world champion and twice Tamura's age, Briggs was approaching the end of her career and was inevitably slowing down. Tamura, by contrast, was young, hungry, and lightning quick. She astonished the crowd by throwing Briggs twice to win the contest and going on to win the final. Tamura later said that she thought she had beaten Briggs "purely by chance."[9] It was the first of three encounters they were to have, each fraught with the drama that ensues when the supremacy of a venerated champion is threatened by a bright new talent.

When both women reached the final of the world championships in Barcelona in 1991, the British champion wrought her revenge on the teenage upstart by nailing Tamura to the floor for a winning score. They met for the last time in the semifinal of the Barcelona Olympics in 1992. Briggs, clearly now the slower of the two, wanted to take Tamura to the ground, where the Japanese girl wouldn't have the advantage of her speed; but Tamura did everything she could to avoid that and launched a series of vigorous attacks, outgripping Briggs and dragging her around the mat. In one exchange she partially dislocated Briggs's still vulnerable right shoulder. As always, the Great Britain squad doctor, Ken Kingsbury, was in attendance and instructed her how to put the joint back into its socket. She managed to get it functioning after a fashion and the fight was restarted, but Tamura, presented with such an easy target, kept attacking the damaged area. In one ghastly moment, clearly visible on the video, Briggs cannot properly defend herself and Tamura drags her to the floor so that Briggs lands on the injured arm.

The pain was so intense that Briggs could scarcely resist, let alone attack. The inevitable followed, the referee halting the contest to penalize her for passivity. Briggs refused to give up and endured a further period of torture before the referee stopped the contest and summoned the two corner judges to the center. After a puzzlingly long discussion, they reached agreement. Briggs was awarded a second passivity penalty that mercifully brought the business to a close; the contest was awarded to Tamura.

Barcelona was the end of the road for Briggs. By now exhausted, she felt she had done what she could and announced her retirement. "I'd been competing at the top for fourteen years," she said. "Your body tells you when it's had enough and in my case I was always a bit afraid I would get an injury that I wouldn't recover from. I wanted to live the rest of my life."

One of the boys Briggs used to train with at Fairholme was Roy Inman's son, Peter. She described him as "a perfect training partner at the time—a skillful teenager who was only a little taller than myself."

They are still partners: they were married in 1994 and have two children.

BY THE SUMMER OF 2005, the University of Bath had assembled the collection of judo-related books, documents, and letters bequeathed by Dickie Bowen, one of the sport's most assiduous historians, before his death in the previous year. Housing this archive is not the only contribution that the university has made to judo. In 2005 it launched a three-year foundation degree course run by Mike Callan, the director of judo, designed for high-level coaches. But most important, the $53 million (£30 million) sports training village on the campus in the Somerset countryside to the east of the city is one of judo's national centers of excellence. I wanted to see the archive, talk to Mike Callan, and catch up with Roy Inman, who had moved out of the London area and come here to be high-performance coach, and who was now technical director.

On the evening I arrived, I joined in a training session for promising players conducted by Inman in the magnificent new dojo, equipped with a sprung floor that must be the envy of almost every club in the country. The opening ceremony had been performed by no less than Yusuhiro Yamashita himself, now education director of the International Judo Federation. The next day I met Roy in the café area on a concourse where tracksuited athletes, fencers, swimmers, and gymnasts moved along the different levels between the indoor track, the pool, and the sports halls. The complex, light and airy and beautifully equipped, was all so very different from the dilapidation of Fairholme. As we sat over a coffee, he reflected on the ups and downs of British judo and his own career within it.

As Inman talked about the development of the sport for women, it became clear that their story was the exact converse of the men's, in which the preeminence of the Japanese was gradually eroded by challengers from the West. The impetus for women to compete came entirely from Europe and the United States; in the beginning, the Japanese never saw the sport as something that females would do and were slow to react.

"In those early days, the British women's team was the best in the world," says Inman. "The Japanese brought twenty girls to the British Open one year just so they could train with us. And we were invited to take a team to Japan. We beat Cuba in the final; the Japanese were wiped out." Looking back on the system he created for the women's squad, he was regretful of the way that the infrastructure that produced the world-beating champions had long since decayed. "Today the most successful women's teams have a full-time training infrastructure—what we used to have before Seoul and Barcelona. But that's gone now. Today the foreigners are fitter and more technically aware than our players."

In 1992, after the Barcelona Games in which Inman's women had won three medals, he had a major falling out with the British Judo Association. Inman, undoubtedly a Cromwellian figure in the dojo, could be a bit of a cavalier when it came to administration and relationships with his masters. He had never made a point of being courteous to those he did not respect, and had accumulated a good number of enemies who now successfully worked to reduce his power. While his eventual departure may have tidied up the administration, it also managed to bring to an end Olympic success for British women's judo. In Atlanta in 1996, Great Britain's women's squad failed to win a single medal.

After Inman had left his BJA post, he and Kate Howey drifted apart. But as the year 2000 approached, she sought him out to be her personal coach again and so he worked with her, this time outside the auspices of the BJA. As he talked I thought back to my visit to the ancient wooden building near Heathrow, when I saw him working with Howey on her preparation for Sydney. And I was reminded how, when her great day came, I went into the sports department of the *Sunday Telegraph* to follow her progress through to the finals on TV. Watching her do battle with the Cuban, I was late for my most important editorial conference and I recalled the blank incomprehension on the faces of my colleagues as I tried to explain why Kate's—and Roy's—silver was more important. I had succumbed to a fan's peculiar sense of ownership in the fortunes of those whom he follows—a sense of ownership swollen by my tenuous connection with the two of them.

In 2000 Inman had moved to Bath and shortly afterward the Bedfont club was closed down. And that marked the end of a glorious era in British judo—the days when a handful of women and one man conquered the world from a little wooden hut called Fairholme.

HOW TO BUILD A FIGHTING MACHINE

The first part of Señor Ronaldo Veitia Valdivie to become visible when he enters the stadium is a substantial stomach. After some moments this is followed by the rest of its moustachioed owner, who is walking with a studiedly casual and superior air. He is leaning slightly backwards to counterbalance the payload he carries up front, which means that the last part of him to arrive is the dark ponytail harvested from all parts of his scalp.

To have a belly like his in Cuba is like hanging a sign across your abdomen that says: "I am rich." While to be this fat in Miami takes indolence, to achieve it in Cuba you have to be smart. Such a girth is evidence of a well-paid job; otherwise, you'd never be able to afford the raw materials to build it. And, in Cuban terms, Valdivie is very well paid, for he is a valuable man. He is an alchemist: he can turn sweat into gold. Valdivie is the chief coach of the national women's judo team of Cuba.

COMMUNISM HAS BEEN GOOD for judo. And it has been good for judoka, for whom success on the mat can bring—quite apart from respect and adulation—privileges of which most can only dream. The fabulous incompetence of the Eastern Bloc's communist-inspired economies has done much to create the ideal conditions for this tender plant.

When players from these countries first appeared on the circuit, they fought so hard that they seemed to be fighting for their lives. In a way that is just what they were doing: they were fighting for their *style* of lives. For a Russian the difference between defeat and victory could be the difference between living like everyone else and having decent accommodation, a good diet including meat, and—that most precious privilege of all—overseas travel. In an egalitarian state it's well worth being part of the elite.

Nowhere in the lands ruled by Marxism has judo thrived better than in Cuba. A desperate desire to improve their living conditions, allied to a passion for sport and a natural athleticism, have produced formidable judoka able to fire their opponents into the air with devastating certainty. Once the island's authorities targeted the sport, other countries had to start paying attention, for here indeed was a Cuban missile crisis.

From the mid 1980s on, little Cuba with its eleven million people and a diminutive judo population of only three thousand females and four thousand males[1] has produced a succession of ferocious competitors who have fought their way out of poverty to throw the rest of the world over their shoulder and scamper home adorned with gold, silver, and bronze. While the country has produced some brilliant male players, it is the women's squad which has made the greater impact, and the architect of their victories has been Ronaldo Veitia Valdivie. For the best view of him in action, we will seat ourselves in the stadium behind the officials' table and opposite the chairs of the matside coaches.

SO HERE HE COMES NOW, bulky and slow-moving, his charge walking a few paces in front of him with a bustling businesslike gait, a little brown face, and crisp white *gi*. There's something gently incongruous, even comic, about the sight of a tiny cotton bundle weighing 105 pounds (48 kilograms) bustling into the arena, followed by this man who weighs more than three times as much.

There is nothing faintly funny about what happens next.

Whoever the Great Ronaldo brings into the arena will unleash a hail of fighting fury. When Cuba's women go onto the mat they bring new meaning to the phrase "state-sponsored terrorism."

"They'll poke you in the eye, throw you on your face—anything to destroy an opponent's technique," one former contestant complained. A British squad woman nursing a nasty elbow injury moaned, "I snapped the medial ligament on a Cuban witch in Italy who did it on purpose." "With a Cuban you know you've got a fight on your hands," says Ronaldo's oldest adversary, Roy Inman, the former coach of the British women's squad. "Cubans don't do footsweeps, so you don't need to worry about that, but you must never let them get on your back because whatever you do they'll always roll you."

To give an idea of just how effective they are, consider the result of a match which took place in April 2006, at the High Performance Center in the city of Cuenca in Ecuador. The Cuban women's team took on a men's team from the host nation and won twenty-eight of the thirty fights.[2]

Valdivie is their inspiration, their Svengali; whatever happens in any major women's contest, the Cuban side of the proceedings will be controlled by him. His fighters obey him to the letter. While so many sometimes seem to pay their coaches scant attention, Valdivie's squad will stand during any break in the fighting like sheepdogs, wide-eyed and panting, their shoulders pointing towards their task but their obedient gaze fixed on their master, searching for instruction.

Valdivie's participation from the coach's chair is so forceful and so closely engaged in the proceedings that you think that at any moment he might make his way onto the mat and engage with the enemy himself. There are those who say this dominance has disadvantages, that his fighters miss him too much when he isn't there. At the 2000 Olympics, his intervention in coaching Legna Verdicia to a gold medal was deemed so excessive that he was banned from matside for twenty-four hours. Unfortunately this occurred the day before he was due to be at the side of the mat for the awesome Driulys González. The twice–world champion was expected to take gold, but it was noted that "without the tactical brain of Ronaldo to guide her, she looked lost,"[3] and she was beaten into second place.

Frequently the conduct of a contest provokes in Valdivie so many cubic centimeters of exasperation forced under pressure into so small a space, so many degrees of fury-induced heat, that he will drape a damp cloth over his face, as if to prevent his head from exploding.

What is it that provokes him so? Why, the fantastic blindness, stupidity, ineptness, and inexperience of any referee who is foolish enough to suggest his fighter was being passive, failed to score *waza-ari,* and was given a ridiculous *koka.* Are they all mad?

And how is this discontent expressed? By pulling out every stop and stamping on every pedal of the Wurlitzer of histrionics. In a scenario seemingly created to intimidate referees, he casts himself as a lone figure hell-bent on fighting the injustice that rages around him. It starts with a modest gesture of complaint, a single palm upturned: "Come *on!*" The behavior is that of a *reasonable* man. If that doesn't work, he turns up the volume. We are given the doleful brown eyes rolled to heaven; the head shaken in despair; the stabbing accusatory finger; but most of all *both* palms turned up and proffered in a cocktail of supplication and disbelief. This is accompanied by a shrug of awesome despair that freezes, leaving his shoulders nearly level with his ears for some time before the stance slowly melts. He makes John McEnroe's famously savage interjections look like good-natured quibbles. However many times you see the Great Ronaldo do the show, you have to admit: It is one hell of an act.

Wherever he goes in the world, whichever hotel room he is allocated, Valdivie's routine is the same: First, he sets up the shrine. In a rich mixture of Catholicism, voodoo, and superstition, he lays a small towel out on the table, around which he arranges a number of items: a red candle, a photograph of the Native American chief Sitting Bull, a hair band, some postcards and plastic flowers, a wristwatch, and a small cup of holy water. These will be joined, once his squad of women have done their work, by the tournament medals. The girls who fought so hard to win these prizes are not allowed to keep them for a moment beyond the medal ceremony; as soon as they come off the rostrum they must hand them over to Ronaldo, who that night puts them on the shrine.

The preparations are often unorthodox. A Belgian coach visiting the Cuban team when they came to Europe was surprised to find that their training center was in the open under a tree and that the equipment consisted of nothing more than a bar, a rope, a tricep machine, and a ladder.[4] At Fukuoka in 2001, the IJF photographer Bob Willingham, who had got to know the team, was invited to come and train with them. "It turned out that they weren't training in a dojo, but in their hotel," said Willingham. "The girls' squad like to train in secret and they want everyone to *know* they are training in secret. We were on the seventh floor doing shuttle runs up and down the corridor and moving *uchikomi* on the landing by the lifts."

Sometimes, as a warm-up exercise before they start training, the Cuban women dance to salsa music for thirty minutes because Ronaldo believes in "uniting the psychological and physical aspects" and finds this relaxes the minds of his athletes.

As well as a doctor and physiotherapist, a psychologist always accompanies the team. Until recently security has not appeared to be a problem, even though dozens of Cuban athletes have simply vamoosed when competing abroad. But when Ronaldo's squad alights from the plane in Havana they are always a full complement—or they were until two of them ran away after the Osaka world championships, when they disappeared during a stopover in the United States. Not long after that, another pair followed suit while they were in Spain. But, given that dozens of Cuban athletes have defected, the loss of four judo players is not bad going.

This could be because of the devotion of Ronaldo's squad, but it must also be said that a Cuban judo star is no more likely to defect to the West for career reasons than a U.S. international tennis champion would seek new riches and sporting opportunity by applying for political asylum in Burkina Faso. While it would be understandable for a Cuban star basketball player or athlete to make a run for it, it would make no sense for a judoka to do so. Judo is paid so poorly in most Western countries that it is little better than voluntary work.

However, it would be fair to say that if a seriously talented American judoka really wanted to improve his prospects, he couldn't do much better than to catch a flight to Florida and—following the example of the Cubans traveling in the opposite direction—climb onto an inner tube and start paddling hell-for-leather the ninety miles to Havana, in defiance of the sharks and the security patrols. In the parallel world of judo the United States is merely a middle-ranking nation, while Cuba is a superpower. How can this be? The United States has produced some brilliant judoka, including Olympic medalist Mike Swain and Jimmy Pedro, who are renowned world champions, but the Americans have never been able to produce an Olympic gold medalist.

In his youth Fidel Castro was an avid sportsman and at one stage even considered becoming a professional baseball player. Like the rest of the communist leaders, he appreciated that sports could provide an international showcase for his nation and a means to achieve international prestige; he lavished money on sports, copying the Soviet Bloc model of early selection and specialist training schools. It worked. The country has won more than fifty gold medals since the revolution, after having won only one medal, a silver, in the previous five decades. It was an East German who developed judo in post-revolutionary Cuba, but Castro added it to the main curriculum, along with volleyball and fencing, pandering to his Russian paymasters' fondness for those particular sports.

Valdivie, an athlete in his youth, has coached the women's judo team since 1986; before he took over they had won no medals—not even at the Central American or Caribbean Games. He soon changed all that. He travels all over the island searching for Cuban girls with the strength and potential to be champions. The chosen ones are then put through a rigorous series of physical, mental, and psychological tests before they are considered capable of joining the squad.[5] The majority of them are from Santiago in the east of the island, where life is harder and where people desperately want to get to Havana. Those who come from Havana are considered to have become soft because they have too much.

The women's squad trains in a dark and dingy gym at the High Performance Center of Cerro Pelado on the outskirts of the capital. Bob Willingham has been to Cuba several times and witnessed the training at their base. He found that the amount of work the girls are expected to do is phenomenal. They start at five in the morning and train until seven. The session begins with a noisy and vehement pep talk from Valdivie. He conducts all of the training but is always accompanied by an assistant who is constantly taking notes and making softly spoken observations to his chief. One of the staff accompanying a group of British junior squad players who went to train with the Cubans in Havana in 2006 was struck by the presence of a psychologist at the training sessions. "It was common practice for the psychologist to take one of the world champions outside halfway through the session with them returning five minutes later looking very fired up."[6] Psychology may also play a part in coaching the women's behavior in readiness for competition. "The Cuban girls have their own mannerisms," one female competitor told me. "When they come out, they just look bored. As everyone else is so hyper, it is rather disturbing."

Valdivie has explained that the first thing he had to do was to change the perception that exercises for men made women lose their femininity. "It is amazing how many of them can now benchpress 90 and even 110 kg [200 and even 240 pounds]," he says.[7] So, apart from all the uchikomi, the girls do rope climbing (sometimes using a rope made of judo collars stitched together) and chin-ups on a bar; they also hang under a ladder propped against the wall, hauling themselves up hand-over-hand. When training is over, the younger ones change into school uniforms and leave for class at 8:30. After this transformation, some find it hard to believe that these demure schoolgirls belong to one of the most dangerous girl gangs on earth.

On my way home after the Munich world championships, I was standing in the airport departure lounge when a triumphant gaggle of variously sized Cuban women in red-and-white track suits swarmed through the duty-free shop. The roguish figure of Ronaldo Valdivie in their midst with his pigtail, girth, and ambling swagger suggested a pirate captain with his rowdy crew who have sailed out from an island lair in the Spanish Main terrorizing all in their quest for plunder. Now, laden with gold and other precious metals, he would take them on a voyage to another once-notorious pirate's nest, the Barbary Coast. The Cubans were off to North Africa to train with the Tunisian squad.

THE INTERNATIONAL JUDO COMPETITION circuit had learned the lessons of their defeats at the hands of Cuba's patrons, the USSR, who had wrought havoc in the 1960s. But in the 1990s they had to face a second devastating wave. The collapse of the Soviet system and the subsequent independence of each of the Soviet states drastically changed the face of competition judo. Suddenly fifteen new competitors appeared in each weight category. This didn't only mean more work for the people who have to stitch all these new sets of initials such as KAZ, KGZ, UZB, and AZE on the backs of the *gis* on the eve of a tournament, or that the organizers had the additional bureaucratic burden generated by more than a dozen new national teams. Its major significance was that suddenly every competitor on the circuit suddenly found themselves facing several extra fighters who attacked with an alarming new array of individual fighting styles. Competitors grumbled, "We used to have one Russian to fight; now we've got fifteen!"

As well as the traditions and religious beliefs to which they had clandestinely clung through the dark days of the Soviet empire, each of these nations had, as we have seen, its own long-established way of fighting. Starved of national glory, subordinated and plundered by Russian sporting imperialism, they were hungry for success on their own terms. The new republics didn't have the resources to train and pamper thoroughbred athletes, buy fine horses, or compete in events dependent on expensive hi-tech equipment, but they excelled at combat, and judo offered an ideal showcase for their ferocious talent.

ALEXANDER IATSKEVICH would one day become an Olympic bronze medalist and three-time European champion and later coach the formidably successful Belgian team, but in 1970 he was a twelve-year-old boy who joined a sambo club in the Latvian city of Riga so he could defend himself on the streets. Three hundred other children started with him that term. They were launched into a furious training routine in which they were made to do repeated push-ups, pull-ups, and other exercises. The first ones to stop were told to go away. "It was totally Spartan," he remembers, "the survival of the fittest."[8]

The sessions continued to be so punishing that within a few weeks the class had been reduced to half. Meanwhile, even at this age they were being taught dangerous leg and arm locks and were using them in competitions. By the end of the year there were just twenty-seven left. Those were the ones the sports commissars wanted. "The idea was to weed out the no-hopers," says Iatskevich, "those who would be unlikely to succeed in competition, and keep just the cream." He thought he was joining a sports club; in fact he was raw material fed into a factory manufacturing competition fighters. Such was the Soviet selection system, but it worked. When he was eighteen, Iatskevich, who had by this time switched to judo, became junior champion of the world. And that ruthless approach would continue to serve the nation well.

But there had been other developments in the Soviet Bloc since the USSR made its dramatic onslaught on judo in the 1960s. As in warfare, so in unarmed combat; every attack has a defense. Japanese and other judo players studied film footage of the sambo techniques that caused them such trouble and they worked to develop counters. Within a few years judo had learned how to cope with Soviet-style attacks and some of the techniques had been absorbed into its repertoire.

What was more, Japanese judoka went on the offensive and took the war into the enemy camp. In 1972 two Japanese judo champions, Katsuhiko Kashiwazaki and Nobuyuki Sato (who was still competing and was yet to become Yamashita's coach), entered a national sambo competition in Riga and beat the best the Soviets could put up. The effect on the appalled hosts was dramatic. They had seen sambo as the superior form, but now they began to reconsider. "I was convinced at that moment that judo had to be something special for judo players to come along and beat sambo players," wrote Alexander Iatskevich. His coach felt the same; in the following years he changed the name of his club to the Dynamo Judo Club, and a number of other Soviet sambo clubs did likewise. And they started teaching judo.

THE ONLY JUDOKA who has ever become known to the general public throughout the world is a Russian. The son of a factory foreman, he was born in Leningrad, now St. Petersburg, in 1952 and took up sambo and then judo in his early teens. Explaining how he came into the sport, he spoke of the frequent street fights among teenagers. "Tough laws reigned there, therefore I looked for various ways to become physically stronger: I tried boxing, wrestling, and so on. I gradually got to judo." He won competitions in Leningrad and gained third place in the Russian junior nationals; he also became the senior champion of Leningrad—all achievements which marked him as a serious player.

He was helped by the fact that he had chosen a career in the KGB, where he was encouraged to keep up his training. Indeed, the organization insisted upon regular attendance at some form of combat class for its members. He rose through the ranks of the organization and it wasn't long before he was running the KGB in St. Petersburg. Now he runs Russia. He is Prime Minister Vladimir Putin.

He may be the leader of a world superpower, but to his fellow judo club members Putin is perhaps more respected for his effective sweeping hip throw (*harai-goshi*). He told one reporter in 2002 that he had a mat at home: "When friends come to see me, we do judo."[9] He had also encouraged his daughters into the sport, but told a group of girls studying judo at a sports education center he was visiting in his home city that, although his girls used to study judo, they were now "lazy."

He abandoned the problems of the economy and Chechnya for a few hours to watch some of the Moscow Grand Prix in 2001. He is president of the Yawara Dojo, the same St. Petersburg club at which he trained in his youth, and he has co-authored, with two club members, a book on his favorite sport, which has also been published in English under the title *Judo: History, Theory, Practice.*

He uses judo as a continuation of diplomacy by other means. On a state visit to Japan in 2000, he was invited to the Kodokan, where he was welcomed by Yukimitsu Kano, the grandson of its founder Dr. Jigoro Kano. Putin changed into a *gi*, demonstrated some throws and groundwork techniques, and was awarded his sixth dan. In spite of his high office, he was confident enough to risk his personal dignity by allowing himself to be photographed with a small girl who, with Putin's cooperation and the audience's approbation, threw the Russian premier over her shoulder.

When asked by a journalist what the sports term "pure victory" means to him, Putin—who describes himself as having a "pugilistic nature"[10]—replied, "It is a very pleasant sensation, it is even hard to convey in words."

He has claimed that wrestling had influenced his character and helped him to remain calm and react quickly.[11] "Judo is not just a competition sport, it is my philosophy. The moment I stepped on mats my life changed." He maintains that the ultimate purpose of practicing judo is "to apply the principles of judo, maximum efficiency and mutual welfare and benefit, to perfect ourselves and contribute to the world."[12]

Well, we'll all drink to that. In Washington. And in the ruins of Grozny.

IN 1998 THE BRITISH JUDO ASSOCIATION appointed as performance director to the British squad the remarkable East German featherweight Udo Quellmalz. He had just retired from competition after winning gold at the Atlanta Olympics; he had won bronze at Barcelona and was twice world champion. He would often bring British squad players to the Budokwai, which gave me a chance to get more, highly prized autographs. It also enabled me to hear something about life for a judoka behind the Iron Curtain under probably the most scientifically intensive training systems that had yet been devised.

Quellmalz was one of the finest products of the Soviet Bloc's cradle-to-grave approach to the selection and training of athletes. He was born in Leipzig and spent most of his career under the East German regime, but moved to Bavaria in 1990, shortly after the Berlin Wall came down. "It was only then that I realized the extent of the advantage I had over many of my main rivals," he told me in one of a series of conversations.

People did much less training than I was used to. The East German approach was much more professional than that of the West. The volume and intensity of the training was so much higher. There were more training camps and they lasted longer. Olympic sports were fully funded by the East German government; there were specialist sports schools and teachers in the training camps who gave you school work (and checked that you did it). Talent was identified early; there was a proper training set-up with three main sports clubs all providing class training partners, well-educated coaches, strong rivals, and a depth of good players throughout the system. The big difference between the two systems was the time allowed for training and the hardness of that training. In the GDR, the athletes spent over twenty hours a week training. In the West a top athlete could do about ten to twelve hours a week. It's not enough. It is really hard for athletes trying to get to the top; they must work, study, go to school and they cannot get enough time to train—especially to attend training camps.

Also the trainers in the East were harder and athletes had to do exactly what they were told. In the West the athlete might say, "I don't want to . . ." and there was a lot of discussion. In the GDR there was no discussion; they used to have to train to keep their job. Now there are more compromises.

One thing we were made to do was climb to the top of a rope without using our legs as many times as we could in one hour. I managed nearly seventy, but I had blisters on my hands for days. I knew that not many of my opponents went to such extremes, so I wasn't frightened to go all out for all of the fight and I could take some pain if necessary.

Even after unification, some of the conditioning work organized by the German trainers could be quite arduous—in all likelihood prompted by learning of Eastern methods.

In preparation for the 1995 world championships we did a ten-day conditioning camp in the Austrian Alps. We hardly did any judo, it was just endurance and strength training. One day we did a bike race through the mountains. I fell quite early on and cut my head and at one point we had to climb some pretty steep rocks with our mountain bikes on our backs. I am a good climber but it was pretty

> dangerous. It took us about four hours. I was completely dead after that. You might say you don't need extreme endurance training sessions like this for judo—after all a fight only lasts for five minutes—but I am convinced it made me mentally harder.
>
> The East German training regime was very strict but, looking back, I would say that we trained too hard for too long.

At first he doubted he would be able to continue at the top level because the West was so much less professional. As it turned out he did even better. He says: "On reflection, I know I used the more limited time for training in a more effective way. It was only by reducing my training volume that I could survive so long—twenty-nine is pretty old to be Olympic champion in a lightweight category."

Quellmalz now feels that the East Germans "could sometimes be too scientific and didn't allow for the spirit." Certainly, no other nation devoted more resources or more ingenuity to the task of winning medals. I had already learned just how scientific they could be.

WHEN I WAS AT the Tournoi de Paris in 1998, I noticed two people at the back of the *tribune des athletes* who seemed particularly assiduous and systematic in their videoing of the contests. I fell into conversation with one of them, Roland Oswald, and learned that he was with the East German squad. He was based in Leipzig, on the staff of the sports science institute (IAT) which had been part of the hugely successful East German judo effort. Now it happened that I had to be in Leipzig ten days later, so I was able to visit the squad at their headquarters and see the work they were doing.

I took a tram from the middle of town which trundled in the drizzle through Leipzig's gray streets. I got off at the entrance to the Sports Forum to find a small group of athletes outside, apparently waiting for me. Oblivious to the rain, they stared across the road, standing in attitudes that I guess their sculptor had deemed heroic. At the reception area I was given directions that took me across a section of the vast campus that includes a stadium, swimming pools, several running tracks, and a number of sports halls. The architecture was early 1960s Eastern Bloc, grim and austere. There was hardly a soul around, which added to the sense of desolation; I was visiting the heart of an empire that had apparently been abandoned.

I found my way to two identical blocks housing the sports science departments on the western edge. One had been the headquarters of the notorious East German banned-drug program. I headed for the other, where the combat sports section was sited. There I found Roland Oswald sitting in front of a TV monitor, analyzing and editing tapes of the Tournoi de Paris. He was ebullient as he stood up to greet me. "Oh, there are some *great* techniques here!"

In the great days of the Soviet empire the institute employed more than six hundred people. But with the collapse of the Warsaw Pact and the crumbling of the East German government, funding suddenly stopped and its existence appeared to be in jeopardy. The doctor and his staff carried on working for months without pay, until the West realized that the institute had some value. Now, down to a staff of eighty and with the judo group shrunk from twelve to two, it was a shadow of its former self. Once members of the East German national judo squad had been summoned here every six weeks to have their fitness measured. These days, the institute had to go out to where the athletes were.

The head of the combat section, Dr. Harold Tünneman, now joined us. He took me across the campus into a large glass-fronted sports hall that was showing signs of neglect. Green slime was gathering on the glazing bars; in places the carpet was rotting. At one end was gymnastic equipment including a set of rings rigged over a pit filled with musty chunks of foam rubber to catch falling gymnasts. The central floor area was occupied by a mat; half a dozen life-size wrestling dummies stood leaning against the wall beside the door.

As we made our way, the doctor explained that the institute had been given two tasks. The first was to help athletes develop their technique, strategy, and tactics by giving them detailed information about their opponents. The second was to make them physically and mentally fit. But fitness could mean many things.

The basic tenet of East German training was that each sport required its own special performance monitoring system. It made no sense, for instance, to put judo players on the treadmill, because it was no indicator of "judo fitness." To measure that, more complex tests were needed. So the institute had developed a special circuit of twelve exercises that had to be repeated in a fixed time, and which included weightlifting, throwing a dummy, jumping over a box, sit-ups, and chin-ups. The circuit, which was repeated several times at three-minute intervals, replicated the range of physical pressures that a typical judo contest placed upon a body. The scientists would measure lactate and heart rate to see how much energy was used and how quickly the athlete recovered. It revealed both his aerobic and anaerobic fitness, as well as various other strengths and weaknesses. Later Quellmalz was to tell me how valuable he found it. "The results gave a really useful guide to what you needed to do in the final stages of preparation for a big tournament."

By now we had reached a door at the back of the sports hall. As Dr. Tünneman unlocked it, he announced melodramatically, "And this is the *Freuderkommand* . . . the dungeon." Beyond lay a small windowless room crowded with sinister-looking pieces of machinery. One consisted of a steel shaft to which had been fixed a stuffed leather dummy roughly in the shape of a human torso with short stumpy arms. "This is Billi," the doctor said. "It was built in 1973 and there was nothing like it anywhere else in the world." He explained that the machines were primarily for wrestlers, but that judoka were also brought in here. "Seventy percent of the effort is to hold the opponent to prepare for the technique, so we developed this electro-hydraulic robot which operates in three axes and measures strength and endurance. The athlete is made to fight against the machine for nine minutes. It is too powerful for him to beat, but the important thing is that you can measure his resistance at every stage." He moved over to a control console and turned the machine on. An engine began to whirr and the dummy started to turn and lean at odd angles. To demonstrate, Oswald grasped it with both hands and tried to resist. The needle on the monitor flickered into life, marking his effort as he fought against the twisting and turning torso.

Next we moved over to another dummy that was fixed horizontally to an axle just above the level of the floor. "In combat sports we have a basic gut wrench—you have to roll your opponent over when you are underneath. The big problem is that you've got to bring power and strength into a technique. We developed this device from an old truck brake. We set it at increasing resistances and the athlete has to break that resistance. Everyone said we couldn't measure the specific movements and specific demands in combat sports. But that's just what we did with this. It was our big secret."

As the doctor explained, "We realized we couldn't extend the amount of time athletes were training—they were already training to the limit—therefore we had to think about the quality of training and develop new methods."

So, here in this land of Zeiss, where Germans had made precision into an art, they had taken the concept of judo fitness, brought it into their laboratory and stripped it down to its components so that they could measure the hitherto immeasurable. While their colleagues had the task of analyzing the single simple action of a weightlifter, they had to cope with the complex movements of a fighter grappling with a shifting, resisting opponent.

The East German managers needed to know exactly about the progress of each of their precious athletes. It was not enough to rely on the anecdotal evidence gathered by a coach as he watched his charges train. The athletes had to improve their performance and that improvement had to be proven. To do that they would use a method of measurement in which the only variable was the athlete himself. They would do this by pitting him against a faceless fighter who was never off form, who knew no fatigue, who could consistently resist at a predetermined level. They would calibrate precisely their athletes' performance against this unyielding benchmark, a tireless, superhumanly strong, short-armed monster called Billi.

No other country ever rivaled the East Germans in the intensity of their efforts to apply the certainties of science to the uncertainties of judo. Outside the rain had stopped and the sun was beginning to shine. As I sat on the tram that took me back into a more ordinary world of life in a city center beginning to brighten after decades of gloom, it occurred to me that there was perhaps some strange inevitability that, in their effort to turn their athletes into virtual fighting machines, they should make them fight real ones.

18

WHEN JUDO GOES INTO THE CAGE

From its earliest days, Dr. Kano's creation has had to struggle against its numerous rivals. Hoplology, or the study of combat, suggests that there are probably as many fighting systems practiced around the world as there are spoken languages. Even if we confine ourselves to the unarmed versions there are still scores of them. They can be divided into striking and grappling. The former include punching styles (Western boxing, Chinese boxing), kicking and punching (karate, savate, taekwondo), and open-handed striking (karate). In grappling there are belt and jacket styles (sumo, sambo, jujitsu, aikido) and bare-chested styles (Greco-Roman, freestyle wrestling). And these are just the market leaders. Many countries have more than one style—the United Kingdom, for instance, has Cornish, Cumbrian, and Scottish backhold wrestling among others. The question hanging over each system is, How would it fare against its rivals?

There is only one way to find out. You have to do what the Tokyo police department did in 1886 when they invited Dr. Kano to send a team of fifteen to the shrine in Shiba Park. In terms of scientific research these numbers constituted a fair if not random sample—both schools sent their best—and the experiment was conducted under what, in this business anyway, passes for laboratory conditions. It was an easy test to run because judo was, after all, merely one more system within jujitsu. To assess other forms of combat against each other is rather more difficult. The boxer versus the wrestler is an obvious and popular contest. But to ask which one would win is like asking the same question about a race between a runner and a swimmer. It rather depends what the rules are; for instance, does the race take place on a track or in a pool? Rules for the conduct of a mixed combat are crucial. When, in the 1920s, little Tani was taking on all comers in the music halls of Britain, he allowed his challengers to use any technique that they wanted, insisting only that they wear a jacket. This gave him the one big advantage that he needed over all the wrestlers and boxers who were invariably larger than he was.

When the striker and grappler confront each other, a great uncertainty enters the fray; they are nervous and respectful of each other's skills. During the occupation of Japan at the end of the Second World War, the mighty Kimura was invited to take part in a private boxing match with the best pugilist in the U.S. Marine Corps.[1] The Japanese thought he would prevail because he had also studied karate. He quickly learned how wrong he was; the American destroyed him. Kimura records how he would shut his eyes every time a glove came toward him; it was, he said, like a fight between an adult and a child. Humiliated, he asked his persecutor to teach him to box.

In the ensuing lessons, his teacher spent most of the time using Kimura for target practice. But once, in a moment of desperation, the judoka resorted to what he knew best: he darted in and lifted his tormentor high into the air. Just when he was about to spin him around and hurl him to the floor, the boxer, "with a pathetic tone of voice," begged him not to. Suddenly it was the boxer's turn to be terrified. Kimura set him back down on his feet. With mutual respect now established, the lessons continued. The Japanese claimed that after about a year he was able to hold his own.

THE ADOPTION OF judo training by police and armed forces around the world occurred because judo was more successful than the existing systems when comparative experiments were conducted. For instance, the introduction of judo into the training syllabus of the Royal Canadian Mounted Police and the U.S. Air Force came about because their wrestling champions were beaten by judo men.

Abiding curiosity as to the relative effectiveness of differing combat styles resulted in an explosion in the promotion of fights devoted to "mixed martial arts," one of the great fight phenomena of the past two decades. It is not a new idea. There was the _pankration_ in the Greek games. The bare-knuckle prize fights of Regency England featured as much grappling as punching until the Marquess of Queensberry appeared with his rules. The jujitsu contests of pre-Meiji Japan, as we have seen, permitted pretty well anything. Later, in the mid twentieth century, Brazil became a pioneer in this bloody field.

Brazil has made two significant contributions to the martial arts menu. One is capoiera, developed by slaves who, forbidden to fight, disguised their combat as acrobatic dancing. The present-day version, neither fighting nor dancing, belongs in the vegetarian section of the menu. But decidedly among the meat dishes is _vale tudo_ (anything goes), in which any kind of throw or joint lock, kick, or (bare-knuckle) punch is allowed in pursuit of a win decided by knock out or submission. Biting is one of just a few actions proscribed. Because a single infringement of any one of these rules could be catastrophic for the victim, it is punished by immediate disqualification. The contests are a lottery for the desperate among the pugilistic poor—a chance to win, in a few painful minutes, wealth that will transform their lives.

It was to such a contest that Kimura, now forty-two years old and in the twilight of his fighting career, was challenged in 1959. The previous vale tudo champion had been his old adversary, Helio Gracie, but he had lost his title in an epic struggle, lasting two hours and ten minutes, which ended when Gracie was kicked so hard in the abdomen that he could no longer defend himself and was knocked unconscious. The victor was a twenty-five-year-old black Brazilian called Aldemar Santana, and this was the man Kimura now had to face.

The Japanese champion had already beaten the Brazilian in a judo contest. However, although he may not have been a match for Kimura's brilliantly skilled Kodokan techniques, vale tudo was something very different and Santana had formidable advantages: he was not only a heavyweight boxing champion, but he was six feet tall and weighed almost 220 pounds (100 kilograms)—this compared to Kimura's five feet six inches and 189 pounds (86 kilograms).

Ten thousand people turned up to watch the contest in the former slave port of San Salvador in northern Brazil. The fight, according to Kimura's own account, began with Santana launching spasmodic high kicks at Kimura's head, which he easily blocked with his hands. Eventually, distracted by these leg attacks, some of which were delivered in spinning roundhouse style, Kimura failed to see an open hand strike which caught him on the temple with "a fire-like impact." The Japanese was badly shaken and the crowd were beginning to smell foreign blood. Kimura realized that in spite of all his own karate training, Santana was the superior when it came to striking; if he was to survive, let alone win, he would have to take the fight to the floor. There followed a brutal exchange of kicking, punching, and headbutting during which Kimura admits he momentarily lost consciousness. His peril worsened after the referee had stopped the contest to bring the blood-spattered combatants off the ropes to the center of the ring. Next came a moment rich in slapstick but light on laughs.

When Santana lashed out with a strike, Kimura caught his arm and spun round into *ippon-seoi-nage*, the classic judo shoulder-throw. It was the wrong technique to try on an opponent without a jacket. The sweat-soaked arm slipped through his grip like greased soap and Kimura's throwing momentum catapulted him into a forward somersault which landed him on his back. Seizing the opportunity, Santana leapt on him. Kimura only just managed to save himself in time by catching the Brazilian with his legs and applying a body scissors in an attempt to crush his intestines.

Santana was able to survive the pressure, but Kimura escaped by striking his face so hard that the Brazilian was forced onto his feet in retreat. There was another fearful exchange of kicking, striking, and headbutting, but now both men were exhausted and, half-blinded by blood, neither could land a knockout strike. After forty minutes the contest was declared a draw. The mob had paid their money and got their blood.

One can imagine the functionaries meeting in conclave at the Kodokan on the other side of the Pacific and deploring Kimura's abandonment of the faith, his forays into the world of prize fighting where he worshipped with that devil (judoka were forbidden to compete in other combat sports or fight for money). But surely his victories over Santana and Gracie were particularly sweet in that they signaled a clear vindication of their creed after a long doctrinal feud that had begun after Carlos and Helio Gracie set up their own school outside the auspices of the Kodokan—a feud which we shall soon learn still persists today.

These Brazilian brothers brought a fresh eye to jujitsu just as their fellow countrymen brought a special new approach to football. The school proved popular and commercially successful. But it was not only a new school of jujitsu that they founded, but also a whole dynasty of fighters—three generations, twelve Gracies in all, augmented by a dozen or more who married into the family.

Kimura's defeat of Helio in 1952 had long rankled with the Gracie family. In 2002, exactly half a century after that encounter, Royce Gracie, Helio's grandson, challenged a newly retired Japanese judoka, Hidehiko Yoshida, an Olympic gold medallist, to a contest under jujitsu rules (which permit leg locks). Yoshida felt he had to justify his participation in the event in terms that "I was only doing it for judo," but it cannot have been entirely disconnected from the fact that, having just retired, he had opened a dojo that was in need of promotion. Billed as "Dynamite" by Pride, the leading promoters of mixed martial arts in Japan, it was staged in the national stadium and attracted ninety thousand people, possibly the largest audience ever for a sporting event in the country.

This time there were no cardboard coffins or prematch hostilities, just intense excitement at the prospect of a foreigner bringing his alien strain of jujitsu to the land where it all began. Giant TV screens relayed pictures of the struggle, which would otherwise have been impossible to follow. It ended after seven minutes when the referee judged that Gracie had been strangled unconscious. He may have been right—the Brazilian did stop moving—or he may have been overcautious. Gracie nevertheless jumped straight up at the end of the contest and protested that he hadn't gone "out." The decision remained highly controversial. They fought again in the following year under the more usual Pride rules, which permitted kicks and punches. That bout ended after two ten-minute rounds, neither fighter having gained a submission.

IN 2000 THE GRACIE ORGANIZATION took over the running of jujitsu classes held in the downstairs dojo at the Budokwai. A number of judoka started training there because of the focus on groundwork in Brazilian jujitsu, while some of the jujitsu people would come upstairs to improve their standing work. Among these was Roger Gracie, five-time world jujitsu champion and son of Helio's niece, Reila.

Roger Gracie was then preparing to enter the world of mixed martial arts and needed to develop his ability to fight on his feet. He would work with Ray Stevens, Barcelona silver medalist and now manager of the Budokwai. Stevens would instruct him in *tachiwaza* while Gracie would school Stevens in advanced groundwork techniques.

Etiquette between the two groups was always punctiliously observed. Whenever we planned to train in their dojo, we would exchange our black or colored belts for a white belt, because we had no status in jujitsu, and they would do likewise. Even Roger Gracie, a world champion, would tie a white belt around his six-feet-four-inch frame before he entered our dojo. Moreover, when it was time to form a kneeling line in grade order at the end of our session, this charming and most modest of men would go down to the far end and take his place among the beginners.

One Saturday afternoon, I had stayed on with a few others after the end of the class, at which Olympic gold medalist Kenzo Nakamura was a guest instructor. Some, like me, were stretching and cooling down; others were engrossed in rope climbing and practicing techniques; some were just gossiping. Suddenly I saw on the floor that a war of the gods had broken out. There, entangled in a mutually murderous embrace, were Gracie and Nakamura. Because there was very little movement it was clearly not one of those cooperative *randoris* used to explore technique, but a serious all-out struggle.

Now this was a rare thing because champions, under some unwritten etiquette, tend not to fight each other. The thinking is that they respect each other too much; they all have hard-won reputations to preserve that they are not anxious to hazard in front of their students. Nakamura and Gracie had perhaps decided to wait until most people had gone before having their semiprivate contest.

The business was prolonged and inconclusive, but nevertheless quite extraordinary. As I looked I realized that I was witnessing yet one more battle in that long war that had begun half a century earlier in Rio when Roger's great-uncle, Helio, fought Kimura in the Maracana stadium. This was an unofficial but nonetheless highly fascinating contest between two scions of Japanese jujitsu: its Brazilian offspring and judo. And the whole thing was happening no more than a few feet from where I, one of two or three witnesses, stood watching and inwardly boasting to myself that earlier that afternoon I had done *randori* with both of these champions.

JUDO WAS GROWING at a healthy pace in the 1960s and its continued popularity seemed assured, when from out of the blue it received a nasty smack on the side of its head. In a whirl of high-spinning kicks, staccato jabbing, and choppy hand strikes, karate suddenly burst onto the scene. The young were dazzled by its theatricality, by its deranged barking and screaming; they also found appealing a certain psychopathic quality in the art. Responsibility for all this can be laid at the door of one man: Bruce Lee.

Lee was a performing genius who, like Elvis Presley, will be preserved in the popular memory by a series of some of the most successful and deeply terrible films ever made. When Bruce Lee isn't fighting, his films are as bad as Elvis's when Elvis isn't singing. With scenery made of cardboard and dialogue fashioned from wood, these movies placed their stars in arthritic plots to convey them from one fight or one song to the next. The difference is that at least Elvis is singing in his films, whereas Lee isn't actually fighting. Nevertheless the stunts are an impressive exercise in close-harmony combat: Lee waves his toes in the air and nine people fall over in perfect and carefully rehearsed unison. The ensuing success at the box office was testament to the fact that the most important parts of the films were recorded in a language that everyone in the world could understand: the language of no words, the language of the body.

Within moments of arriving in the United Kingdom and elsewhere in the West, karate and kung fu seemed to have brought thousands of relatives too. They all had short choppy Oriental names like *jeet do* and *wush ann*, and few knew what they were or how they differed; they all looked alike, they all came with rice. Their effect was to divert a steady stream of people away from judo into karate and its numerous cousins, although, as many karate classes were held in judo dojos, they provided a valuable source of income to clubs that always faced financial struggle.

These Eastern kicking and punching disciplines have always had one particular and peculiar appeal for the general public: The skills they demand are so dangerous that they cannot be practiced properly. They are designed to injure, so practicing them must consist largely of drills against a notional opponent. This presents possibilities for a new kind of student. Classes which concentrated on endless drills conducted by lines of students stomping up and down the dojo demanded no physical contact but offered the chance of martial posing and shouting. Certainly there was no shortage of full-contact schools for those who enjoyed a proper fight, but the appeal of karate for many was that it offered all the contact of a boxercise class—which is to say it was enticing to those who didn't actually like fighting but liked the movements and the *idea* of fighting.

These arts also appealed to teachers because they were much more profitable: while judoka needed quite a bit of space to do their free-moving *randori,* you could cram many more karate students into a room, packed in tight ranks and attacking thin air.

Combat sports and martial arts constitute a sizeable industry from which many people in the West are earning an income, if not always a living. They are all locked in perpetual combat with each other, struggling for customers, and one of the factors in the sales pitch is the efficacy of their product—the effectiveness of their particular method, school, or style of fighting. But they need evidence to demonstrate this. It is partly here that the origin of mixed martial arts contests lies.

IN 1993 EIGHT LEADING martial artists were invited to compete in a series of no-holds-barred, bare-knuckle fights. This was the latest of a long line of events designed to answer the nagging question, What would happen when kickboxers, wrestlers, karate men, and sumo champions came face to face? The advance publicity seemed to be written by a ghoul high on splatter flicks, who warned that bouts could end only by "knockout, submission, doctor's intervention, or death."[2] And so Ultimate Fighting Championship (UFC) was born.

It was very different from Dr. Kano's idea. He had done everything he could to remove the impurities in fighting and reduce it to the crystalline springwater of "the attack-and-defense form of movement." But for the ultimate fight crowd the impurities are a delicacy to be savored; promoters work hard to put them back in. An octagonal chain-link cage around the arena created a sensationalist atmosphere: a suggestion that the crowd was about to bear witness to a confrontation of animal-like savagery from which there could be no escape. This was, of course, merely the psychology of cheap theater: in reality, a cage presents no greater menace to fighters than does the chain-link fencing surrounding two players on a municipal tennis court.

Eventually mixed martial arts contests produced a style of their own that drew on a number of disciplines. However, in the early days before that cross-fertilization occurred, it was one discipline against another. The strikers—boxers and karate men—were shown to be extremely vulnerable to the grapplers, and judo proved itself in two different ways. The winner of the first Ultimate Fighting Championship in 1993, and on two subsequent occasions, was Royce Gracie—the man whom Hidehiko Yoshida, the judoka, was later to beat in their first encounter and hold to a draw in their second. Moreover, the origins of Gracie's jujitsu technique lay in the judo that Maeda had brought to Brazil in the 1920s. Gracie thus owed his victories substantially to early Kodokan judo; in essence Gracie jujitsu was judo. These events confirmed judoka in their belief that their discipline was constructed around immutable principles that could handle a whole spectrum of threats. Even here, in prize-money-fueled contests against the world's hardest men, exponents of "the gentle way" could more than hold their own.

19

THE LITTLE EMPRESS

One evening during the 2003 world championships in Osaka, I find myself having dinner with Nicolas Soames, the *Telegraph* judo correspondent, and Katsuhiko Kashiwazaki, the 1981 lightweight world champion, at a small restaurant close to the castle with seating for no more than twenty. The decor is far from luxurious—some torn beer posters on the grubby white walls—but the food prepared in a tiny kitchen and served on the chipped plastic tables is superb: smoked goose breast, raw chicken, small barbecued kebabs—liver or beef interleaved with leek. Translucent pink shavings of dried fish curl and uncurl in the flame under their dish in a way that makes me wonder if they are still alive.

Towards the end of the meal, Kashiwazaki suddenly leans across the table and takes a collar-and-sleeve grip on my jacket. He is explaining to Soames some principles of technique. The discussion, which is way above my head, concerns the difference between the emphasis on the collar arm and that on the sleeve arm. The sleeve arm is for speed but the collar gives control, and you use that to throw big people. Our table is littered with beer bottles and jugs for hot and cold sake that in vain I have vowed to avoid. They constitute a hazard for even the mildest demonstration. So Kashiwazaki stands up and moves me into the middle of the restaurant, which is almost empty, and continues demonstrating various grips and attacks accompanied by a complicated technical running commentary. The staff, which is to say the chef and the owner, seems unflustered by their premises' change of use from restaurant to dojo.

The conversation has turned towards the prospects of Japan's Ryoko Tamura, who is to fight in a couple of days' time. In the bantamweight category, speed is everything, and it is this subject that has prompted an impromptu master class from Kashiwazaki, himself a bantamweight world champion.

There's a lot of talk of Tamura around town, speculation that she is slowing down. This has been prompted by her recent surprise defeat in the Kano Cup at the hands of a high school student—an eerie echo of her own schoolgirl victory over the veteran Karen Briggs of Great Britain. When such an event happens at this stage in a career, the speculation starts. So people have been wondering: Is this little moon on the wane? But Kashiwazaki is absolutely confident that she will win.

AFTER THEIR DRAMATIC contest at the 1992 Barcelona Olympics, when Briggs was defeated by her dislocated shoulder, Tamura reached the final. She had now dismissed her most significant opposition and the gold medal was almost within reach. But in a close contest, she lost to Cecile Nowak of France, who twice caught her leg and took her down for a small score. Tamura ended up with silver.

The gold may have slipped from her grasp, but the little fireball from Fukuoka was on her way to glory. In the following year, again at Barcelona, she became world champion for the first of many times. She was still only seventeen and she would soon exceed Karen Briggs's record, becoming in the process the most famous female judoka the sport has ever known. Four-time Olympic medalist and six-time world champion, Tamura has become the biggest smallest fighter in the world—the biggest because of her achievement and her fame in her home country; and the smallest because she fights among the lightest, at bantamweight, under 105 pounds (48 kilograms).

This tiny bundle of spring-loaded aggression and dazzling technique caused many to dread seeing her name paired with theirs on the draw sheet. Her astonishing record is marred by a mere handful of defeats, and it is her great misfortune that two of them occurred when the stakes were at their highest. But in most tournaments she leaves the tatami strewn with the bodies of her opponents, whom she destroys by a rich repertoire of techniques. A superstar in her native Japan, it is hard to comprehend the popularity she enjoys. A British girl who was at the same training camp with her in Kamaishi, in a remote part of northern Japan, was astonished to find people of all ages along the route halfway up a mountainside at six o'clock in the morning waiting to cheer Tamura as she passed by on her morning run.[1] Often known as "Yawara-chan" (the name derived from a popular *manga* comic strip featuring a small schoolgirl who, when changed into her judo kit, becomes an action heroine), Tamura has video games based upon her and some 350 web sites devoted to her adulation; her contests are followed by a private army of shrieking teenage fans who see in her an exemplar of irresistible girl power, an inspiring model of modern femininity.

BORN IN 1975, TAMURA was eight when she was taken by her parents to watch her brother doing judo at his school. She was immediately entranced. "I saw girls throwing guys," she says. "It was *so* cool." Her mother refused Tamura's pleas to take up the sport. "She wanted me to play the piano, or maybe take tennis lessons—something more girl-like. She said judo was a sport for boys and was too dangerous. I think it was because the first time we went to watch a training session one boy broke his arm. But my father encouraged me. To begin with I won a few bouts and lost a few. But in my first competition I received a gold medal for beating five boys in a row."

Tamura was still at elementary school when she first saw Karen Briggs in action, and the English girl made a deep and inspiring impression upon her. Struck by her power and technique, she sought to emulate Briggs, never guessing that one day she would meet her on the tatami.

Judo's little empress competes with extreme aggression, and is seldom on the defensive. "She is a born fighter," commented one Japanese judo correspondent.[2] "She is a contestant who hates losing. She changes color when it comes to a match." During combat, her expression remains impassive but for a hint of mild irritation. Her attitude appears domineering, workman-like and perfunctory: it says, "OK, let's get this over with quickly." Her judo, however, far from workman-like, is recognized as stylish, inspired, and technically brilliant. Her trademark technique is *seoi-otoshi*, a shoulder throw in which, gripping a sleeve and a collar, she spins and drops under her opponents to whip them through the air and bang them flat. She seems to carry out the entire maneuver slightly faster than the flick of an eyelash.

"Tamura is poetry to watch, bouncy and lightning fast," was the description of Miriam Blasco, the under–123 pounds (56 kilograms) Olympic gold medalist, who has monitored Tamura's progress over the years. "She has an unrivaled range of techniques—she can score *ippon* with eight of them. Her sense of balance, posture, and feet position are near textbook. As well as technical purity she has tactical capability—she's willing to wait for the perfect moment."

Those who have coached Tamura speak in awed tones of her powers of concentration and dedication to training. A typical day begins with a dawn run and some work in the gym. From nine till midday she goes to work on her academic studies or her job. After lunch she practices judo for between three and five hours.

BY THE TIME the Atlanta Olympics came around in 1996, Tamura had established complete dominance of the bantamweight class. She had won the world championship three times; she had beaten everyone every year at the Fukuoka Cup. The numbers in her fan club were swelling; she was their princess. There was almost an unspoken assumption that she would have to do little more than step onto the tatami and bow a few times before collecting the gold. The weight of the heavy flagpole she had to carry in her tiny hands round the stadium at the head of her countrymen in the opening ceremony procession was nothing compared to the burden of Japanese expectations on her shoulders.

Judo can be as cruel as any sport. In the preliminary rounds everything went exactly as predicted; Tamura stormed through the opposition, quickly destroying everyone in her path, but when it came to the final she was confronted by that recurring phenomenon of international competition: the Unknown Korean.

The North and South of the politically divided peninsula of Korea, about 125 miles from Japan, both produce top-class fighters by the truckload. Competition to represent each country is incredibly intense and new faces are constantly making their appearance. The latest little horror they had produced for the delectation of the other bantamweight contenders was a sixteen-year-old called Sun-Hui Kye, an unseeded player from the Democratic People's Republic who, in her isolated world, had never even heard of Tamura. Although from the start the Japanese girl bombarded her with a series of ferocious attacks, Kye dealt with them all. Late in the contest she lured Tamura into an attack; the Korean was ready and waiting with a counter. Tamura was brought down for only a small score—but it was enough. The Japanese was unable to claw back the fight in the time remaining. Kye had won. The crowd was stunned; the Japanese were aghast. Tamura's teammates were so distraught that the team managers hustled them away from the arena to the warm-up room and gave them what can only be described as "counseling" to steady their morale.

The defeat plunged Tamura into despair. She simply was not used to losing—for the last four years she had won every single one of her eighty-four matches; but this had been the most important one of all and had been witnessed by more people than all the others put together. When she got back to Japan she couldn't face putting on her *judogi* and resuming the daily grind of her fierce training routine. She quit.

It was two months before a memory stirred in her mind of a conversation with her old rival, Karen Briggs, some years earlier. "I remember her advising me never to give up as long as I was enjoying it." And the simple truth was that she *was* enjoying it. To the visible relief—if not complete surprise—of her coach, she reappeared one day at the dojo. With her mind gazing at a dauntingly distant horizon four years away, she re-embarked on her exhausting training schedule.

HAVING NOW TWICE FAILED to win Olympic gold, the pressures on Tamura four years later at Sydney were horrendous. This was surely her third and last chance for the one medal she passionately wanted—she had won everything else worth winning. The omens were not good; her preparations had been dogged by injury. In December she broke a finger in the course of winning Fukuoka for the tenth time by beating her Cuban arch-rival Amarilis Savon. She sprained another finger in March and, just a month before the Sydney Games, badly bruised her left calf.

When the big day came at the Darling Harbour stadium, it would have been hard to say who was more tense—Tamura herself, or the large crowd of Japanese supporters, which included her boyfriend, Yoshi Tani, a Tokyo baseball star. In her early fights she demonstrated that she was still in a class of her own, but in her semifinal she came face to face with the North Korean competitor. This time it wasn't Kye, who had moved up to the next weight category, but another unknown quantity called Hyon-Hyang Cha. Tamura could seem to do nothing to overcome her challenger, even when she increased the pressure. In the last half-minute she gave it everything she had but, with no score on the board at the end of five minutes, the result went to a decision: the judges agreed that Tamura had marginally dominated the fight and all three flags went up for her.

The final presented her no problem and the result was rather more decisive. She took a mere thirty-six seconds to bang her Russian opponent to the floor for *ippon* with an *uchimata* and end her Olympic jinx. "I felt like I was dreaming," she said after she had been presented with the gold medal. "It was like meeting one's first love after eight years." She stayed up until 3 A.M. doing television interviews, after which she locked the door of her bedroom in the Olympic village. One account has it that "Alone at last, she burst into tears and then placed her gold medal on her pillow and fell asleep."[3]

TAMURA'S CAREER MIGHT well have ended there but, in 2003, she was only twenty-eight and was determined to go to Osaka and win her sixth world title. The Japanese camp, like Kashiwazaki, seemed confident that she would do it even though she had now been a world champion for ten years, which is a long time to be at the top. Before setting off for Osaka myself, I rang her old adversary Karen Briggs, now living in Hull, to ask her about Tamura's prospects. "I must admit when I've seen her recently she's tending to slow down a little bit, which is only natural because if you don't you would be a robot," she told me. "In Japan they start much earlier so I hope Tamura doesn't run out of steam, because it does take its toll."

In Osaka, Tamura was on top of the world. She had just announced her engagement to Yoshi Tani. She talked ebulliently to the press about her plans to compete in Athens and how she had been driving some formula cars and wanted to take up motor racing after she retired from judo competition. She had acquired this taste for the track through working for Toyota. Her arrangement with the motor manufacturer—it employed her in its PR department—demonstrates how the Japanese system finances top players. From her earliest days Tamura received every possible kind of help. While she was employed by Toyota, Tamura was studying literature at Teikyo University in Tokyo, where she could spend as much time as she wanted in the dojo. Then, in the run-up to the Sydney Games, she moved to Nippon Sport Science University's graduate program to study physical education. Before the Athens Olympics, Toyota helped finance the $88,000 (£50,000) cost of her preparations; these included having five training partners, each with a distinct style, replicating the various kinds of opposition she might encounter.[4]

The women's bantamweight competition was scheduled for the fourth and final day of the tournament. The stadium balconies were adorned with Yawara comic posters, which fans were already beginning to harvest as souvenirs; the whole place was abuzz with excitement. I watched Tamura's supporters file through the doors and take their seats early so they had plenty of time to rehearse their routines. Most of them wore white and were armed with pink banners; the elite—the cheerleaders—wore pink tops and red skirts and waved pink pompoms in a series of routines conducted by a slim, sleek young man in a white jacket. This courtier-like figure was the most loyal and selfless supporter of them all, because he had to stand with his back to the mat and so seldom saw his idol in action. When Tamura's name was announced and she entered the arena, the shouting thickened into a wall of sound. At the call of *hajime,* they went mad.

I found it hard to believe that Tamura could be so small. She is *tiny,* weighing less than 105 pounds (48 kilograms) and standing just four feet nine inches. From halfway back in the stadium seating, you think you are watching a child's doll. She is a bonsai fighter; she is miniaturized. The ends of her little black belt do not hang, but point out to the side like starched ribbons. She has a bossy, bouncy little strut. Her movements are so precise that she's like a little wind-up toy; when she turns around, you half-expect to see a key sticking out of her back. But all that's there is a big white patch with her name and a number. And that's pretty much the last thing on earth that her victims see before their symbolic death. They see it in a high-speed action sequence as she spins around for a throw, then there's a blur as several thousand spectators turn upside down in their seats, and it ends with a sudden jolt, immediately followed by a cut to a wide-angle shot of the stadium roof, which is held for several seconds.

It is the awesome suddenness of Tamura's attacks that so impresses. She moves so fast that often you see no movement, only an adjusted position. It is as though there are some frames missing from this movie. Sometimes she will snatch an opponent into the air as if they were weightless. When an opponent has stumbled under her pressure, she is adept at the trick of bouncing them back onto their feet so she can attack again and knock them over for good. Tamura is not above performing little tactical tricks to convince the judges that she is dominating a contest. I have watched her drag an opponent across the mat and discard the load with a disdainful shove as if she was getting rid of a sack of rubbish—a little bit of theater seemingly designed to make the victim look, in the eyes of the referee, helpless, inept, and—more significantly—passive.

Tamura's working expression of stony determination is unsettling to behold. You feel a great sense of relief when, as her medal and ribbon is placed around her neck, it melts into the delighted soft smile of a woman whose lover has just surprised her with the gift of a beautiful necklace.

BEFORE THE CONTESTS had started, I was in the press room to collect the draw sheets detailing the pairings and the order of contests. There I found Bob Willingham, the IJF's official photographer, preparing his gear. We discussed Tamura's prospects for the day and he told me something about the challenge of photographing her in action.

Every photographer wants to capture the action in mid-throw. Heavyweights, who move slowly, are quite easy; the lighter weights are much more difficult. Tamura was a nightmare. Even with his Nikon on motor drive, the Japanese girl's incredible speed presented a tough test. The dawn of the digital age, which coincided with the early part of Tamura's career, presented Willingham with special problems. He had ordered one of the first batch of digital Nikons that came into the United Kingdom, but they were slower than film cameras, whose motors managed eight frames a second. "They were doing five frames a second, which is just not enough for someone like Tamura—it leaves a big gap in the action and you can miss the very best bit of the throw."

Even now that the digitals have caught up, he says he still finds her difficult. "The problem is not only that she's just so fast, but there's no warning at all. As soon as you even *sense* a twitch you have to click the button and keep your finger down on the motor."

Willingham's task was simple but difficult. It was akin to watching a lizard for five minutes and trying to catch it with its eyes shut—catching the lizard blink.

TAMURA MARRIED IN 2003. The wedding, which took place in Paris and cost a reputed $3 million, was shown on national television. A lot of people thought that would be the end of her competitive career, but when the Athens Olympics came round in 2004, she appeared again. She took the gold. In the following year she announced that she was pregnant, which kept her out of the Cairo world championships, and on the first day of 2006 she gave birth to a baby boy. She said that she had absolutely no intention of retiring from judo. "I won an Olympic gold under the name Tamura and also under Tani and I would like to win another as a mother."

There is evidence to suggest that women are physically stronger after they have given birth. However, will Tamura really want to forfeit a prosperous career of commercial sponsorship, personal appearances, and public adulation, along with the pleasures of a full motherhood, for hours of merciless training every day at the dojo, at the same time risking the inevitable diminution of her reputation that would follow her defeat at the hands of some new and hungry sixteen-year-old? It seems she did. In the 2007 world championship in Rio de Janeiro, Tamura took the gold, and at the 2008 Beijing Olympics, she defeated Lyudmila Bogdanova of Russia to win the bronze.

The names Tamura and Tani will long be remembered. Her country once lagged behind the West in women's competition and, although Tamura-Tani was by no means the only Japanese to change that, the rule of the little empress has done more than anything else to transform the status of women's judo in Japan and the rest of the world.

20

DAVID THE GOLIATH AND INOUE THE PRINCE

When they climb up the steps into the belly of a jumbo jet, most sound-minded people know that if this thing gets into the sky it will only be by a combination of massive collective faith and magic. Regardless of how many times someone shows you diagrams of the little arrows going under and over the curved profile of a wing, you have only to look at the great steel beast, stitched with rivets, its thin wings sagging under engines the size of mobile homes, to know that it can never fly. Even if, instead of several hundred tons of passengers and their luggage, its cargo consisted entirely of extra-lightweight Ping-Pong balls, it would not stand a prayer of becoming airborne.

You reach the same sort of conclusion when you encounter close up some of judo's heavyweights.

Consider Shinichi Shinohara of Japan. He is a giant of a man. He has a noble countenance, but before you can see it, you must wait for any low clouds to clear, for he is truly tall. One wonders in which forest in Japan they felled the trees to build him, or indeed how many had to be slaughtered. His jawbone alone would require a team of four men to carry it to the nearest museum of anthropology.

Can such a man be made to fly? Or, for that matter, can Chechenborn Tartaroglu the Turk, with a girth of several kilometers? Or Aythami Ruano, the truly awesome 485 pound (220 kilogram) Spaniard, whose dimensions approximate those of an upended London double-decker bus?

One man could make them all fly: the Frenchman, David Douillet. In France judo is loved and adored: its fans gratified, its players well rewarded, its heroes worshipped. With well over half a million active players, judo is the most popular participation sport in the country after soccer and skiing. French judo has been a triumph of organization, promotion, and state intervention on a scale that might have been the envy of even the former Eastern Bloc. The outcome of this passion for the sport has been the creation of an environment in which potential champions can be discovered and nurtured. The greatest of them has been their heavyweight, David Douillet, whose succession of world victories across the divide of the centuries turned him from successful judoka into a sporting superstar, recognized in his country wherever he goes. Moreover, by winning four world championships and two Olympic gold medals he exceeded Yamashita's record and has, by this measure at least, become the most successful judoka of all time.

Born in 1969, Douillet started judo at the age of eleven at a club in his native Brittany. He came to martial arts through the study of Dr. Justice, a comic-book character whose exploits transfixed him as a young boy. More precise inspiration came when, aged six, he saw Jean-Luc Rouge become France's first world champion in 1975 and later when, awestruck, he watched the opening ceremony of the Moscow Olympic Games. His teachers tried to discourage the sport that was diverting so much of his attention from academic study, but the boy and his parents thought his love of judo was more important. It was at this point the French grassroots system came into its own.

A key element in this system is the number of specialist sports schools scattered throughout the country that permit pupils to train twice a day. At the age of fifteen Douillet was accepted by the school at Rennes, and while there was spotted by Jean-Luc Rouge, now a leading figure in the French Judo Federation. Rouge immediately arranged a place for him at INSEP, the training center for France's sporting elite.

Inevitably, Douillet's fellow trainees were intensively competitive and sometimes ruthless in asserting their superiority. He remembers one vicious youth who used to humiliate him every day. "It was purgatory," he said. "If I met him on the mat today, I would behead him." But he persevered. He stopped growing when he reached six feet five inches, but his skill and fitness improved all the time and his progress was inexorable. In 1991, aged twenty-two, he became champion of France and in the following year took bronze in the under–209 pound (95 kilogram) category at the Barcelona Olympics. His first world title came in 1993 at Hamilton in Canada, where he beat the powerful Olympic champion David Khakhaleichvili from Georgia. By 1995, when at the Mukuhari world championships he became the first Westerner to hold both the world heavyweight and openweight crowns, he was beginning seriously to rival Yamashita's record. In 1996 he equaled it by defeating his Japanese opponent to take gold in the over–209 pound category at the Atlanta Games.

The hosting of the 1997 world championships was awarded to France, a well-deserved reward for the nation's contribution to the sport. The stadium at Bercy in the west of Paris was to provide a brilliant showcase for world judo as the contents of the French Judo Federation's fat coffers were poured into putting on a fantastic show.

The climax of the occasion should have been the openweight category, in which Douillet was to encounter the reigning world champion, Shinohara. Sadly, after four days of beautiful judo, stylishly presented, the contest was a slow and pitiful anticlimax. In combat the very act of attack makes the attacker vulnerable and courts disaster. When the stakes are high, as they were here, there is a strong temptation to be defensive. Both men succumbed to that temptation and the fight went nowhere; it consisted of little more than a series of passivity penalties, a game that Shinohara lost by dint of having been awarded the first one. When he got a third, he received _hansoku-make_—disqualification. Many believed that the decision had been unduly influenced by the pressure of the French home crowd and that the fight ought to have gone to the Japanese. That controversy was a mere shadow of what was to follow.

Three years later, when Douillet arrived at the Sydney Olympics in 2000, he was one of France's great hopes for a medal, but not one of the certainties. Having been away from competition for long periods because of various judo injuries and a motorbike accident, this was only his third competition since the 1997 world championships. But he reached the final of the over–220 pounds (100 kilograms) category on September 23 to defend his Olympic title, demolishing the finest the world could throw at him. His opponent in the final was once again Shinichi Shinohara. For both men, this was to be the last fight of their career. The result was to cause one of the most controversial and acrimonious rows over a referee's decision ever to take place in judo's history.

This final encounter between the two greatest heavyweights of their time was far from being a great contest. As in their previous meeting, any excitement derived from the tension of the occasion rather than the cautious, tactical judo to which they resorted. One minute and forty seconds into the contest, Douillet's huge frame came hurtling in for a leg throw against the Japanese giant. Shinohara's left leg was lifted high into the air, at which point Douillet toppled forward and they both went over, the Japanese landing on his side and the Frenchman on his back. Shinohara got up and raised his hands in triumph. He had not only escaped from the throw but had countered it, bringing down Douillet.

To the astonishment of many, the New Zealand referee, Craig Monaghan, thought otherwise and awarded *yuko* to Douillet. Of the two corner judges, one signaled *ippon* for Shinohara and the other abstained. The referee stuck by his decision and restarted the fight. In the remaining time Douillet picked up two penalties, one for passivity, but he also scored a second *yuko* with a counterattack. Ahead on points when the time was up, he was accordingly awarded the contest. Without the first, contentious score he would have lost.

When the contest ended, the retiring French champion was declared the victor. His supporters roared with jubilation and the Japanese camp was stunned.

For anyone in the crowd who might have been in some doubt about what happened, there was to be no big-screen replay; Jim Kojima, referee director of the IJF, prevented it. He had learned his bitter lesson three years earlier at the Paris world championships when repeated replays on the big screens had revealed to an increasingly angry crowd a mistaken decision against the Korean lightweight.

The scene by the officials' table in Sydney became bedlam. Shinohara's matside coach, a man ending his eight-year rule as chief coach, was none other than Yasuhiro Yamashita, Japan's greatest champion. He had got hold of a video camera and was trying to replay the incident to any senior IJF official he could buttonhole. A phalanx of security guards had to be deployed to prevent this formidable figure from getting through to them.

Once the fighters and judges had left the contest area, the opportunity for protest was over. Insisting that the referee had "clearly made a misjudgement," Yamashita said that the Japanese Judo Federation would appeal to the IJF. "We do not expect the judgment will change, but we want the IJF to recognize just who was thrown." The forlorn figure of Shinohara stood trying to control his emotions as "the rowdy French fans in a full house of 6,500 spectators sang La Marseillaise and filled the auditorium with flying French flags where the Hinomaru once flew."[1] Shinohara was in tears throughout the press conference. Douillet, meanwhile, was taking calls on his mobile phone from the French president, Jacques Chirac, and the prime minister, Lionel Jospin.

According to the *Asahi Shimbun,* "IJF spokesman Michel Brousse said the rules of judo favored the attacking player, and in the move in question, the Frenchman had clearly attacked. The question is, Did Shinohara use the technique of his opponent to counterattack, or did he block or avoid the move? The referee thought he didn't block the first attack, so if there is no defense the score goes to the attacker."

The argument exercised people for months—indeed years—afterwards. The action of a technique can look so different from different vantage points. Each time you look at these tapes you can come to a different conclusion—and that is after you have had plenty of time to study and consider the evidence. Poor Monaghan and his two judges had only seconds.

A few months after the events in Sydney, the International Judo Federation's referees' commission gathered for a special meeting during the world junior championships at Nabeul in Tunisia. After repeated scrutiny of the video footage and long discussion, they came to their conclusion. They decided that Douillet had lost control in executing the technique and that Shinohara had lost his balance in countering the throw; their verdict was that neither contestant should have been awarded any score.

KOSEI INOUE LEANED ON the crowd barrier at the edge of the contest area and began to sob violently. Minutes earlier, at the National Indoor Arena in Birmingham, England, he had become champion of the world. The year was 1999 and the awesome twenty-one-year-old was the latest wonder to come from Japan. He had flattened all his opponents in the course of the day's under–100 kilogram (200 pound) category and now, having just stepped off the mat after winning the final, he was over-come with emotion. Next to this hunched and sobbing figure stood Yasuhiro Yamashita, who himself had won the title three times and was now chief Japanese coach; he knew all about the intensity of emotion that can follow a contest, so he stared into the middle distance waiting for this storm of grief, relief, and elation to pass. He soothed Inoue, patting him consolingly on the back. For most people this would have felt like being whacked with a shovel; the pounding blows from that powerful paw would have felled a mortal. But Inoue was, in any case, no longer a mere mortal.

When the moment came for him to go back into the arena and climb onto the rostrum, he held in front of him for all to see a framed photograph of his father and his beloved mother, who had died from a stroke just four months earlier. Here was the truth of his tears. He was dedicating his victory to his lost parent.

Inoue, born in 1978, is a psychology student from Tokai. Quiet, serious, and obsessive in the pursuit of perfection, he follows, like Yamashita and many others, the samurai custom of cleaning his room until it is spotless before any big contest. As a child he studied judo with an unnerving intensity. One of his coaches, Hidetoshi Nakanishi, himself a world champion, remembers Inoue at the age of eleven when he would practice every day until his teachers forced him to stop. Nakanishi once remarked, "I knew he was someone to be looking forward to."

In a private and invisible gesture, Inoue would on occasion sew his mother's name in black cotton on his black belt. "It is all because of her that I am here," Inoue would say, "I wanted to make her the world's number-one mother this way."

Two years after Birmingham I saw him win the world title at Munich. These two world championship golds and his successive victories in the All Japan confirmed him as the new prince. At the Osaka world championships he was again in devastating form, destroying everything in his path. I watched him execute a beautifully graceful strangle when, having got a grip high on the other man's lapel, he drew the cloth down and out to his side like a bullfighter performing a low pass with his cape. As it reached hip height, he whipped the collar under the chin of his now kneeling opponent and throttled him into submission. A member of the Japanese contingent later told me that it takes hours for most people to learn to perform this strangle effectively, but when they had taught Inoue the technique, he had mastered it in minutes.

ATHENS, AUGUST 17, 2004. After nearly ten years of sweat and tears, of early-morning runs in the park, of weight training and endless stretching, of going on the mat two or three times a week, this devotion to my sport has finally paid off. I have secured my place in the Olympic Games. It is Seat 7, Row 15, Section 118, in the Anio Liossia Stadium on the northwestern outskirts of the cradle of democracy. This is day five, the day of the men's under–198 pound (90 kilogram) competition.

The Greeks, who had come up with the idea in the first place, finally managed to bring the show back home when they secured the 2004 Olympic Games for Athens. The world's finest judoka made their way to the ancient city, bringing a sport rooted in the ancient East to the homeland of a sporting ideal founded in the ancient West. Athens was to be the latest battlefield in judo's own unending world war, which had begun with Japan's total domination of every territory on the globe, from the lightest weight category to the heaviest. Then Geesink of Holland seized the largest and most precious piece of this territory: the openweight division. The giant and his successor, Wilhelm Ruska, held it for some years while other states fought Japan for other territories, seizing them one by one. Increasingly threatened by the encroachments of the Eastern powers of the USSR, China, and the Korean peninsula, as well as France, Germany, Britain, and Cuba in the West, the Japanese would rally and recapture some of their lost lands as they did during Emperor Yamashita's reign as contestant and coach.

Now all the nations had come to face each other in Athens in a tournament which would be a stark reminder of the changing nature of the fortunes of war—a reminder that empires fall as well as rise, and so indeed do princes.

I had not been able to get to Athens in time for the lightweight competition on the first day and so missed the surprise defeat in the second round of Britain's great light hope, Craig Fallon, a brilliant young British bantamweight whom I had interviewed during his preparations at the National Sports Centre at Bisham Abbey in Buckinghamshire.

I am pleased that I know quite a few people here who are taking part in the Games or who have competed in previous Olympics. And there are those who are connected with the event in some other way—like Bob Willingham, the official IJF photographer, and his brother-in-law Simon Hicks, who runs the Fighting Films team that is recording the judo event. Simon is also a personal coach to Winston Gordon, whom I know from the Budokwai where he trains regularly. After Craig Fallon's defeat, it is on Gordon's shoulders that U.K. hopes for a men's medal now rest; to support him, a contingent of us from the Budokwai are in attendance.

While most people buy their tickets months in advance and secure a phalanx of seats to form a choral block that might be heard by the contestants they have come to support, Budokwai people are incapable of such organization. We all book individually or in small groups, mostly at the very last minute, and are consequently scattered all over the stadium. However, in spite of years of planning by the Olympic organizers, color-coded tickets, and frequent patrols by the armbanded officials, in an entirely unplanned action several of us have made our way to some vacant seats in the front row of the arena right opposite the mat where Gordon's next contest will take place.

We are full of anticipation. Gordon has done really well in the past year, taking a number of major tournament medals, and is looking very dangerous. In his first contest he threw and strangled the Australian contender within twenty seconds. He then strangled the man from the Dominican Republic. His third fight was to be against the formidable Brazilian Carlos Honorato, an Olympic gold medalist.

Honorato is a dangerous proposition. Immensely strong ("like a bull," Gordon later told me), it was this Brazilian who hurled the Japanese hope, Hidehiko Yoshida, out of the Sydney Olympic final. The throw was so hard that when Yoshida put his arm out to save himself, he dislocated his elbow. And Yoshida was no mean player. He was the Barcelona gold medalist who went on, after his retirement, to defeat Royce Gracie in that all-in Pride fight in Tokyo in 2002. Remarkably, Gordon not only holds his own against Honorato, but beats him by a couple of *kokas*.

As the day progresses, Mark Earle, one of the Great Britain squad's coaches, joins us. He has been scrutinizing the opposition and is on his phone to Gordon, who is in the practice area with Udo Quellmalz, performance director of the British team. I hear Earle urgently warning Gordon about the dangers that Zurab Zviadauri from Georgia will present. "He does left *uchimata*—high right hand to you," he says, before exhorting: "Punish him, and punish him again."

Winnie didn't manage to get a medal but when I watched him fighting hell-for-leather out there, I couldn't help thinking of the occasions—perhaps he needed a breather, or some light entertainment—when he would call me out for a *randori* and throw me all around the dojo with stylish grace, causing me a great deal of mental alarm but leaving me physically unscathed. This small connection with our local hero out there in the greatest arena in the world makes me feel preposterously proud.

I MADE A LATE START on Thursday, the day of the under–220 pound (100 kilogram) category in which Kosei Inoue was fighting. The Athens sun was warming and it was uncomfortably hot standing in the queue for the security check. By the time I entered the stadium, the three referees had removed their shoes and were climbing the steps onto the mat area; I reached my seat just as *hajime* was called.

The expectations resting upon the Prince that day were enormous. As the reigning Olympic champion and three-time world champion, he was supreme in the world. And as Japan's greatest hope and pride, he had inevitably been chosen to captain their entire Olympic contingent. When he started to fight, it was almost as though the weight of all this responsibility and expectation turned from the abstract and bore down upon him physically. He made his way through his first two fights, but for the most part they were colorless performances. The spectators were expecting to see explosions but there were almost none.

When he met Dutchman Elco van der Geest, Inoue seemed in a torpor, underpowered and lacking in spirit as if someone had put the wrong fuel in his tank. The spectators felt as though they were watching a play where the actors had completely forgotten their lines: Inoue had definitely lost the plot and van der Geest, who was meant to lose, seemed not to have read the script he'd been given. He caught Inoue with a last-minute shoulder throw to relegate the three-time world champion and Sydney gold medallist to the repêchage, where he was picked up and thrown onto the floor and out of the contest by the Azerbaijani Movlud Miraliyev. Inoue was later to say of those two defeats, "I have never tasted such humiliation and frustration before."

That may have been the case, but he still managed to produce at least one great moment in the course of that terrible day. In his third round fight against the Australian, there was a long moment when both had secured their grip and were almost motionless, but for a slight tuning of the tension and angle of their arms as the signals skeetered up and down the bio wires. Inoue knew what he was going to do, his opponent knew what Inoue was going to do. Half the spectators knew what Inoue was going to do. Because of this he was surely not going to be able to do it. The static deadlock continued. Then the Japanese's hands seemed to bounce very gently before he suddenly spun round, sinking and then rising into a huge exploding *uchimata*. *Ta-ka-ta. Whooooosh! BANG! Ippon*. And it was all over. The best part of over 220 Australian pounds lay flattened at his feet.

Inoue had made this huge throw out of *nothing*. That slight bounce from his arms provoked all the reaction that he needed.

Such an act of destruction is the judoka's act of creation. Engineers like to talk of an "elegant solution" when describing a design that achieves its function with economy and efficiency. Inoue has drafted many elegant solutions, and his many successes represent a victory for purist classical judo. To watch him lay low those who come to bow before him is to be reminded that this martial sport can indeed be called an art. Judoka across the world believe that he—along with so many Japanese—is always worth watching for the utter beauty of his judo.

And not just because it is beautiful but because, for the most part, it works, as events in Athens were to demonstrate. By the end of the Games Cuba had won six medals, five of them gained by the women for Señor Ronaldo Valdivie to place on his hotel-room shrine. Without Douillet, France's eminence crumbled; the largest judo nation in the world came back with just one medal—a result that would provoke a major domestic row within the French judo authority.

Only one country won more than one gold medal: the Japanese squad left Athens with eight, as well as two silvers—and all this without a contribution from Inoue, their greatest champion. Five of their trove of medals were taken by women (Tamura-Tani won her second Olympic gold), convincing testimony that Japanese women, after a late start, had not only caught up with their rivals in Cuba and the rest of the world, but had overtaken them and were now supreme.

The Japanese had never done so well in any of the forty years since those first Tokyo Olympics when Anton Geesink had thrown their greatest hope on the floor. For them the natural order of things was restored. They had absorbed the lessons of their enemies, recaptured vast swathes of lost territory, and demonstrated their superiority. They achieved all this by sticking to the tenets of the true faith, Kano's pure Kodokan judo.

21

WHITE-COLLAR WORKER

So, how are we doing so far? Are you managing to keep up? Handling the names OK?

Take a breather. You probably want some water. Nowadays everyone wants water all the time. It was not always so:

> The famous masters of old Japan required intense and long hours of judo training. It was thought that if the trainees did not perspire blood and water, the training was inadequate. Kishimoto trained himself daily for six consecutive hours beginning at five A.M. Kotani recalls that during his student days there was never a chance to rest. The drinking of water was forbidden. After one and a half hours of steady exertion, perspiration would cease to flow, and at around two hours, salt would form on the lips and tongue.[1]

AT THE BUDOKWAI I PRACTICED under the eyes of several different senseis, including the celebrated Kisaburo Watanabe, who has sat there with his thumbs tucked into his black belt watching over the proceedings ever since they hung his portrait on the wall of the main dojo. Alongside him is the club's founder, Gunji Koizumi, and little Yukio Tani who after his feats in the music halls became the club's first instructor. I sometimes feel the three men watching, even though they are not present, and I wonder what on earth they think.

I saw Watanabe in person once when he visited the Budokwai in the late 1990s. In spite of an artificial hip, he demonstrated a series of changing grips as he waltzed solo around the mat in a beautiful flowing movement before showing us some techniques, throwing his _uke_ so hard and with such tidy precision that he hit the floor each time with the noise of a pistol shot. Ben Andersen, who was that _uke_, teaches at the club himself now. He remembers hearing about when the great man first came to live in Britain and instruct at the Budokwai in the 1960s. At first Watanabe could speak no English, but he was known to be studying the language hard. Everyone was curious to know what jewel of judo knowledge he would choose for his first public utterance in his newly acquired tongue. What was it that he would most want to impress upon his students' minds? At last the day came when he felt he was ready. The sublime technician, whose mastery had overcome all opposition by the sheer perfection of his movement, finally spoke his first words of English. "First," he told them, "you must _smash_ your opponent!"

AFTER SOME FIVE YEARS I COULD find no diminution in the symptoms of my obsessive condition. But my job on the newspaper gave me some diversion. From my vantage point in the midst of a large information-gathering machine, in frequent touch with foreign correspondents, I had good seats for the greatest show on earth. The plot at this stage concerned the aftermath of the mighty convulsions that Mikhail Gorbachev had unleashed in the Soviet Union. I saw the ice of the Cold War political landscape shift and crack. I tried to understand why Yugoslavia had exploded and why South Africa hadn't. But, throughout, the question that haunted me was not some great issue such as, Would Russia ever be a fully functioning free democracy? but rather, Would I ever be able to throw anyone with _tai otoshi_? The answer to both these questions was the same: "Possibly, but not in the foreseeable future."

At the beginning I was relieved to discover that the practice of judo did not entail any study of Eastern philosophy. It was just another sport, although I became aware from my more cerebral brethren at the club that Zen and Confucianism did inform the Japanese approach to judo. I could never really get on with the sort of Zen Buddhist budo-babble that says things like, "When you seek it, you cannot find it. When you no longer seek it, it is always with you." I can see that may be true of the car keys, but how does it help me to do *ouchi-gari*? And there was "Your opponent is not as weak as you think. Your opponent is not as strong as you think." Which means so much. Which means nothing at all.

Perhaps it is *because* I was reluctant to absorb these sorts of ideas that I could never make any really significant progress. The "mental tranquility" that was meant to sharpen my concentration somehow eluded me, though I was deriving a huge amount of pleasure from *randori*. I was presumably getting high on endorphins as well as judo. Even if a training session went badly, I always came away from the dojo feeling as though I had just consumed three-quarters of a bottle of extremely good champagne.

Apart from the judo itself, I enjoyed the crazy mixture of people from more than two dozen countries with a variety of jobs and backgrounds. Although some of them could hardly speak English, everyone could speak judo—which was all that mattered. Meanwhile I was discovering that, as with any other language, the better one spoke it, the more interesting were the conversations one could have. And all the time, I measured my progress in this language against that of my peers, who came and went as fitness, injury, and family and work commitments decreed.

I also had the splendid privilege of training alongside judo players who were among the best in the country, the best in the world. Here I could see the champions in action up close—closer than any of the spectators at a tournament. I could hear what they could never hear: the soft hoarse whisper of tatami brushed by skillful feet. Not only that, I was able to practice with the great contestants myself and find out exactly what it was like to be on the receiving end of their craft. I have already explained the

good
line!

course such encounters would inevitably follow, but my "auto-
graph book" was forever filling with the signatures of the great.

Regardless of the odds I faced in *randori*, I always believed I
might just prevail. This self-delusion has been a crucial element
in sustaining me through the whole enterprise as I sought to defy
gravity in all its forms—age, fitness, health, and the pull of the
earth that would so often drop me on the floor. Self-delusion has
stood by me like a loyal friend. Perhaps not *entirely* loyal. I noticed
that whenever I went to one of those dreaded gradings it would
cut and run. Then I would be left alone with an awareness of the
grim reality of my inadequacy. To be honest, our friendship has
been wearing a little thin with the passage of time.

Seven times thrown, eight times rise. If only it was just the
seven. Given the level of judo at the club, I was more thrown
than throwing. It didn't matter to me. I'd occasionally throw
someone; the smallest success would keep me going for days. I
found it quite tiring being chucked on the floor. To be thrown
is like doing a bungee jump with a rope that is a little too long.
There are many different ways of landing. Sometimes the mat
comes rushing up to greet you and slap you on the shoulder like
an old friend; sometimes, when things go wrong, it'll just punch
you in the face.

I trained quite hard outside the dojo to get fit for what I had
to face inside it, but I still found *randori* fantastically grueling.
At times my whole system was on the verge of a work strike. The
lungs would put down their tools, the legs and arms were ready
to come out in support, and, up on the management floor, pride
and will couldn't do a thing about it. Sometimes, in my oxygen-
deprived state, I became light-headed, overcome with a cocktail of
emotions—three parts frustration at my technical shortcomings,
two parts anger that I did not try this thing when I was younger,
and a large dash of self-pity for my physical decline.

One Sunday morning I was training at the Judokan in Ham-
mersmith when a familiar figure caught my attention at the other
end of the mat. He was in a terrible state; with his sweat-soaked *gi*,

he looked as though he had just been dragged half-drowning from the sea. His face was frighteningly gaunt and he appeared to be in the final stages of exhaustion. As I saw the look of desperation in his eyes, I wondered what was driving the poor fellow. I also began to question the wisdom of having a mirror in a dojo.

Even in the depths of fatigue, my attendance at training sessions was never an act of will. I found that this ridiculous pastime had got its talons into me and was dragging me along regardless of my need to rest. I was puzzled by friends who would ask, "Are you still doing the old . . . ?" and applaud me for my persistence. Does one admire the alcoholic for his unflagging attendance at the bar? Does one congratulate the crack addict on his habit—"Well done, it's just amazing the way you've stuck with it"?

But as time went by, my once dark-brown belt was growing paler and more frayed. I wanted another color, the only color that mattered to me. I wanted to get my dan grade and be a black belt. Apart from the obvious reason that I rated it as some sort of an achievement, I wanted it because there was something comically incongruous in the notion of my getting it that appealed to me. It would be a good joke to play on judo, which had played so many jokes on me. There was something else. Although the enterprise was essentially an act of supreme selfishness, I felt heavily indebted to a number of people who had put an awful lot of personal effort into teaching and encouraging me. When one of them might ask with studied casualness, "Are you going along to the grading this Sunday?" I sensed their expectations.

HAVING CONSIDERED the notion that combat is a metaphor for life, I began to wonder about the nature of that combat. Surely life, though not without its punches, is more of a wrestling match than a punchup. Certainly, life can deliver some punishing blows—bereavement, acute illness, accident, sudden financial collapse—but most of life is a slow struggle with business rivals, the mortgage, school fees, employers, or health. Our problems get their grip on us as we try to get a grip on them; they try to drag us down while we fight to stay on our feet. Progress in this contest is a slow and hard-fought struggle for advantage interspersed with a few sudden surprises, shifts of position, setbacks, and gains. Much as we'd like to deliver a knockout blow, it is more likely that we'll gradually force them into submission—and if we don't they will do the same to us. So judo, which is a style of grappling, rather than pugilism, is perhaps a better metaphor for life.

If the saying, "As in judo, so in life" holds good, was Dr. Kano right to claim that judo is a training for life and should be widely taught in schools? To make that happen would be an uphill battle. In this new age of "issues," which include an abhorrence of competitiveness and an obsession with health and safety, judo stands a slim chance in the United Kingdom. But it could be argued that, since the grotesquely misguided decision to sell off school playing fields was made, the building of a dojo would be a wise use of any school's remaining real estate. It forms an all-weather 24-hour "field" which, square meter for square meter, delivers incredible value. If some of the nation's increasingly obese, distressed, and dysfunctional children could be coaxed through a dojo door, they would lose more weight more quickly; would get fitter; would acquire more confidence, manners, and self-esteem; would learn more about concentration, about persistence, about winning and losing—and therefore life—than in any other endeavor that they could pursue in so small a space.

IN FRANCE, if you tell someone that you do judo, they don't raise an eyebrow. If you tell someone in the United Kingdom, they raise both. Among friends, I noticed a nervy bewilderment at my chosen entertainment—they looked at me as though I had run off to join the Moonies.

If it wasn't bewilderment, it was mockery. I have had to put up with a lot of that narrowing of the eyes and expulsion of the breath from the back of the throat that passes for Oriental impersonation. Two *Telegraph* editorial writers, both destined to become in their own ways figures of some significance in British politics, would sometimes weary of telling our government where they were going wrong. For diversion they would circle around me, singing in its entirety, complete with gong sounds, the title song of *Hong Kong Phooey* in flat, nasal *we-are-Siamee-eese* voices. "*Hong Kong Phooey, faster than the human eye; Hong Kong Phooey, number-one super guy.*" I tried to feign laughter, but I was amused to note the point at which my sense of humor failed.

Often people were curious to know if I had ever had to use judo in self-defense. I would explain, luckily no, but the whole point was that it had been specifically devised *not* to hurt people. It was all very well for Brian Jacks to say to a journalist, "Say I was out in the street and you attacked me. All I'd have to do is throw you on the concrete and most likely you'd die."[2] I prefer to think of Kashiwazaki, who when asked what *he* would do if he was threatened by an assailant, said, "I'd look for a piece of wood."

THROUGHOUT MY ENDEAVORS, the question of "the spirit of judo" was ever present.

It is possible for a lesser player to have some success against a much better player. Although good for the morale, such a triumph can be thoroughly misleading. An experienced judoka has to make huge allowances for an ordinary club player if he is to keep the practice interesting for both parties. How much to give is a fine judgment. Because opponents are so close, there is very little time or space to allow the superior player to recover his advantage.

It applies at all levels when there is a disparity. As a brown belt I was once doing groundwork with a blue belt who was smaller and less experienced than me. I had never trained with him before and I gave him several advantages before I realized that he was better and stronger than I had calculated. Too late: he was on my back and very close to strangling me. Mortified at the prospect of defeat at the hands of a lower grade, I struggled furiously to escape, but in vain.

In these circumstances a player must accept the situation, tap in submission, and then put things right in the ensuing struggle— *that* is the spirit of judo. That's what any mature, sportsmanlike, or decent judoka would do. At that moment I was none of those things. Instead, realizing I needed "another arm," I surreptitiously slipped his sleeve into my mouth and clamped it firmly between my teeth—in the hope that he wouldn't realize what was happening. This would free my arm to get the problem sorted.

Unfortunately, as I sank my teeth into the cotton fabric there was a terrible scream just behind my right ear. I had not reckoned on the flesh of his forearm being so close to the sleeve. The blue belt slid off my back onto the floor, where he lay for some moments looking at me reproachfully while clutching his partially eaten limb. On hearing the commotion, the instructor wandered over to investigate and raised a quizzical eyebrow. But explanation was too complicated; he wouldn't have been interested. I apologized to my opponent profusely, but nothing could spare me from looking at best like a bad sportsman or, at worst, like a psychopath.

I was victim as well as perpetrator. At the Budokwai I once found myself facing a large Algerian dan grade whom I'd never seen before. He was thirty or forty pounds heavier than me and it wasn't long before he was on my back fishing for my elbow. I did what I could to defend myself against the inevitable armlock, but it never came. Instead I suddenly felt him working on my right hand and, even though attacking individual fingers is forbidden, he bent the diminutive digit in on itself. It was agony and I quickly tapped. As we disentangled ourselves and I rubbed the sore joint, he explained, "Deez one very good. Zer referee, he no can see deez ting!" Again, this is not what Dr. Kano had in mind when he talked of "the spirit of judo."

One evening I was training with one of the Budokwai's heavier members and an exemplar of that spirit. As he was ten years younger and eighty pounds heavier I always had to work hard with him, whereas he would always go very light. At one stage I turned in for a throw and two hundred and eighty pounds went sailing over my shoulder to land with a pleasing smack on his back in front of me. An experienced club member standing on the edge of the mat asked in astonishment, "Did he really throw you?" My opponent just smiled. But we both knew what had really happened. I had made a reasonable attempt at a throw and, in "the spirit of judo" and "mutual benefit," he had decided to indulge me and go with it. He could easily have blocked the throw and flattened me with a counter, but instead he "jumped." And he did it so subtly that he momentarily fooled even an experienced observer with this skillful piece of physical acting.

The incident made me understand that the real problem with the desperate antics of professional wrestlers is not that they don't fight, but that they can't act. It also made me realize how complete is this language of combat: it is even possible to tell a lie.

THE TIME IS FAST APPROACHING when we have to abandon the friendly familiarity of the club and set off to one of the great tournaments in order to see its rituals and its workings. This almost certainly means that we'll have to go abroad for a few days, but it will give us the chance to enjoy the sport at its apex.

After I had been doing judo for a couple of years, I started to cover some of the major events for the *Daily Telegraph*. Apart from the pleasure of seeing familiar faces from the club in distant locations, there was also the surprise of seeing someone come into the arena whom I would recognize because I had trained with him or her at the Budokwai. The experience of watching the best competitive judo in the world was elating—and also depressing. When it was all over I would hurry back to the dojo thinking that, by some sort of osmosis, my judo would have improved. Of course it hadn't and I would become disconsolate. There was no connection between what I had seen and what I could do. They were two entirely different sports, both of which were called judo.

Inevitably, the trip to Osaka for the 2003 world championships was an important moment, because it would give me my chance to do judo in the land of its birth. I'd been told about the dojo in the grounds of the castle where anyone could train, but I got there to find that it had been closed to the public and divided into small curtained sections to serve as a practice area where the tournament competitors could train in some secrecy. I am probably the only judoka who has taken his *gi* all the way to Japan and never gone on the mat—like a pilgrim who reached Rome but never made it to St. Peter's.

On these trips I enjoyed being an occasional member of that tiny contingent of journalists who followed the circuit, almost all of whom were active judoka. Often we'd meet up with champions and coaches of the present and past, for a drink or a meal and a tireless exchange of memories, comment, and gossip.

I became aware of one newcomer to the group who, unlike most of the others, had clearly never been a serious competitor. I found something irritating about his presence—the way he was clearly pleased to be in this exalted company. I noticed how members of the group would greet some naïve question from him with an amused and world-weary patience, but seemed prepared to tolerate him nonetheless. What irritated me most of all about this intruder was that he was me.

In the little writing I have done on judo, I have always taken immense care over what I have written. I would never criticize any competitor—partly because I had too little knowledge or authority and too much respect for anyone who goes out into the arena. But also because, while a theater critic can savage his victims from the safety of a box seat, those who write about this sport are rather more at hazard. They may one day find themselves on the same mat as one of their offended subjects, who might come up to them when it's time for *randori* and utter those worrying words, "Would you like the next practice?"

Anyway, we'd better get going. We need to find our hotel, which we hope is as near the stadium as the map suggests so we can get there by the time the first contests start at 9 A.M. I don't want to miss a thing.

THE TOURNAMENT

A Fistful of Collars

One of the crucial differences between boxing and judo in much of the world is that, while boxing offers people a chance to fight their way out of poverty, judo offers people a chance to fight their way into it. Throughout their competition lives, judo players look enviously at their friends in other sports and occupations. All of them are much better off, because they are paid in dollars, while the judoka is paid only in glory. That glory is earned through success in combat in the great tournaments.

IN STRONG JUDO COUNTRIES such as Japan or France the selection process is a desperate business. There are so many high-caliber players in each category battling for their place that some of the most memorable contests have been those fought between rivals to represent their country. Shozo Fujii, four-time middle-weight world champion in the 1970s, maintained it was easier to win the Olympic Games than to qualify for it. Foreigners were easier to beat than the Japanese.

With more and more countries piling into judo, the struggle to compete in the Olympics is now harder than ever. After Barcelona, the authorities, having decided that the event was becoming too unwieldy, imposed a limit on the number of contestants in each weight category. Regrettably, this means that many nations do not get to take part. That may be in the spirit of neither judo nor the Olympics, but it is the price of judo's success.

For a contestant, the tournament begins at dawn on the scales. For some it can end there too. On the morning of August 7 at the Sydney Olympics in 2000, Great Britain's Debbie Allan, the twenty-four-year-old European champion from Surrey, was suffering from more than her usual competition nerves when she arrived at the weigh-in at Darling Harbour. She had been selected to represent Britain in the under–114 pounds (52 kilograms) category, but the practice scales revealed she was still too heavy.

The official weigh-in took place between 7 A.M. and 8 A.M. Allan left it as late as she possibly could to attend and, clad in sweat gear, spent the time skipping frantically. She couldn't have left it any later. At 7:58 A.M., two minutes before the close of the authorized weigh-in period, she stepped naked and shaking with nerves onto the official scales: just before she did, women's team coach Diane Bell cut off Debbie's shoulder-length brown hair. It was a sad and pointless sacrifice. She was still a little over a pound (fifty grams) overweight and was disqualified from the competition.[1] Allan was moved out of the Olympic village so that her demoralization did not infect her teammates.

The Debbie Allan fiasco was distressing for Britain but hardly as disastrous as the fate of Chung Se-Hoon, the Korean who had taken bronze at the Barcelona Olympics. In March 1996 he was struggling to make the weight for the under–143 pound (65 kilogram) category of the Atlanta Games. He had managed to lose 17 pounds (8 kilos)—an eighth of his body weight—and was still sweating it out in the sauna when he had a heart attack. He died on the way to hospital.[2] David Khakhaleichvili, the heavyweight from Georgia and a serious contender for the heavyweight gold medal, reached Atlanta in 1996 but became lost after being given the wrong directions to the weigh-in, failed to meet the deadline, and was disqualified.[3]

Some make the weight and get as far as the mat before the system says enough is enough. One man competing at Crystal Palace for selection in the British squad before the Tokyo

Olympics in 1964 came on and bowed for his first contest. To the watching crowd it was rather a slow bow; then, to their horror, he toppled over and lay unconscious on the mat. In those days the perils of dieting were not well understood and he had starved his body to the point of extreme dehydration. Given his parlous state, perhaps it was just as well that he had collapsed *before* the contest started.

Today these hazards are appreciated, but the lives of those whose weight hovers around the upper end of their category remain tyrannized by the scales. Once they have weighed in they can consume as much as they want; sadly, by this time it is only a couple of hours before they have to compete and many are too nervous to eat.

The scene now moves from the weigh-in to the practice area, a large space close to the arena laid with mats around which the teams can pitch camp. Here they change, warm up, and practice until they are called to the arena. They can use the time to assess, impress, or unnerve the opposition.

Everyone seems to be walking around looking like the lone gunman who's just come through the swing doors of the saloon. Syd Hoare offers precise advice on how to signal confidence. "Off the mat, walk tall; do not slump. Hold the back of your neck straight, let your shoulders drop down, feel strong in your stomach and do not hollow your chest. If you meet a rival do not avoid their gaze or look at them. Just see them without focusing."[4]

Hair—or the shaving of it—occupies an important subsection in the manual of combat psychology. Consider the case of the six Japanese high school pupils disqualified from a tournament in June 2002 because "their eyebrows were too thin."[5] In devising a refinement to unnerve their opposition, five girls and a boy plucked their eyebrows until they became two needle-thin lines. "We have banned thin eyebrows," an official explained, "because they are intimidating to opponents and cause displeasure."

The practice room offers a chance to show off and intimidate. I once watched a tiny Japanese featherweight girl at the Tournoi de Paris throw her male training partner all around the practice mat over and over again in quick succession. Each time he hit the floor like a pistol shot, a fraction of a second after her little high-pitched war cry. It was an impressive tour de force and for its duration she was the center of attention, however much her rivals practicing nearby pretended not to notice.

Others prefer not to use these kind of psy-ops but to practice more discreetly, or even to take the opportunity to spread some disinformation. Ray Stevens told me how, at the Barcelona Olympics, he became aware that his preparations were being watched by the first contestant he was to meet. His response was to make a show of rehearsing a series of left-handed techniques. As soon as their contest started, Stevens took the left grip that he knew his opponent was expecting but caught him completely by surprise, coming in suddenly for a right *uchimata* and throwing him for *ippon* within the first few seconds. It was a morale-boosting start to a day that was to see him take the silver medal.

COMPETITORS CAN BE BESET by very mixed emotions before a contest. In the course of the Athens Olympics, Dennis van der Geest, the Dutch heavyweight, told his father and coach, Cor, "I don't want to go any more. I am finished. I want to go back to the Olympic village and have a beer and some chips and I want to sit in front of the telly." He later explained, "This was not really coming from inside but . . . one moment you are thinking 'Yeah, I want to fight' and the next you are thinking 'No man, just leave me alone.'"[6]

Some judoka have been surprisingly frank about their nervousness and fear. One wrote, "Feelings like 'I just want to run away' or 'I'm frightened' are always felt to a certain degree." Another athlete revealed:

> If I may be permitted a personal confession, never in the countless tournaments in which I have participated have I had a feeling of perfect security.

I am always pursued by an uneasiness that I can only describe as fear directed toward the opponent I must encounter. When I reach the hall where the tournament is to be held, I always experience a vague sense of bleakness. Though I cannot ascribe exact causes to the feeling, I am perfectly aware of its manifestations. The blood drains from my face, and tears well up in my eyes. I cannot carry on coherent conversations. Even when I eat nothing in the early part of the day, in the afternoon I am not hungry. I begin to have doubts about myself: perhaps I am a coward. But I realize that I must not let others see that I entertain such fears. Often I long to pray to something. In fact, on one occasion I did break away from the people around me and find an isolated place where I put my hands together in a prayer to some power. I do not know to what I addressed the prayer; it was simply the last resort of a person pushed to the limits of tension.[7]

Both authors were Japanese. The first words were those of Yasuhiro Yamashita, the last came from Isao Okano. Both were great champions and the most feared men of their day.

Neil Adams said, "I never know until I step on that mat, whether I'm going to feel sharp and alert or, for some unaccountable reason, as weak as a kitten with legs like jelly."[8] Another player spoke to me of his nerves and fear. "You'd have to wait so long it was awful. There was this loneliness. You just wanted to go home."[9] Because most competitors—though not all—prefer to be distracted by company, good coaches never leave a contestant by himself for long.[10] And they have to know when to speak, when to be quiet. "Sometimes you may have to say something very obvious, just so you're saying something," says Roy Inman. Sometimes, if the contestant is very nervous, he will constantly push and joke with him or her to stop the tension from building up—as one coach put it, "to get them out of their minds and into their bodies."

Coaches can, however, seriously demoralize their charges. One player described how, feeling extremely nervous before his Olympic debut, he was training with his coach, a former champion. When the coach spotted two old friends approaching, he suddenly threw his man in front of them in a showily dismissive way. It may have impressed the friends but it left the competitor in despair and wondering to himself, "If I've been thrown by this guy who has been retired ten years, what chance have I got out there?" It was a shameful display by the coach, who still felt he had something to prove and could not subordinate his ego to his task.

WHEN THE TIME COMES, the coach takes his contestant to the tunnel leading into the arena where he checks in at the control desk, sheds his shoes, and waits in line for his name to be called. As each contestant comes forward, the sleeves of his jacket are measured by an official with calipers to make sure they are the minimum length and width. If they are too narrow, they will give the opponent less of a chance to get a grip, putting him at a disadvantage.

Nerves are stretched to the breaking point and the tension in this part of the arena is palpable. Standing in the tunnel at the Paris world championships in 1998, I saw the French middleweight Djamel Bouras waiting to go on in his semifinal. Occasionally he would look up at the TV monitor to watch the current contest. His hand would suddenly go into a spasm and his face into a fearful grimace. He was a frightening sight, his skull shaven, his face gaunt and hollow-eyed and a terrible gray color; he paced backward and forward like a big cat in its cage. I would have felt more comfortable if there had been bars between us.

So now the time has come. Out in the arena the crowd is thickening and the buzz growing, and the announcer calls on the first contestants. All those weeks of assiduous preparation, pitiless dieting, dedicated training, working through injury, painstaking practice—unending effort—are about to be put to the test.

Here comes the moment of truth.

The Four-Ring Circus

The procession of a competitor to the mat sometimes looks uncannily like the arrival of a prisoner and firing squad. Almost as if to make sure he can't make a break for it, the contestant is sandwiched between two people—an event official walks in front and his mat coach close behind. Bringing up the rear is the team doctor or physiotherapist.

The mats, arranged in a line down the center of the arena, are divided by color into four contest areas. In judo the ring is square. Along one side are the officials' tables, laden with enough electronic equipment to make them look like Mission Control at Houston. Around these swarm the officials themselves, wearing ill-fitting yellow blazers and puffing out their chests. Actually, they aren't puffing out their chests; they are retired judoka whose pectorals haven't receded as quickly as their hairlines. And there's nothing wrong with the blazers: it's their thick-necked, swollen-shouldered occupants who are ill fitting.

The competitors proceed down the other side and wait beside their allocated mat, while their coaches take their seats. Those who have sustained themselves through the awkward wait with external stimuli must now take out their earphones and face the real soundtrack, or remove the chewing gum that is believed to promote aggression. All sorts of firing-up techniques are deployed on the edge of the mat. Some leap into the air and bounce down on bended knees, executing sumo-esque crouches and stamps. Some slap the floor; some slap themselves. A few rub their ears, which stimulates the flow of adrenaline.

When all the officials are ready, the referee beckons the contestants forward. They make their way in opposite directions around the edge of the tatami where they wait facing each other just outside the contest area. On the referee's signal, they step onto the mat and bow. Then they walk up to their marks, which are taped in blue and white in the middle of the mat. The referee calls them to bow each other: "*Rei!*" And then to engage: "*Hajime!*"

Within seconds of this call something really terrible can happen: a very quick and very sudden death. These tend to occur early in the day when weak judo countries face strong ones; when, for instance, South Africa tries conclusions with North Korea.

A soccer team can suffer a humiliatingly quick goal, but at least the game goes on. In judo, when a fighter is thrown flat on his back and the ref gives an *ippon,* it's like a knockout—that's the end of it. A judoka can train for years and cross half the globe to compete in a major competition like the world championships or the Olympics. Then he steps onto the mat for his first fight, bows twice as etiquette demands, and suddenly some shaven-headed psychopath from the Asian steppes hurtles across the tatami and bangs him over and out of the competition within a few seconds. He has spent more time bowing than fighting. What can this man tell the folks back home?

Got Butt Kicked.

MOST FIGHTS BEGIN WITH a battle for grips. This may appear to be merely small-arms fire, the placing of pawns, but grip fighting is an art in itself. As Neil Adams put it, "Those who haven't tried judo seldom realize how much can be transmitted through the initial exchange of grips: volumes of subtle, tactical information . . . picked up . . . in just a few seconds."

The bantamweight women move like insects. They jump and flutter. You can hear the meows of little Oriental fighters: yowls and high-pitched yaps and barks that sometimes make them sound like Yorkshire terriers. The lightweight men are cats; the middleweight are monkeys; the heavyweights are bulls.

The contests differ widely in character, they have so many variations in pattern and cadence. Some are skillful, some are tactical, some are brutal; there are the slow and dull as well as the fast and furious. They also vary in mood—from bad-tempered and ugly to fine-mannered and sublime.

Who fights whom will have been decided on the eve of the tournament by an electronic draw into which is programmed an ironic knowledge of politics and history that likes to see old adversaries do battle with each other all over again. Colonies fight their conquerors. Police states are pitted against liberal democracies. Communists grapple with capitalists. Of course, this happens in every sport, but here they're not just running and jumping against each other, they're fighting each other. This is never truer than in the case of contests between adversaries on the brink of hostilities, such as Israel and its neighbors or North and South Korea.

Novice spectators can find the vehemence of the contests frightening. One Budokwai member who went with his wife to see the Mel Gibson film *The Passion of the Christ* told me that while she had remained unperturbed, he had spent most of the time wincing in horror at all the flailing and nailing. A few days later he took her to a judo tournament for the first time. Much to his embarrassment and the amusement of nearby spectators, she put her hands over her head and cried out in horror every time someone was thrown.

BY THE TIME he appears in his second or third bout of the tournament, the athlete may become conscious of what Isao Okano calls "an imaginary membrane" separating him from all outside influences, including the spectators:

> Perhaps this state can be called a kind of hypnotism; perhaps it is something very near absentmindedness. But surrounded by that imaginary membrane, I find that my mind is alert and cool. I am like an animal standing alone. The voices and shouts of the crowd have no effect on me. My excitement leads

my body into a separate realm where winning and
losing are the only important things. My hands and
feet sweat, and I tremble. At such times, pats on the
back or words of encouragement from friends tend to
bring me back from this realm. Consequently, I avoid
meeting people I know. I am fighting my own battle
alone. It is not a matter that concerns other people.
My strength is the only thing that can lead me to victory, and no words of encouragement are helpful.[11]

SOMETIMES A THROW comes from out of nowhere. Sometimes
it builds like the music in a film thriller when the vulnerable
heroine goes into the dark and empty building; you know something horrible is going to happen—the music tells you it is going
to happen—then it happens and you still jump out of your seat.
So it is with certain contestants. This man wants his grip, a deep
grip which he seizes from over his opponent's shoulder to the
back of his belt, like a mongoose leaping onto the neck of a cobra.
And when he gets it, which he usually does, the knowing crowd
begins to roar; the victim tries to wriggle free but he is trapped.
They all know exactly what is going to happen next. Yes! *Ta-ka-ta.
Whoosh. Kerboooom!*

The sheer agility that allows these athletes, by twisting in
the air, to avoid being thrown is wondrous. I see one, caught by
a shoulder throw, who is now airborne and seems to be done for.
But he performs some extraordinary simian aerobatics and he has
escaped. They replay his maneuver three times on the big screen
but you still can't work out what happened, other than that he
managed to find a patch of thin air into which he could dig his
fingers and toes to arrest his flight before slipping back down to
land on both feet and carry on fighting.

The dominated seem to ricochet off invisible walls. Rever-
sals of fortune can be rapid and frequent. A contest can ebb
and flow, back and forth, with brain-numbing rapidity. A player
suddenly changes grip and seems to roll his opponent to the

floor, the referee signaling the small score of *koka* because he lacked the force and control to achieve more. But the attacker has gone down with his adversary, who now becomes the aggressor by using the momentum that brought him to the ground to roll the other man smoothly into a hold-down. The captive is wrapped and trapped, going nowhere. He is pinned for an *ippon*-winning twenty-five seconds. And just when he was on the brink of victory.

Referees are instructed not to let groundwork last for long—it makes for a poor spectacle. But some contestants nevertheless take their opponents to the floor, for the same reason that alligators drag their prey under water—they can finish the job more easily down there.

The little lightweight women are quite disturbing: in their white outfits they look as demure as milkmaids, but once they're out there they fight like alley cats. All that's missing is the sound of crashing trash-can lids. At the other end of the scales, the heavyweights in action can look like articulated trucks competing for a parking space; when they go to the floor one seems to be witnessing some maritime ecological tragedy. As the two great mammals lie there struggling, one can do nothing but wait and hope that the high tide will come to their rescue, refloat these poor beasts, and carry them back out to sea.

There are victories that seem to be the result of massive effort, and others which come with insulting ease. A perfectly timed footsweep can make its recipient look fantastically foolish: with a sudden subtle gliding of the foot, the angled sole smacks the load-bearing ankle and the victim collapses like a deck chair. But sometimes the sweep can take his legs so high that, for one exquisite moment, he lies horizontal in mid-air—before the crash to earth. *Keerrrbbbooohhhm!*

Like a bird of prey, the attacker works on his floored victim, plucking and tugging at the cloth of the *gi*. Fingers tap in hurried submission to avoid broken arms. When time runs out there is a blast on a klaxon; it sounds like the despairing honk of an ancient mule that is still smoking sixty cigarettes a day. The number of bodies flattened on the tatami begins to look like road kill on a country lane in autumn. The finality of this symbolic death means there are moments when, looking at the fallen, one imagines one sees not a floored judoka in a *gi* but a corpse wrapped in a shroud.

Even the dead must observe the niceties of etiquette. I see a man who fails to bow before leaving the mat. Ordered back by the referee, at first he refuses with a dismissing wave of his hand, before bowing without returning to the mark. When the referee again insists, he carries out the order. But his belt wasn't done up, so he is made to retie it and bow again before being finally allowed to go.

Spectators, too, enjoy the niceties of etiquette and manners. A defeated Cuban girl is booed when she refuses to shake her victor's proffered hand. A little Ukrainian girl suffering from an injured shoulder can walk only slowly and leaves last; nevertheless she stops to make a painful bow to the empty mat, then shuffles off amid a burst of warm applause.

Of course, it is hell losing in any sport. It's grim for an outwitted goalkeeper sitting on his backside with the net still twitching behind him while the opposing team are having group sex on his front lawn. But judo inflicts its own special indignities. Contestants are thrown around like bags of laundry, tortured into submission, and clamped to the floor where they can do nothing but thrash around like dying carp. The end can be sinister, making for a grim tableau: the body of the defeated spread out on the floor while the victor stands over him, arms raised in triumph. This death seems much more than symbolic. One sometimes wonders why they don't just go the whole hog: allow the winner to rest his foot on the corpse of his vanquished enemy and hold aloft his severed head.

For all this, victory can be sweet to see: white or blue, a body in flight is a wonderful sight. The whippy acrobatics and darting feet form a choreography of such intricate beauty that here is cause for Balanchine to blanch. All that dedication, all that training culminates in this one moment—a moment of ephemeral calligraphy written by a body whirling earthward through the sky.

The Day of Judgment

One day God and the Devil are talking about judo, which apparently they do quite a lot, and the Devil challenges God to a judo tournament. God says, "Don't be stupid. You wouldn't stand a chance. In my team I've got Kano and Yokoyama as well as Kimura. And, of course, I've got the Heavenly Lords."

"I know," says the Devil with a sly grin, "but I've got all the referees."

Pity the referee in any sport—but the judges of judo have an especially hard task. The rules are so complicated, the judgment so subtle. Shozo Fujii found the pressure of being a referee more daunting than that of being a contestant. "As a fighter I was responsible only to myself," he said, "as a referee I am responsible to everyone else." He said that if he ever made a big mistake he would stop.[12]

Unlike his counterpart in boxing, the judo referee has to score the fight as well as conduct it. From the swirl of entangled cotton bundles he has to decide whether a contestant landed clearly or perhaps slightly on his side and consider the degree of speed, force, and control in awarding the right score. If both contestants go over, he must decide who initiated the throw. In the tangle of groundwork he must ensure that an attempt at a legal armlock does not turn into an illegal shoulder lock (and the difference is subtle) or that out of his sight one contestant isn't attacking the other one's face.

Referees have some thorny problems to solve. Consider the dilemma of the strangle on the bell. The man who is clamped in a strangle is winning on points, but when the bell rings marking the end of the contest, he has not tapped. The reason that he has not tapped, it turns out when the bodies are disentangled, is that he is unconscious. But the question is, Did he lose consciousness before or after the twenty-five-second signal sounded? If he goes out before he is the loser, if he survived until the bell, he is the winner.

One of the duties of referees is to stimulate fighters if they falter. Contestants who are fearful of each other can be overcautious and reluctant to get on with their work. It can be difficult to persuade them to fight, short of using electric cattle prods, and so he can award penalties for passivity to a competitor who fails to attack for twenty seconds. If this happens four times to a fighter, he is disqualified.

A throw in judo, like a punch in boxing, can look very different depending on the viewpoint, and so judges work in threes. The referee conducts the contest, the other two judges sit in diagonally opposite corners. In the event of a dispute, majority rule prevails. Referees have a vocabulary of hand signals with which to confirm the score or penalty they shout out. In judo as in cricket, the bigger the gesture the bigger the score. An *ippon* is announced by a single hand raised straight and high above the head, like a referee holding a victorious boxer's hand aloft and similar to a cricket umpire's two-handed signal for six. A *waza-ari,* the second highest score, is signaled by sweeping an extended arm, palm down, from side to side at hip level, like a cricket umpire signaling four for a ball that has rolled over the boundary. The referee signals a passivity penalty by circling his hands around each other and then pointing at the offender.

One gesture sometimes puzzles the novice spectator—when a referee approaches his two judges in order to confer with them, he places his flattened palm over his heart in what seems to be a formal gesture of respect; in fact he is covering the microphone clipped to his lapel in order to prevent the entire crowd hearing their deliberations.

The rules of combat through the centuries are expressions of the prevailing culture. The crossbow was once considered a cowardly weapon. More recently the planting of explosives in the ground, once completely accepted, has become frowned upon, although it is acceptable to drop explosives from the air. You can shoot at the pilot who is trying to drop those explosives, but you must not shoot him once he has left his aircraft (for example, by parachute) or landed on your territory. You can shoot an enemy soldier if his hands hold a gun, but not if his hands hold no gun and are raised above his head. You may ask an enemy combatant in civilian clothes the whereabouts of the time-detonated bomb that he has planted to kill your people, but you are not permitted to force him to tell you. And so on.

The rules are there to reduce the unpleasantness inherent in war. Judo, which is a sort of war in microcosm, has rules for similar reasons.

Putting your fingers or thumbs inside the sleeve of your opponent's jacket is forbidden (in case you break your fingers). "Grapevining"—entwining your leg around your opponent's leg as you fall backwards—is forbidden, although it is permitted when you fall forwards. You may choke an opponent's windpipe but you must not endanger his spinal column; you may strangle him with your jacket but you must not attempt to do so with your belt.

There are pages and pages of this stuff. It is not just the number of rules in the sport that make the judo judge's task so hard, but the frequency with which changes are made. Sometimes rules—such as those to reduce passivity—are introduced to make the sport more interesting to spectators, but often the motive is safety.

Some rules are put in place to protect the aggressor. At one time competitors were doing *uchimata* with such dynamism that they would fire themselves headfirst into the mat and buckle their necks, resulting in a number of cases of paralysis: so, in 1978, the IJF introduced legislation disqualifying a combatant if he failed to turn his head when executing certain forward throws.

One change has made the life of referees a little easier: the golden score. Until 2003, if a fight came to time and the scores were equal, the three judges would decide to whom to award victory by judging which contestant was the most dominant. Under the golden score rule, the contest goes to extra time and the first person to score any point is the winner.

One thing has made referees' lives much harder: the video camera. Judo is, of course, not the only sport in which the camera's pitiless and perfect vision, not to mention 20/20 hindsight, makes the spectators better able to pass judgment than the referee.

I saw a terrible incident in the world championships in Paris in 1997. In a desperate bid to turn the tables in a medal match he was losing, Myong Chang Kang, an under–145 pounds (60 kilograms) player from North Korea, managed to catch his opponent with a shoulder throw, but the score, *waza-ari*, was given to his opponent. Most of the spectators, however, knew for certain that the referee had made a mistake. Because this was France, the crowd was knowledgeable and very voluble, and fourteen thousand people immediately began to complain vociferously. The referee wouldn't change his mind, even after consulting with his fellow judges.

Then the inevitable happened.

The TV director and his team in the outside broadcast unit did what they had to do for every fight: they ran back the tape, found the highlight, and replayed it. It cut into the live camera signal on the two giant screens and there it was for all to see: it was clear that it was the Korean's score. Presented with this incontrovertible supporting evidence, the crowd went mad with fury. The Korean was sitting disconsolately on the mat, holding his head in his hands as if saying, "I cannot believe this." His raging coach, along with various members of the Korean delegation, were arguing with the referees and the officials at the table. Yamashita, the manager of the Japanese team, tried to intervene on the Korean's behalf. Meanwhile the TV technician replayed the throw, again and again and again, each time provoking a further roar of fury from the crowd. The tumult was deafening, but the authorities would not yield.

The Korean had been cheated—and was shown to have been cheated. Eventually he stood up and walked off the mat, the furious roar of the crowd turning to applause for the victim of this miscarriage of justice. The incident had soured the day and would rankle for a long time.

Referees are only noticed when they get it wrong: it is their fate to be asked to play God and forever to be accused of acting for the Devil.

THE BANE OF the referee's life is the matside coach who seeks to cajole or bully him instead of carrying out his true task, which is to instruct and encourage his players. Cuba's Ronaldo Valdivie is not the only one to get so excited that you think he is going to get caught up in the fray. The Dutchman Cor van der Geest, head coach of the Netherlands team that has included his sons, is a notorious figure. On the single occasion I met him he seemed to be the most gentle of men, with kindly blue eyes, soft voice, and avuncular manner. But the coach's chair has the same effect on him as the concoction that turned the kindly Dr. Jekyll into the monstrous Mr. Hyde. If van der Geest disapproves of a decision that has gone against one of his sons, all hell breaks loose. He bellows in fury as his giant frame rises out of his chair, his head swaying like an angry elephant just before it charges. Every score awarded against any of his boys is as if a spear has been plunged deep into his flank. His sonorous roaring—in a language that no one is able to understand—can be heard over the din of any crowd. You wonder if the authorities are going to have to bring him down with tranquilizer darts before he runs amok. He did once.

At the world championships in Birmingham in 1999, Shinohara, who was fighting van der Geest's son Dennis, was awarded an *ippon* by the referees. Infuriated by the decision, van der Geest senior broke loose, lumbered onto the mat—wearing his shoes—and kicked the coach's chair. In the event, the authorities didn't use darts, but they did ban him from the matside chair for the rest of the year and put him on probation for a further twelve months. They have kept a close eye on him ever since: At the Athens Olympics, I saw an official receiving a message on his radio that prompted him to approach and restrain van der Geest and make him get back in his chair.

Defeat rather than victory reveals most about the relationship between a coach and his charge. Although a coach will usually console his contestant as he comes off the mat and accompany him out of the arena, sometimes he will deliver a lambasting lecture while still in full public view. This may be because he is cross, or because it has been established that a fighter is at his most receptive to information in the moments immediately after a contest. But sometimes a coach will say nothing, putting his hand firmly on the back of his defeated charge and ushering him quickly out of the arena, as if to get him out of public view in order to proceed with the execution. The Central Asian coaches, particularly, can appear to be so disgusted with their competitors' performance that they'll walk out of the arena before their charges have even left the mat and will leave them alone in the misery of their defeat.

In the highly charged atmosphere of the arena, a coach's self-control can fall apart. At the Athens Olympics a South Korean coach was thrown out of the Games after being seen slapping a female contestant, a lightweight, across the face. This may sound unpleasant by normal social standards, but given the number of offences of assault and battery committed against a judoka in the course of a typical tournament day, a whack on the cheek is neither here nor there. As the authorities might have put it, however, "It's the thought that counts."

A GOOD COACH WILL understand that some competitors need loud, vociferous assistance and others prefer subtler guidance. Either way he will give short, clear, intelligible advice: for instance "Hold the left hand higher," or "Pull his head down." Some individuals react with defiance when a trainer tries to control them too much. The judoka has to have his independence.[13] Most coaches will agree that "You can only tell a player two things without confusing them."

And you have to be careful how you tell them. Not a few fights have been won because one contestant has heard the instructions of his opponent's coach—and acted upon it.

In the awe-inspiring final in the Munich world championships of 2001 between Yusuke Kanamaru and Vitali Makarov, Hirotaka Okada, the former double world champion (once my nemesis at the Budokwai) and now a coach for his national squad, was sitting in the matside chair. During a brief pause towards the end of the contest, the exhausted Japanese looked over to Okada to see if he had any instructions. Okada could only clench his fist and half punch it in the air. It seemed to signal "budo spirit." The coach knew Kanamaru was doing everything he could; there was simply nothing else for Okada to do or say.

In Harm's Way

Back in the practice area, the athletes are awaiting their turn. Some warm up, stretching and tumbling. Some spar with their coach or training partner, who might mimic the style of their next opponent, others are doing their *uchikomi*. Here is a large pile of clothes that, on closer inspection, turns out to be the Italian women's team huddled together for warmth and moral support.

By the end of the morning, some are so swathed in bandages and strapped with tape and Velcro-fixed wrappings that, were it not for the occasional patches of flesh, one would suppose these are not people but neoprene-encased humanoids. Physiotherapists move among the wounded, dispensing diagnosis and treatment. The amount of ice in all the packs strapped to shoulders, elbows, and knees would be enough to bring down the *Titanic,* while a cursory examination of the more serious cases by a veterinary surgeon would prompt him to have them humanely destroyed.

Injury is the bane of any judoka's life. The good Dr. Kano did everything he could to make judo safe, but it is safe only in the sense that our roads are safe: people strapped in steel containers hurtle past each other a few feet apart at combined speeds of 140 miles per hour without incident—until someone makes a mistake. The high velocities reached by players in Formula One judo mean that accidents will happen. For the most part these are merely collisions of upholstery, but there are a number of hard surfaces flying around the arena during a contest; these include shins, knees, elbows, and skulls. Inevitably the pressures of high-grade competition drive people to operate at the extremes; sooner or later every player will take his turn to be the one confined by injury to watching a practice from the side of the dojo in a state of frustrated and impatient envy.

In one way judoka are more fortunate than other sportsmen in that, so long as an injury is not too bad, they can adapt their techniques to it. Many competitors have been forced by injury to develop new techniques and have gone on to be world champions, Toshihiko Koga, Udo Quellmalz, and Katsuhiko Kashiwazaki among them. If a tennis player has a damaged playing arm or shoulder, he's done for. The downside of a judo injury is that one's opponent can exploit it. Just as a boxer will keep working on an opponent's damaged eye, a judo player can keep working on the other man's damaged limb. A player may, for instance, manage to escape from an armlock that has injured his elbow joint. If the opponent realizes it is painful, he will try to attack it. The injured party feels vulnerable and tries to protect it, and in doing so opens himself to other attacks.

Nevertheless, judo is in some ways safer than games where players accidentally collide because they are so focused on the ball that they do not always see each other. Because in combat the other man *is* the ball, judoka watch only each other and have turned safe collision into an art form. And because the consequences could be dire if a contest got out of control, it is hedged about by a mass of rules and closely monitored by judges who outnumber the participants.

Injuries in the course of a tournament are not infrequent and the barefoot doctors have to be called onto the mat. Novice spectators are often puzzled that when this happens the doctor does not touch his charge, but merely kneels beside him to discuss his injury while occasionally pointing and gesturing to the damaged area. He can only suggest that the injured player try to move the injured limb in a certain way. Unless the damage was clearly the result of an action by the opponent, doctors are forbidden to touch an injured competitor if he wants to be able to continue. Even in these circumstances he is only allowed to examine the injury. No ice or spray is allowed.

Sometimes an injury is too bad for the player to continue. If this is a result of his own action, the other man is awarded the contest—likewise if neither can be blamed for the injury. A competitor who has clearly caused an injury to another player, rendering him unable to carry on, is disqualified and the contest awarded to his injured opponent.

Injury can provide desperately needed breathing space for an exhausted fighter, so the ability to fake one is a useful skill in the repertoire of a tactical player. Referees are ever on the lookout for this, though, so some skill is required. This may be why judo contestants go for a much less operatic, over-the-top style than their soccer colleagues.

Although treatment on the mat is forbidden, all sorts of things can be done to patch up a competitor between contests. Koga went into the Barcelona Games, according to one account, "carrying a knee injury that practically prevented him walking, let alone fighting." He had *six* injections of anti-inflammatory solution in his knee just before his first contest and a further series before his winning final.[14]

When a player takes drugs to keep him going like this, the relief is only a loan and the interest rates are punitive. Drugs may conceal further damage sustained to an injury in subsequent contests, so that when they wear off players may suffer more badly and for longer. As happens in soccer or rugby, injured players appear to be in such agony that it seems impossible they will continue. But somehow they do. At the 1998 Tournoi de Paris, I saw one contestant suffer terribly when, in a fight for grips, his opponent's finger jabbed deep into his eye. The victim hunched in pain and then exploded in a series of violent convulsions. Bent double, clutching at his face with one hand, he thrashed the air with his other. In his agony, he leapt about in a terrible dance; he skeetered and staggered across the mat; he crashed to the floor, rolled, arched, twisting and bucking like a shark on the end of a line. Eventually he collapsed on the mat and lay there, quite still.

It is at moments like this that you learn the full extent of judo officials' sympathy. As the injured man lay there, the referee came across and stood over the still-gasping heap of damp white cloth, pointing insistently with his open palm back towards the center of the mat where his opponent stood waiting to finish the job. The referee's body language resembled that of an impatient maître d'hôtel hurrying a customer to his table. The opponent looked like a hungry predator waiting for the human in the socks to move away from his carrion.

Eventually, just when it appeared that the injured contestant was incapable of getting up, let alone fighting, he rose and began to walk off the mat. As he did so, something seemed to click in his mind. Another moment and it would have been too late; he would have crossed the red area, thus automatically ending the contest. But just before he reached it, he paused and exchanged a few words with his coach, who had come forward to lead him away. The coach shrugged and nodded at the referee. His contestant then turned round, adjusted his kit, and stood at his mark to continue the fight. He seemed reinvigorated by the possibility of revenge.

Whether or not he was fired up by the injury, in quite a short time he came in with an *ippon*-scoring shoulder throw to flatten his opponent, an Olympic medalist and the favorite to win.

THERE ARE NO RECORDED cases of death in judo through strangulation,[15] but many who witnessed the semifinal of the under–143 pounds (65 kilograms) weight category of the European championships when they were held in Liège in the mid 1980s were convinced that a fatality was only narrowly averted.

In life, it falls to some to be brain surgeons and some to be plumbers. You could say that on the morning of May 4, 1984, Steve Gawthorpe, although at the time employed as a mechanic by the Highways Department of South Yorkshire County Council, had to be a bit of both. His immediate task was to close down a control unit that was presenting him with problems and to shut off a supply pipe in the system. The control unit was a brain belonging to an East European judoka; the pipe by which it was supplied with oxygen was his carotid artery.

Gawthorpe was never bathed in ice-cold water as a baby like Yamashita. He didn't need to be: he was born and brought up in Barnsley, Yorkshire, where it falls out of the sky almost all the year round. He has the kind of physique that R. S. Surtees described graphically in one of his tales of nineteenth-century hunting folk when he referred to a particular horseman as being "just like so many feet of galvanized gristle."[16]

I had encountered Gawthorpe when he brought various squad members to train at the Budokwai, but it was only when I spent a day at the National Sports Centre at Bisham Abbey, where he was coaching, that I heard from him firsthand an account of the unfortunate incident in Belgium.

With his loping gait and taut, sparse frame, Gawthorpe has the demeanor of a wolf at the end of a long winter. He has cropped blond hair and restless eyes that seem to be forever scanning the vicinity for prey. He deploys a deadpan delivery with Barnsley twang, occasionally omitting the definite article as he tells the events of that day two decades earlier.

"I got this Romanian, Illie Serban, to fight in semis," he recalls. "I armlocked him and he tapped and the referee stood us up. I thought that was that, but Serban complained and said that he'd never submitted—that he'd never given in.

"When they set us off again, we weren't in the best of moods." There is an unnerving mixture of twinkling comedy and deep menace in this piece of gentle understatement. "So when I knocked him down again, he stayed down. I were on top. I had him in *tati shiho gatam*" (which is to say he was straddling the chest of the Romanian, who was lying on his back with one of Gawthorpe's arms encircling his neck and pinning his upper arm hard against his ear). "And I'd also got him in a strangle. He starts dribbling but he won't tap. I weren't bothered. I'd tucked my legs in and I were pushing up and he still weren't going to give in. After what had happened before I thought he were trying to work me a trick and I kept squeezing and squeezing. When we watched on video replay he were unconscious after about three seconds 'cos you could see his legs just stop moving."

It must be said that, long after he retired from competition, Gawthorpe's power is frightening when he is merely doing light *randori*—and he gives no quarter. I have done groundwork with him several times and each occasion has been a near-death experience. The pressure applied to the unfortunate Serban's frame when the stakes were high and when, moreover, this python in his prime was "not in the best of moods" is a chilling thought. Imagine the tableau: Gawthorpe from the Highways Department causing catatonic arterial blockage as he lay clamped on the apparently lifeless form of the unfortunate Romanian like some ghastly death-support machine marked Made in Yorkshire.

"When he stopped struggling I thought, 'There's something not quite right here. But there's no way I'm stopping; I'll let this run on.' Crowd got a bit agitated. They were booing at referee. Eventually he stopped it. Serban were still unconscious."

One of the corner judges had called out to the referee, to no avail, finally standing up to intervene before a reluctant Gawthorpe was pulled off the inert body of the Romanian.[17] Attempts were made by another of the judges to revive him. When that failed, a medic came on, but the Romanian remained unconscious and was carried off on a stretcher.

Serban eventually came round and apparently suffered no ill effects. But IJF officials had been so rattled by the anger and distress of the spectators that they felt compelled to offer some reassurance. And so, as Gawthorpe gleefully reports, "Next day they brought him back into stadium to prove he weren't dead!"

JUDO ABHORS BLOOD. Its appearance is seldom the symptom of serious damage; it's likely to be a cut, a bleeding nose, a torn finger nail—a mere scratch on the bodywork or a small leak in a fuel pipe. Nevertheless the authorities possess an almost comic aversion to the stuff. A newspaper sportswriter sent to cover a tournament for the first time watched incredulously as the referee, seeing a speck of red from a cut on a contestant's face, stopped the fight and called for a doctor who removed his shoes, scurried onto the mat with his box of tricks, and dabbed at the offending wound before elaborately taping it up. By the time the medic had finished, the fighter's head was so swathed in tape and bandage that, although he had suffered only a small cut on his temple, he looked like the visible version of the Invisible Man, or as if he had just emerged from the serious burns unit. "What a bunch of poufs!" the reporter jeered. "It's not like this in boxing—there's blood everywhere!"

Even a small blob of blood on the mat prompts everyone to behave as though there's been a toxic spillage. The contest is brought to a halt. The referee points to the offending patch and a functionary immediately appears with a cloth and a squeezy plastic bottle of some fluid, proceeding to dab at the plastic tatami with the concerned precision of a paramedic cleaning an open wound.

Why the fuss? It probably goes back to Kano, who was so keen to distance his version of jujitsu from the sanguinary combats of the old schools. Judo's more serious injuries hardly ever involve bloodshed; most are caused by "twisting out." When a player is thrown, he will spin in the air to avoid landing on his back and conceding a score. This high-speed contortion, this twist against the force of the throw—a bit like wringing a towel—puts a huge stress on a body's joints. Frequent repetition of this action can cause lasting damage, leaving the body with the same sort of problems as a car with a twisted chassis.

If there have been fatalities in this very safe form of combat, they have probably been the result of overexertion leading to heart failure. Death in judo is entirely symbolic. However, at worst, a judo injury can be catastrophic. In the course of a British tournament in the late 1980s, a player broke his leg. The leg was put in plaster but later found to have bled so badly that the limb had to be amputated. In September 1987, the victim's friends staged a benefit tournament at a Merseyside sports center. One pairing was between Nigel Donahue, a former amateur wrestler who switched to judo and would compete in the Atlanta Olympics, and eighteen-year-old Owen Lowery, a talented player who had already won a number of British titles. In the course of the contest Donahue threw his opponent, who landed badly, breaking his neck and paralyzing all his limbs. Soon after the tragedy the first Fight Night Wales appeared on the judo calendar—now it was the turn of his friends to organize a benefit tournament for the unfortunate Lowery.

The Cinderella Syndrome

The preliminary rounds are completed by lunch time. The spectators have started to drift away, often leaving the last contests to be conducted in an uneasy silence. Now people can wander around the concourses at the back of the arena seating to browse among the stalls selling *gis* and books. Here they can buy a belt and have their name embroidered on it. Over there is a bookshop selling laboriously illustrated books devoted to a single technique, while a selection of DVDs such as *101 Judo Ippons* plays on the monitor: that's sixty-seven minutes of *Ta-ka-ta. Whoosh. Splat! Ta-ka-ta. Whoosh. Bang! Ta-ka. Crump!*

The air is stifling in the stadium. Someone had warned me, "Going to a judo tournament is like spending four days in an airport." They were right. You've just got to get out of there into the fresh air, away from the crowd. Perhaps, depending on where in the world we are, we might grab a hot dog or some cold sushi. Out here in the stadium grounds we can ask ourselves the question, If judo is really such a wonderful thing, why don't more people want to watch it?

JUDO WOULD LOVE TO be rich and famous. It is wearying of poverty and semi-obscurity. It is tired of the sort of barb that appears in the smart-alec Olympic television coverage: "7:30 P.M.: Judo—the sport that's so boring everyone wears their pajamas just in case they doze off." Or, "Where the action isn't—Olympic events we save you the trouble of watching."[18] It resents being called a "Cinderella sport" and longs to be at the party along with soccer, baseball, golf, and the others, feted by the public and fawned upon by the media.

Judo has been unceasing in its attempts to seek fame but its efforts at seduction have been poignant, misguided, and at times even comic. The sport's authorities want to pursue the path that took their sport into the Olympics—to slip into that benign spiral in that spectacle brings spectators, who bring television, which brings sponsorship, which brings stars, who bring more spectators and so on. They have an uphill battle on their hands. Judo's potential as a spectacular, full-contact, high-speed combat sport is diminished by Japanese terminology, complex rules, terrible staging, and an impenetrable scoring system. It is a broadcaster's nightmare, and mainstream television has never made a serious attempt to tackle the problems it presents.[19]

After the world championships took place in Rio de Janeiro in 1965, a Londoner called Charles Palmer became the first non-

Japanese to be elected to the highest office in judo, succeeding Dr. Kano's grandson as president of the International Judo Federation. Some described him as "forceful and outspoken," others chose "slightly overbearing and confrontational."[20] Either way he was a colorful figure who spoke four foreign languages, smoked cigars, drove a Rolls-Royce, piloted his own plane, excelled at skiing, and played both the drums and poker with considerable skill. He was to have a profound and lasting influence on the sport.

Born in 1930, Palmer started to learn judo at school in Ealing at fourteen. He joined the Budokwai to be taught by Gunji Koizumi and Trevor Leggett and was selected for the British team while still in his teens. He went to Tokyo in 1951 to study judo at the Kodokan and stayed for four years, earning his living as a security guard at the British Embassy. Having returned to the United Kingdom to captain the British team to some notable successes, after his retirement from competition he started to teach at the Budokwai, became an international referee, and, armed with the fluent Japanese he had acquired while in Tokyo, immersed himself in high-level judo politics. As chairman of the IJF he instituted a series of dramatic reforms.

Exasperated by those aspects of judo which made it incomprehensible to outsiders and dull as a spectator sport, Palmer set to work with vigor on the rule book. He struck off arcane rules such as the one that permitted contestants interlocked in groundwork near the edge of the area to be dragged back into the center: when this occurred with heavyweight players and a diminutive referee, it caused understandable mirth among Europeans. For similar reasons of dignity, he decreed that referees must remain standing throughout the contest and should not get down on the floor to monitor groundwork more closely. His critics say that this emphasis on detached dignity has often restricted the referee's view and resulted in injury to contestants.

Palmer believed in the spectacle of the throw and instituted new regulations governing the cut of jackets. The traditional *gi* was replaced with a new looser sleeve design, resulting in bigger and more impressive throws which looked better on camera; it is true to say that judo has been tailored for TV.[21]

Competitors who lacked aggression were a particular source of irritation to Palmer. When he refereed the heavyweight (under–205 pounds [93 kilograms]) final at the Tokyo Olympics between Isao Inokuma of Japan and Canada's Doug Rogers, both contestants were being tediously cautious. Stopping the contest, he gave a loud warning that both would be disqualified unless they went onto the offensive. All this in front of the emperor. To legislate for this he introduced the passivity rule (an idea taken from amateur wrestling),[22] which penalized a contestant if he failed to attack for twenty seconds. He also brought in the small scores, *koka* and *yuko,* to reduce the number of contests going to a decision. (He did however retain the use of Japanese terms, which many now see as an obstacle to understanding.) For all that he did, Palmer has been described as "the father of modern judo."[23]

Palmer modernized not only the rules, but also the Federation itself; he was crucial in securing judo's place in the Olympics and considerably reduced the influence of Japan. He refused to allow international politics to play any part in the sport, fighting to defy Margaret Thatcher and send a British team to the 1980 Olympics in Moscow despite her desire for a boycott following the Russian invasion of Afghanistan. To his dying day he believed this intransigence cost him a knighthood.

None of this was achieved without deep resentment from the Japanese, who felt that their control of the sport was slipping away along with its traditions; they were more than relieved when he fell from power in 1979 and the post reverted to one of their countrymen. But the struggle to modernize judo did not end with the defeat of Charles Palmer; it persists to this day.

THE HEART OF traditional judo, once housed in that little hut in the grounds of the Eishoji temple, now occupies a large eight-story building in Tokyo. It has offices for administrative staff, accommodation for visiting judoka, a library, and five mat areas, culminating in a large rooftop dojo with a four-mat competition arena and seating for nine hundred.

The Kodokan has some of the characteristics of a multinational corporation: it promotes the product, protects the brand, and manages finances; it also bears some resemblance to the spiritual center of a worldwide church. The Kodokan's cardinals spread its faith, train its priests, welcome pilgrims, and guard the flame of Kano's vision. Moreover, some might say, its rigid hierarchy, arcane traditions, and relentless conservatism make the Vatican seem, by comparison, as happy-go-lucky and progressive as a 1990s dot-com startup.

As each successive proposition for the modernization of the sport is presented, at the back of the collective mind of the Kodokan's broad-shouldered priests lies the question, Is this really in "the spirit of judo"? They debate that any move to popularize their art takes it ever further from its altruistic roots. They are unceasingly watchful for signs that judo is being changed for the benefit of spectators rather than its participants. They live with the undying tension that exists between the notion of mere sport and some grander idea. And nothing has symbolized this schism between modernizers and traditionalists better than the Battle of the Blue Gi.

The struggles of Anton Geesink against Japanese hegemony did not end with his Olympic triumph in 1964. Like Charles Palmer, the Dutchman believed that the sport had to change if it were to be popularized in the West, and that one of the most necessary changes was to introduce colored judo suits.

In judo, the players are in a state of almost constant entanglement, whether on their feet or on the floor. When both contestants are in white, groundwork is by no means easy to follow from a distance. It is very hard for a spectator to establish from a knotted heap of bodies, both clad in white and struggling on the floor, just who is the rightful owner of which limb. The issue of contrastingly colored *gis* was not about show business, but about helping the spectator.   •

Geesink campaigned doggedly for colored *gis* and, in an action that was to make him many enemies in Japan, went ahead and introduced them in 1967 in his native Holland. This was anathema to the old guard in the Kodokan, who put up a furious resistance and refused to allow them in international competition. They felt that the demise of the all-white contest would symbolize judo's loss of purity—a purity already compromised by the introduction of weight categories and other innovations pushed through by meddling Westerners.

However, some Japanese wanted to make the change, and the row spilled over into the whole judo fraternity. Among the enthusiasts for change was Isao Okano, the world champion who had also won gold in the Tokyo Olympics and was twice winner of the All Japan. These achievements did not save him from being cast out by the Kodokan; his fall from grace was the culmination of an extraordinarily acrimonious row. It was prompted by a photograph that appeared on the cover of a French judo magazine, showing the combatants wearing red and blue judo outfits.[24]

It took decades of constant pressure before eventually the IJF agreed to conduct trials. After these proved highly successful, colored *gis* made their appearance at the world championships in Munich in 2001.

IF, IN THE COURSE OF the Second World War, someone had run into Hut Six at Bletchley Park and dumped an International Judo Federation approved electronic scoreboard on the table instead of one of the German Wehrmacht's Enigma machines, those eccentric pipe-smoking geniuses in their tweed suits would still be sitting there today, trying to disentangle the peculiar mathematical principles that determine the sport's scoring system.

These scores neither have numerical values nor are they cumulative—the player who has scored one *yuko* is ahead of his opponent who has scored four *kokas*. The scoreboard has spaces by the name of each player in which to record the number of *waza-ari, yuko,* and *koka* he has scored. The equivalent three penalties, *keikoku, chui,* and *shido,* are also shown. You cannot just glance at the display; it takes almost as long to absorb as a tennis scoreboard. But in a tennis match the ball is in play for a mere ten to fifteen minutes an hour, so there is plenty of time to look at the board. A judo contest is so fast and so short that you can miss the crucial action while merely taking even a quick blink.

Finality

First come the repêchage contests (depending on how it is structured, all those who were defeated by, say, the semifinalists are brought back to fight for a bronze medal), then the quarter-finals and semifinals, culminating in the finals. The tickets are more expensive. Contests are confined to two mats instead of four and the tension is building—but nowhere more so than in the minds of the competitors who have fought their way through, have survived the carnage, and are still on their feet. As Okano wrote:

> When the tournament reaches the semi-finals or finals stage, a tension of a completely different kind wells up inside me. I am entirely enclosed in a veil of transparency; I feel that I can see through everything. The opponent with whom I must fight has become for me nothing but a physical object. The sense of doing battle with myself becomes clearer and clearer in my mind. Perhaps, because I feel that my heart has been laid bare, I sense a unity with all of the spectators, no matter how many of them are present. I am concerned that the bout, win or lose, be a good one because the moment seems to be climactic, a time when I must show myself to best advantage.

Not every final lives up to the promise of its tensions; they can be something of an anticlimax—unexciting struggles won by the combatant who has put in more attacks. Those who saw

Yamashita fight in his final contest at the All Japan must have been disappointed by a sense of inconclusiveness. And sometimes it all happens too fast. In the Sydney Olympics, Tadahiro Nomura threw his opponent for *ippon* in fourteen seconds. If you'd seen that, you might have wanted your money back.

However, the utter excitement of other finals lingers in the memory forever. Mike Callan was twenty years old when he went to a world championships for the first time. The year was 1981 and the place was Maastricht—a tournament that many remember for the victories of Yasuhiro Yamashita and Neil Adams. Callan remembers it for the performance of another champion. "For me the player of the tournament was Katsuhiko Kashiwazaki. In his semifinal he did two of the greatest techniques I have ever seen. Torsten Reissmann, the current European champion, had looked very strong in the early rounds, throwing with *uchimata*. Kashi was ready for him. As Reissmann attacked, Kashi stepped sideways and Reissmann threw himself up into the air before being thrown with a wonderful *uchimata sukashi*, for which amazingly Kashi only received *waza-ari*.

"Not content to sit on his lead, Kashi then proceeded to skip sideways across the mat, feinting a huge *ashiwaza* which saw him launch himself up into the air—no one, least of all Reismann, knew what he was doing—before he dropped onto his back for *yokotomoe nage*, appearing to flip Reissmann off to the wrong side, for *ippon*."

Callan wasn't the only person who'd never forget this leap by Kashiwazaki. His magnificent flight through the air is engraved on the memory of many others, among them Ray Stevens, who was a sixteen-year-old spectator that day at Maastricht. He remembered how, as in boxing, people tended to follow the heavy-weights while the lightweights never drew much of a crowd, but he noticed Kashiwazaki, who kept winning his contests. "He'd do something like a *ko-uchi*, but it wasn't for real and from there he would make a terrific leap. It was astonishing. He'd cover a huge amount of space—it was like something out of *Crouching*

Tiger. He'd use this to launch himself into a *tomoe* and take his opponent to the ground. Once he'd got them there, he'd sacrifice a leg then tie up an arm. Next he'd kick his leg out and then hold them down.

"But I can never forget that leap. Nor could anyone else. They couldn't believe what they had seen. They kept playing it on the big screen over and over again. Everyone was trying to see exactly what he'd done and afterwards people were talking about it incessantly. It was fantastic! It was Kashiwazaki that I remember most of all."

SOMETIMES A LITTLE EXTRA context can make sense of a contest. Budokwai member Edward Ferrie, a former bodyguard who also used to work the doors of clubs in the United Kingdom and Spain and then became an English teacher in Newcastle, England, told me of going to Essen in 1987 for the *Guardian* newspaper. He had never been to a world championships before and didn't know many of the competitors. Wandering around in the warm-up area, he came across a group of Korean judoka doing *uchikomi*. "One had so many tracksuits on that he looked like a spaceman and he was doing sets of *uchikomi*, throwing on the tenth each time. His five training partners kept encouraging him and I was struck by what superb technique he had. He was practicing only one throw, *uchimata*, and his technique was flawless. Perfect hand action, dancer-fast feet, and he performed his *uchikomi* with a metronomic rhythm and precision that was fascinating to watch. "Equally impressive was his fitness. He must have performed over three hundred *uchikomi* as I watched but showed no sign of tiring or slowing down, resting only at three-minute intervals to peel off a tracksuit top or sweatshirt, then grip and start again.

"I was so enthralled by this striking combination of focus and technical excellence that I lost track of time. Eventually the last tracksuit came off and he put on his jacket, gave a little shout and proceeded to throw his partners one final time. Each one sailed over at lightning speed: grip, *uchimata*, *ippon*, roll over, up, grip, *uchimata*, *ippon* . . . and so on until all had been despatched. Then he stood up, sweat pouring off him, straightened his *gi,* and gave the ends of his black belt a little tug. At this moment another Korean arrived and called the group to follow him; they gathered up their things, slipped on their flip-flops, and began to trot to the competition arena."

As it was time for the final, Ferrie returned to his seat in the stadium just in time to see the man he had been watching step onto the mat. It was Kim Jae-Yup, who was about to fight Shinji Hosakawa for the world under–132 pounds (60 kilograms) gold medal. Ferrie had just been watching his last-minute preparations. "The two had met before; it was expected to be a bit of a grudge match but the Japanese was the favorite. There was some gripping and a few feints as both felt each other out for thirty seconds or so, then Kim smacked Hosakawa flat on his back for *ippon* with a lightning-fast unstoppable *uchimata*—just like he'd been doing to the training partners back in the warm-up area." For Ferry the contest itself seemed almost unremarkable; the dress rehearsal was better than the show.

A JAPANESE MAN ONCE described an extraordinary contest to me, saying that it was his favorite of all the contests he had seen. It was a titanic struggle between a small man and a very large man, and he spoke of it with such marked reverence that I made a point of watching it on tape.

Once he had become world champion in 1989, Toshihiko Koga decided that in the following year he should set himself the supreme challenge and compete in the open category of the All Japan championships. In a series of ten-minute contests Koga beat a 350-pound (160-kilogram) competitor, and then a 285-pound (130-kilogram) opponent, followed by one weighing 340 pounds (155 kilograms). Finally he came face-to-face with the world openweight champion, Naoya Ogawa. Koga is under

156 pounds (71 kilograms) and five feet seven inches tall; at 264 pounds (120 kilograms), Ogawa stood head and shoulders above him. Two boxers with such a weight disparity would never be allowed in the ring together.

It's an extraordinary video to watch. Koga is constantly on the attack; once, when a *seoi-nage* fails and he drops to his knees, he becomes entangled in Ogawa's legs like a dog. For much of the time the big man looks unsettled and confused in the face of a series of desperate attacks by Koga, who can never quite shift his bulk. When he is not on the offensive, Koga is desperately trying to avoid his opponent's grips. But, exhausted by his efforts through the day, he is too tired to stay out of trouble. Eventually the heavy man wrests control and forces down his head. The situation is irredeemable; Koga is now at the mercy of Ogawa, who unleashes a huge but very skilful *oguruma* ("major wheel"). His thigh sweeps across the front of Koga's legs like a great beam and his giant arms flip him over and onto his back. *Ippon*! But, for all he had done in winning three out of his four contests, those who saw him held little Koga to be victorious in spite of his defeat.

The event was a sensation in Japan. Here was proof that the essence of the sport still held true. Judo was not about size but about skill. Height and weight were of no more importance in a judo contest than in a chess match. The Japanese who first related the story to me was Shinro Fujita, an official of the All Japan Judo Federation. Transfixed by the mere memory of it, his face was alight with joy as he told me, "A fight like this . . . this is our dream!"

ONE PERFORMANCE-ENHANCING stimulant which competitors are permitted to ingest in unlimited quantities without infringing any rule is the noise of the spectators. Their support is so valuable that its home crowd is reckoned to be worth at least one medal to any nation that hosts a major international tournament. Pity, then, those who are called to fight at the tail end of the morning when the majority have drifted off to get something to eat and wander round the *gi*-stalls. Seeing a great judo contest without a crowd is like watching a great film without its soundtrack. How the judo fan envies the soccer follower, for whom there is scarcely a week in the year when he cannot be watching his sport in the middle of a roaring crowd. Even in a strong judo nation such as Japan or France or Germany, there is little of the formal chanting of the soccer crowd because support is not focused on the two teams, but distributed among many national groups scattered around the stadium. Some of the greatest moments in judo are when these disparate interests are united in a chorus of praise. It's a wonderful sound—a great, impassioned, but strange choral work of crescendos and sudden crazy cadenzas. Spectators shouting instructions that will never be heard. Cheering, baying. Here, the atavistic thump of a drum in the mob, along with the horns. There, brass instruments playing hurried rabble-rousing riffs.

It isn't always so spontaneous. At the Osaka world championships in 2003, I saw about a hundred and fifty North Koreans suddenly appear in the cheapest seats in the top tier. They had all been shipped in to Osaka harbor to spend the nights on board ship and were bussed to the stadium to cheer for any of their fellow countrymen who appeared in the arena.

There was something peculiar about their support. They chanted in unison and waved huge banners, but only came to life when someone from the People's Democratic Republic of Korea was fighting. Their cheering bore no relation to anything that was happening on the mat—the soundtrack was completely out of sync with the movie. There they were, chanting in a well-drilled kind of way, but their support was devoid of understanding: they didn't seem to have a clue what was happening. Oblivious to what was going on in the world around them, their disconnected presence was a poignant metaphor for the bleak oddness of North Korea itself.

SOMETIMES GREAT CONTESTS stand for something, represent part of a greater battle. Koga's appearance in the All Japan openweight final represented a triumph for judo. Other contests represent rather less happy situations.

Japan and Korea have not been the best of neighbors over the years and relations reached a nadir with Japan's repressive occupation of Korea in the first half of the twentieth century. Even today, relations between the two peoples at a social level are uneasy.

This ancient hostility became grimly manifest among the crowd at the world championships that, in 1985, were held in Seoul, the South Korean capital. And as if by the contrivance of a scriptwriter, when it came to the climactic final in the heavyweight category, the contestants were the Japanese and the South Korean. The former was the mighty Hitoshi Saito, the country's greatest heavyweight now that his old rival Yamashita was retired. Saito, who was much larger than his opponent, was the clear favorite and the Korean, Jong-Jul Cho, very much the outsider. Steve Gawthorpe, who was to compete later in the tournament and was among the spectators, recalls, "We thought the Korean had done well to get to the final." He was struck by the discrepancy between the two contestants. Not only was Saito so much bigger, he had a strong competition record. Cho, however, was to have the invaluable support of the home crowd. As it turned out, he didn't need it.

This was a drama that did not unfold, but exploded into a climax within moments of the start. Gawthorpe remembered how relaxed Saito had appeared. "He walked out very casually and confidently and put his arm on Cho's shoulder. But as soon as he did that Cho just snapped on an armlock and dived down to the floor." Their champion's plight was terrible for the Japanese to behold. Saito was on his front with Cho pulling on the already damaged arm, confronted with a humiliating defeat in a contest that had lasted but seconds. Cho continued to apply the pressure but Saito, who refused to tap, eventually managed to extricate his arm. The referee stopped the contest and got them both to their feet. With Saito's whole face clenched in agony, his arm was inspected, but when he tried to explain to his coach—Nobuyuki Sato, Yamashita's former mentor—that it was damaged beyond use, he was angrily told to get on and fight.

When the contest restarted it was clear that Saito was quite unable to use his arm and the referee soon stopped it again. The Japanese contingent now pressed their appeal against the decision, arguing that the armlock was an illegal move, the rules being that a standing armlock has to take effect in the standing position before it can be continued on the ground. Moreover it has to be carried out under control. The Japanese argued that Cho had just seized the arm and dived to the floor with it.

According to Syd Hoare, "The murmurings in the huge crowd began to grow really ugly. I seriously thought there would be a full-scale riot if the decision was given to the Japanese."[25] In the event the referee awarded the fight to Cho. The mood in the stadium suddenly switched and the home crowd burst into ecstatic cheering. (Saito was to have his revenge when the Olympic Games came to the same city three years later. He conclusively beat Cho on his way to taking the gold medal.)

IN 2001, I WENT TO the world championships in Munich. They were held on the site of the 1972 Olympics, with its swooping tent-line structure of glass panels anchored by steel hawsers over an arena sunk deep into the earth. The tournament was memorable, among many things, for Inoue's magnificent victory in the under–209 pounds (95 kilograms) division. However, the contest at Munich that I found hardest to forget was the under–161 pounds (73 kilograms) final between Vitali Makarov of Russia and Yusuke Kanamaru from Japan. It made a similar impression on other witnesses who spoke to me about it.

With the seats packed for this, the third day of the competition, excitement was high and the rising temperature in the stadium had prompted a series of freak Mexican waves. The contest started with a series of explosions that never stopped. There was no plot, no careful unfolding of a strategy, but instead there came burst after burst of rapid-fire attacks. Although both players often went over, the encounter never properly went to the ground for any length of time—so there was nothing to slow the pace. The contest was fought at whip-tip speed—a pace that was unrelenting. Towards the end one expected it to flag; surely the contestants would run out of ammunition. But still they kept firing attacks at each other, still at breakneck speed, in a dialogue that will always get lost in translation: words just can't keep up. But the elemental forces they both unleashed had coincided to create the perfect storm, and one of them was going to go under. With fifty seconds to go the Russian produced a sudden and powerful surge, catching his opponent with an *uchimata* that whipped him over for *ippon*.

Both men deserved to win, but it was Makarov's hands that reached up to touch the heavens. The exchange of greetings by the two players at the end of the contest was so genuinely good-natured that it was difficult to conceive how they had been able to fight so hard. But, of course, it wasn't a *fight,* it was a *contest;* it was what Dr. Kano forever sought—a pure test of skill in "the attack-and-defense form of movement." There can have been very few Japanese and Russians present, so the cheering was quite unpartisan; the crowd was shouting for them both in an ecstatic roar that acknowledged their skill. This was the sound of a jubilant crowd cheering for judo itself.

"The cheers of the spectators swell into a roaring chorus in celebration of my victory," wrote Okano of the moment of winning. "But, behind this almost abnormal excitement and intoxication, I realize another sober self, coolly observing everything I do. Then the world seems to belong to me, and the single moment of intensely concentrated meaning is unforgettable."

WHAT DO YOU THINK OF IT SO FAR, DR. KANO?

Our struggle is nearing its conclusion: out of the corner of my eye, I see there are but seconds on the clock of this, our last *randori*. The fact that you are reading these words means not only that you still have your grip on my collar—but also that I still have my grip on yours. I have learned much in the course of a practice; I only hope you have, too.

I have described this book as "a journey into the world of judo," but I now wonder if that is perhaps too rich. I merely stepped onto the mat, did some judo, went to some tournaments, talked to some people, and went home. So maybe this was more of a luxury cruise, during which I came down the gangplank in various lands, did a little sightseeing, and returned safely to my own cabin. Perhaps I am one of those tedious tourists who see themselves as "travelers" and boast of "getting to know the natives and the *real* country—not just the sights the tourists see."

Whatever the case, I know I was ashore long enough to catch some fever that wracked my mind, that made my whole frame sweat and ache. And I know that the locals sold me something called *randori*, which I have found impossible to forsake.

I liked the idea of "the spirit of judo" but, sadly, I was never very good at conjuring it. I wanted to walk in processional triumph, with rose petals scattered in my path. All I got were banana skins. I discovered only a shadow of a fragment of a whisper of the truth, and even that was more than I could handle, more than I could work with. Anyway, I am grateful to have learned what I will never know.

Although my brain was not up to it, physically I got fitter. Certainly my fingers are stronger than they were, but I can still have an embarrassing amount of trouble opening a packet of cashews. I would not say judo has changed my outlook on life as it has for others whom I know. I have seen no signs to suggest that my approach to life has become a continuation of judo by other means. Yet, although it may not have changed my attitude, it has adjusted it.

The experience has left me with a deep respect for anyone who competes in this sport at any level. It has also given me a glimmer of insight into other sports; however uninterested I may be, at least now I have some respect for them. But when you proudly tell me your tale of how you know someone who knows someone who had a friend who once got to hold Nick Faldo's golf bag, I nod dutifully at your proclaimed proximity to your sporting idols; I feign to be impressed. But as you talk, inwardly I will scoff, for I have encountered countless heroes of *my* sport. I have fought great warriors by the dozen; I have done battle with giants, champions of the world, Olympian heroes, men who between them have acquired through conquest mule-loads of bronze and silver, more gold than all the Incas. I have talked to an emperor who fought before an emperor, I have been taught by a man who was taught by tiny Tani of the Halls. I have fought a man who fought a man who fought the great Kimura. I have touched the very collars of my gods.

I fear this sounds like double-brandies talking, but one becomes light-headed with elation. A sense of the sheer grandeur, this heady spirit, exhaustion, and oxygen starvation of the brain inflates one's sense of sentiment, intensifies emotionalism, and makes for language with its chest puffed out—hyperventilating prose.

This is what happens when you swim with the endorphins.

I MADE IT clear at the start that I had little time for sportsmen. I loathed their obsessiveness, the way they took it all so seriously; I despised their pathetic little superstitions. More than anything I despised their tears.

Five years after my journey began, on the day of my most important grading, I made absolutely sure that I had with me my talisman, the Budo University phone card that Kashiwazaki gave me at the Balthazar in Paris. And before I left the soft comfort of home I folded my *gi* in exactly the same way as I had always done.

The day went according to hope and when I won the last of the contests I needed to accomplish what seemed to be the most important task in the world, I found myself in a state of bewildered exhilaration. Then a nagging pain in my slightly injured hand reminded me to hurry to get some ice to prevent it swelling. Just before reaching the dojo door, I was struck by a strange smothering blow to my brain that almost stopped me in my tracks. It was as if someone had suddenly slackened the guy ropes that held in place my self-control. I hurried on downstairs and there, alone in the changing room, I began to sob like a teenage girl.

This, then, the final lunacy. Tears.

WE MAY NOT KNOW what Dr. Jigoro Kano, from his present vantage point, thinks about the state of judo today, but many who hold high office in the sport *think* they do. His influence is never far from their deliberations, nor is the presence of his grandson, Yukimitsu Kano, who is president of the Kodokan.

There are doctrinal divisions among those who run judo, at the heart of which is the perceived threat to the future of judo posed by international competition. Some argue that Dr. Kano was always in favor of competition, because he was convinced it promoted "mutual benefit and welfare" and because there were rules for competition from the earliest days of the Kodokan. They point out that it was through competition that judo proved itself on that day in 1886 when Kano's pupils fought their rivals at the shrine in Shiba Park.

Trevor Leggett insisted that Kano was against competition. And in a letter to me shortly before his death, Dickie Bowen wrote, "Do remember, no matter what others may say, Jigoro Kano did not want judo in the Olympics. He was in favor of the Games, but not for judo, which for him was a martial art." Bowen argued that Kano would have hated this need for "medals at all costs."

Perhaps the lure of fostering internationalism through sport overcame the doctor's qualms about competition. Kano thus not only became an important part of the Olympic movement, but began to accept the idea of judo being part of the Games. Visionary though he was, could he really have foreseen what a monster the Olympics were to become, how they would change his creation? To have the nations fight each other in the spirit of judo would surely have been his ultimate vindication.

The last testament of Dr. Jigoro Kano can be found in an article by an American sportswriter who interviewed him shortly before his death in 1938. He wrote that he found the doctor, who was an avowed pacifist, in despair at Japanese militarism and his country's preparations for war. And he reported that Kano made clear to him that he saw international sporting competition as a means to a universal humanity.[1]

THE STORY WE HAVE FOLLOWED in these pages has told of great combats between champions, but it has also traced the struggle between ideas. There has been judo's battle with rival forms of unarmed combat. A struggle between judo's purists and judo's sportsmen, between the idea of hobby judo and serious judo. A battle for recruits between judo and other sports. A battle between classical judo and those alien and mutant versions that threw down their challenge. And it has been about Japan's struggle to retain its superiority and the attempt by every other nation to end it.

It all began, you remember, with the samurai. Their tradition is far from dead and can be traced through the decades to the present day. The code of honor that governed behavior on the battlefield still holds true in our twenty-first-century world. It certainly held true in the Tokyo offices of the Tokai Kensetsu, a construction company fighting a losing battle with insolvency whose leader felt he must pay the price of his shame. That leader was Isao Inokuma, the first heavyweight Olympic gold medalist—by all accounts a wonderful man, but one whose later career did not sustain the success he had achieved on the contest mat. "A great judo man but a bad businessman" was how one rueful Japanese informant told me as, with a quick movement, he drew his fingers across his stomach to mime *hara-kiri*—ritual suicide. In this terrible way ended the life of a fine champion for whom the crowd had once roared. Sad that when he most needed them, those supporters could not be heard. Had they known his plight, surely they would have urged him to keep fighting. Perhaps he *did* hear them, perhaps their roar still echoed in his mind, but still he felt his shame was too great. So, there in his office above the din of the Tokyo traffic, the vestigial code of honor would be observed. The samurai did what he felt he must.

I WOULD LIKE TO THINK that during the time we have spent together I have thrown you with a fact or a notion, or forced you to submit to my argument. Certainly I have to admit that many times you have countered me with your silent challenge and I have been left staring at the ceiling before getting up to try a different technique. No matter. What is important is that we have both tried to use our skill in this dialogue of attack and defense.

I fear that in the course of our *randori* you have been splashed with sweat and tears, but I hope that you have also heard the sound of laughter, that you too have felt the sensation of endorphins leaping in the surf. Perhaps it has been a strange cacophony for you to sit through: the yelps of alarm, grunts of effort, groans of pain, the skeeter of feet like brushes on a snare drum, the thump of bodies on the tatami like tympani. But, rising from this eccentric orchestra above the choir that is the crowd, I hope you have also heard the sound of elation in the notes of a triumphant trumpet dancing in the sky above the staff.

Our struggle is about to end. It has been a close and hard-fought encounter. It has not been easy for me to get here, and I appreciate your effort in doing the same. In this encounter there appears to be no final outcome. My guess is that the judges will declare *hikiwake*—a draw. Because, if I have failed to throw you, to pin you, I have made you go the full distance to the final klaxon on the final page. And you in your way have made me get here too. But the result on the scoreboard is not important to us; what matters more is what we may both have learned through our effort.

When the referee calls *matte*, we must stop and bow as we did at the beginning of our encounter. This time we do it in mutual respect, to thank each other for the privilege of training together and for what we have learned.

In the final minute the pace of our struggle suddenly increases as we make a last attempt to achieve the decisive score of *ippon*—the incontrovertible argument. The danger is that in the frantic effort to do so, our technique will become ragged and uneven, so we must still remain cool. We need to control our breathing and make sure we are not carried away by the terrible emotionalism engendered by sport. We are all engaged in a quest for the sublime, but we must be wary of any falseness in our celebration of judo. We must ask ourselves if we are succumbing to the desire to see art where there is only violence—if we might be guilty of trying to exalt what is nothing more than the athletic antics of some cotton-covered thugs.

Perhaps Kano's great achievement was merely that, rather later than the rest of the world, he discovered sport. For here is an extraordinary thing: *there was no sport in Japan*. There is no word for sport in the Japanese language. Astonishing as it may seem, although they had got hold of the wheel, the Japanese completely forgot to invent the ball. (The one ball game there was, called *kemari*, was confined to court circles.)

Even in the savage lands of Afghanistan, the tribesmen had the *idea* of the ball when they played *buzkashi*, their horseback rugby, using the carcass of a calf. But the Japanese came to the idea very late and, without a ball to kick around, they had only each other. Their concept of sport was trying to slice each other into pieces with swords or tear each other's limbs off with their bare hands. Kano admitted that the introduction of baseball at his school was a revelation to him; he said he loved the spirit of it.[2] Of course he did. This sporting spirit was an entirely unknown phenomenon in Japan. The concept of competition without loss of life or limb, let alone face, was a mind-boggling innovation.

This child of the new age leapt upon this weird foreign idea called sport; he made sportsmanship an element of the philosophy of judo. But does Kano's system of sporting combat really offer any more than baseball, soccer, or whatever? Is the spirit of judo little more than sportsmanship served in a rice bowl? Did the doctor merely come up with a slightly different way to create an adrenaline rush, an endorphin trip, a buzz? When Isao Okano says "judo is the true essence of human life," surely you could be listening to a Italian talking about soccer or an American rhapsodizing about baseball.

And was Dr. Kano's gift to the Western world really so extraordinary? Did he achieve much more than take a Japanese activity and redesign it as a sport? Perhaps he merely did what a generation of postwar Japanese industrialists did, which was to copy, restyle, and efficiently manufacture Western products from TVs to cars to motorbikes, and sell them back to Europe and America. Maybe his trick was simply to use that Japanese skill in packaging to present his sport to the West as though it was an exotic gift.

Whatever the truth, nothing can detract from Dr. Kano's great achievement, which was to build a system of techniques around a series of underlying principles that he had identified as crucial to the art of unarmed offense and defense. These principles gave judo its resilience against the depredations of the Russians and the hazards of the cage. And the sheer effectiveness of the system became recognized and practiced everywhere. It was not Koresh from Kazakhstan or Cornish backhold that spread round the globe, but judo that became a worldwide industry standard, like the dollar and the English language.

We must also credit the doctor with advancing the novel and intriguing idea that the practice of "the attack-and-defense form of movement" would make for self-improvement and would instill virtues—that if we threw each other about a bit it would help us in our everyday lives, that we'd all get on so much better if only we tried to throttle each other into unconsciousness or submission.

We should conclude by asking if Kano's creation is coping in its struggle with those ugly handmaidens of international competition: commercialism, corruption, nationalism, and egotism. It has at times been a closely fought contest, but surely we can argue that, so far, judo is clearly ahead on points.

We should also ask if Kano's desire that judo should be a means of personal development—a way to build not only physical strength and agility, but also mental resilience and self-discipline—has been fulfilled. Has modernity jeopardized the survival of Kano's idea of "the spirit of judo"?

One can only observe that in all those dojos across the globe, in the poorest quarters of the desperate cities, in prosperous suburbs, in the little towns in the mountains and the plains, in the tropics and the tundra, in the lands of sand and ice, every encounter is preceded by the shout of "*Rei!*" at which every judoka bows and after which, for the most part, good-natured euphoria prevails. And at the end they bow again. The conclusion must surely be this pleasing truth: that all across the judo world, even in the ferocity of international competition, the original spirit of Dr. Kano's great vision still shines bright.

Soré-madé!

Rei!

NOTES

Chapter 3. To Walk the Talk
1. *The Times*, April 24, 2004.
2. Bruce Lee, *Tao of Jeet Kune Do* (Santa Clarita, Calif.: Ohara Publications, 1975).

Chapter 4. The Crucible
1. E. J. Harrison, *The Fighting Spirit of Japan* (Middlesex, U.K.: Foulsham, 1955).
2. Allen Gordon, Judo Information Site (www.judoinfo.com).
3. Donn F. Draeger and Robert W. Smith, *Asian Fighting Arts* (Tokyo: Kodansha International, 1969).
4. John Keegan, *A History of Warfare* (London: Hutchinson, 1993).
5. Draeger and Smith, *Asian Fighting Arts* (Berkeley, Calif.: Berkeley Publishing Corps, 1974).

Chapter 5. The Incredible Dr. Kano
1. Brian N. Watson, *The Father of Judo: A Biography of Jigoro Kano* (Tokyo: Kodansha International, 2000).
2. Jigoro Kano, "The Contribution of Judo to Education." Speech given at the University of Southern California at the 11th Olympiad, 1932.
3. Jigoro Kano, *Kodokan Judo: The Essential Guide to Judo by Its Founder Jigoro Kano* (Tokyo: Kodansha International, 1986).
4. Trevor Leggett, *The Dragon Mask and Other Judo Stories in the Zen Tradition* (College Station, Texas: Ippon).
5. Kano, "The Contribution of Judo to Education."
6. Watson, *The Father of Judo*.
7. Michel Brousse and David Matsumoto, *Judo: A Sport and a Way of Life* (International Judo Federation, 1999).
8. Tony Reay and Geoffrey Hobbs, *The Judo Manual* (London: Tiger Books International, 1993).
9. Watson, *The Father of Judo*.

Chapter 6. Beauty and the Beast
1. Lafcadio Hearn, *Out of the East* (Boston: Houghton Mifflin, 1895).

Chapter 7. How the West Was Won

1. Richard Bowen, *Britain and Japan: Biographical Portraits*, vol. 5 (London: Japan Society).
2. Brousse and Matsumoto, *Judo: A Sport and a Way of Life*.
3. Ibid.
4. *The World of Judo* (Spring) *The World of Judo Magazine* (Winter 2004).
5. Donn F. Draeger, *Modern Bujutsu & Budo* (London: Weatherhill, 1974).
6. Masahiko Kimura, *My Judo* (1985), Judo Information Site (www.judoinfo .com).

Chapter 8. The Renegade

1. Watson, *The Father of Judo*.
2. Much material in this chapter is drawn from the Judo Information Site (www.judoinfo.com), which includes Jim Chen and Theodore Chen's "The Man Who Defeated Helio Gracie" and material from Masahiko Kimura's two autobiographies, *Ghost of Judo* (1969) and *My Judo* (1985).
3. Robert W. Smith, *Martial Musings: A Portrayal of Martial Arts in the 20th Century* (Erie, Penn.: Via Media, 1999).
4. Ibid.
5. Watson, *The Father of Judo*.
6. *Historia do Jiu-jitsu atraves dos Tempos*, a monograph written by three students from Escola de Educacão Fisica e Desportos at the Universidade Federal do Rio de Janeiro.
7. Helio Gracie interviewed in 1994 by Nishi Yoshinori, translated by Yoko Kondo; published in *Kakuto Striking Spirit* (May 1, 2002); accessed on Judo Information Site (www.judoinfo.com).
8. Smith, *Martial Musings*.

Chapter 9. The End of Supremacy

1. Nicolas Soames and Roy Inman, *Olympic Judo: History and Techniques* (Wiltshire, U.K.: Ippon/Crowood, 1990).
2. Haku Michigami in an interview in *Nihon Keizai Shimbun,* July 2002 (www.haku-michigami.com/top_e.htm).
3. George Kerr, *The World of Judo Magazine*, 41 (Winter 2004).
4. Nicolas Soames and Simon Hicks, *Fifty Great Judo Champions* (College Station, Texas: Ippon, 2001).
5. www.haku-michigami.com.
6. Anton Geesink, *My Championship Judo* (Middlesex, U.K.: Foulsham, 1996).
7. Ian Buruma, *Inventing Japan: From Empire to Economic Miracle* (London: Phoenix, 2003).
8. Soames and Inman, *Olympic Judo*.
9. The Way, Incorporated (www.winningyourway.com).
10. Geesink, *My Championship Judo*.

11. Buruma, *Inventing Japan*.
12. *Sankei Shimbun* (April 29, 2003).
13. Buruma, *Inventing Japan*.

Chapter 10. The Club
1. *The World of Judo* (Summer 1996).
2. Geof Gleeson, *Judo Inside Out: A Cultural Reconciliation* (Wakefield, U.K.: Lepus, 1983).
3. Syd Hoare, *Judo Strategies* (College Station, Texas: Ippon, 2002).

Chapter 11. The Soviet Menace
1. Peter Seisenbacher and George Kerr, *Modern Judo: Techniques of East and West* (Swindon, Wiltshire, U.K.: Crowood, 1991).
2. Soames and Inman, *Olympic Judo*.
3. Brousse and Matsumoto, *Judo: A Sport and a Way of Life*.
4. Andrew Moshanov, *Judo: From a Russian Perspective* (College Station, Texas: Ippon, 2004).
5. Ibid.
6. Ibid.
7. Seisenbacher and Kerr, *Modern Judo*.
8. Brousse and Matsumoto, *Judo: A Sport and a Way of Life*.

Chapter 12. The Emperor
1. Gary Smith, *Sports Illustrated* (July 13, 1984).
2. Steve Lohr, *New York Times* (February 26, 1984).
3. Philip Nicksan, *Independent* (December 13, 1993).
4. Yasuhiro Yamashita, *The Fighting Spirit of Judo*, trans. Sarah Cousens (College Station, Texas: Ippon, 1993) (first published in Japanese in 1991 by *Baseball* magazine as "Tokon no Judo").
5. *Asahi Shimbun* (November 1999).
6. Yamashita, *The Fighting Spirit of Judo*.
7. Gary Smith, *Sports Illustrated*.
8. Comment made by Jim Woolley.
9. Steve Lohr, *New York Times* (February 26, 1998).
10. Soames and Hicks, *Fifty Great Judo Champions*.
11. John Goodbody, *The Times*.
12. Gary Smith, *Sports Illustrated*.

Chapter 13. The Arms Race
1. Yamashita, *The Fighting Spirit of Judo*.
2. Isao Inokuma and Nobuyuki Sato, *Best Judo* (Japan: Kodansha, 1979).
3. Ibid.
4. Budokwai Web site (www.budokwai.org).

Chapter 14. Zen and the Art of *Uchimata* Maintenance

1. Kodokan Institute Web site (www.kodokan.org).
2. Neil Adams with Nicolas Soames, *A Life in Judo* (London: Willow Books, 1986).

Chapter 15. Hell on a Very Hot Mat

1. Adams, *A Life in Judo*.
2. Smith, *Martial Musings*.
3. Adams, *A Life in Judo*.
4. Ibid.
5. Benjamin Raphael, "Falling About for a Title," *Daily Telegraph* magazine (February 25, 1972).
6. Benjamin Raphael quoting Inman, in "Falling About for a Title."
7. Leggett, *The Dragon Mask*.
8. Adams, *A Life in Judo*.
9. Robert Twigger, *Angry White Pyjamas: An Oxford Poet Trains with the Tokyo Riot Police* (London: Phoenix, 1997).
10. Inokuma and Sato, *Best Judo*.
11. Adams, *A Life in Judo*.

Chapter 16. How the Women Fought to Fight

1. Brousse and Matsumoto, *Judo: A Way of Life*.
2. Ibid.
3. Roy Inman, *Judo for Women* (Wiltshire, U.K.: Crowood Press, 1987).
4. International Judo Federation (IJF) seminar report.
5. Seisenbacher and Kerr, *Modern Judo: Techniques of East and West*.
6. *The World of Judo* (Autumn 2004).
7. Personal interview with Don Werner, coach at Pinewood judo club.
8. Karen Briggs, *Judo Champion* (Wiltshire, U.K.: Crowood, 1988).
9. International Judo Federation (IJF) interview, 1999.

Chapter 17. How to Build a Fighting Machine

1. Interview with Ronaldo Veitia Valdivie at International Judo Federation (IJF) coach seminar (Munich, February, 19, 1998).
2. *Prensa Latina* (April 29, 2006).
3. Soames and Hicks, *Fifty Great Judo Champions*.
4. Roberto Mendez Rodriguez, *Olympic Review*, XXVI: 31 (February–March 2000).
5. Simon Hicks, report of International Judo Federation (IJF) coaching forum (2001).
6. Darren Warner, *Matside*, British Judo Association (October 2006).
7. Rodriguez, *Olympic Review*.
8. Alexander Iatskevich, *Russian Judo* (College Station, Texas: Ippon, 1999).

9. *Interfax* (January 27, 2002).
10. Paul Starobin, "The Accidental Autocrat," *The Atlantic Monthly* (March 2005).
11. Interview with Putin televised by NHK TV of Japan (May 30, 2003), reported by Itar-Tass.
12. Judo Information Site (www.judoinfo.com).

Chapter 18. When Judo Goes into the Cage

1. Kimura, *My Judo*.
2. David Plotz, "Fight Clubbed." *Slate* online magazine (www.Slate.com) (November 1999).

Chapter 19. The Little Empress

1. Karen Harrison, *The World of Judo* (Spring 2004).
2. Yasuhiro Muto, *Chunichi Sports*, quoted in Time.com (August 9, 2004).
3. www.olympic.org.
4. http://web-japan.org/trends/sports/sp0041006.html.

Chapter 20. David the Goliath and Inoue the Prince

1. *Yomiuri Shimbun*.

Chapter 21. White-Collar Worker

1. Takahiko Ishikawa and Donn Draeger, *Judo Training Methods* (Rutland, Vermont, and Tokyo: Charles E. Tuttle, 1961).
2. Dudley Doust, *Sunday Times* (December 1, 1968).

Chapter 22. The Tournament

1. John Goodbody, *The Times*.
2. David Wallechinsky, *The Complete Book of the Summer Olympics* (New York: Overlook Press, 2000).
3. Soames and Hicks, *Fifty Great Judo Champions*.
4. Hoare, *Judo Strategies*.
5. *The World of Judo* (Autumn 2002).
6. Bob Willingham with David Matsumoto, *The Thrill of Victory and the Agony of Defeat* (The World of Judo Publications, 2007).
7. Tetsuya Sato and Isao Okano, *Vital Judo* (Tokyo: Japan Publications, 1976).
8. Adams, *A Life in Judo*.
9. Inokuma and Sato, *Best Judo*.
10. Ulrich Kloche, *The World of Judo* (Winter 1998).
11. Sato and Okano, *Vital Judo*.
12. Soames and Hicks, *Fifty Great Judo Champions*.
13. Kloche, *The World of Judo*.

14. Soames and Hicks, *Fifty Great Judo Champions.*
15. E. K. Koiwai, M.D., "Deaths Allegedly Caused by the Use of Choke Holds," Judo Information Web site (www.judoinfo.com/chokes5.htm).
16. R. S. Surtees, *Mr. Facey Romford's Hounds* (London: Bradbury and Evans, 1865).
17. Katsuhiko Kashiwazaki, *Shimewaza* (College Station, Texas: Ippon, 1992).
18. *Guardian Unlimited* (September 21, 2000).
19. *The Daily Telegraph* online (September 4, 2003).
20. *The Times* (August 20, 2001).
21. *The World of Judo* (Summer 2000).
22. Soames and Inman, *Olympic Judo.*
23. *The Daily Telegraph* (August 20, 2001).
24. David Finch, "Okano Isao's Impact on Judo Since the Lausanne World Championships," *Journal of Asian Martial Arts,* 12: 4.
25. *The World of Judo* (Winter 2004).

Chapter 23. What Do You Think of It So Far, Dr. Kano?

1. Royal Brougham, *Seattle Post-Intelligencer* (May 6, 1938).
2. Brousse and Matsumoto, *Judo: A Way of Life.*

Jillian
Melissa

Owen
Chris
Graham